SEXUAL IDENTITY

The Bible Study Textbook Series

NEW TESTAMENT

The Bible Study New Testament Ed. By Rhoderick Ice	**The Gospel of Matthew** In Four Volumes By Harold Fowler (Vol. IV not yet available)	**The Gospel of Mark** By B. W. Johnson and Don DeWelt
The Gospel of Luke By T. R. Applebury	**The Gospel of John** By Paul T. Butler	**Acts Made Actual** By Don DeWelt
Romans Realized By Don DeWelt	**Studies in Corinthians** By T. R. Applebury	**Guidance From Galatians** By Don Earl Boatman
The Glorious Church (Ephesians) By Wilbur Fields	**Philippians - Colossians Philemon** By Wilbur Fields	**Thinking Through Thessalonians** By Wilbur Fields
Paul's Letters To Timothy & Titus By Don DeWelt	**Helps From Hebrews** By Don Earl Boatman	**James & Jude** By Don Fream
Letters From Peter By Bruce Oberst	**Hereby We Know (I-II-III John)** By Clinton Gill	**The Seer, The Saviour, and The Saved (Revelation)** By James Strauss

OLD TESTAMENT

O.T. History By William Smith and Wilbur Fields	**Genesis** In Four Volumes By C. C. Crawford	**Exploring Exodus** By Wilbur Fields	**Leviticus** By Don DeWelt
Numbers By Brant Lee Doty	**Deuteronomy** By Bruce Oberst	**Joshua - Judges Ruth** By W. W. Winter	**I & II Samuel** By W. W. Winter
I & II Kings By James E. Smith	**I & II Chronicles** By Robert E. Black	**Ezra, Nehemiah & Esther** By Ruben Ratzlaff & Paul T. Butler	**The Shattering of Silence (Job)** By James Strauss
Psalms In Two Volumes By J. B. Rotherham		**Proverbs** By Donald Hunt	**Ecclesiastes and Song of Solomon** — By R. J. Kidwell and Don DeWelt
Isaiah In Three Volumes By Paul T. Butler		**Jeremiah and Lamentations** By James E. Smith	**Ezekiel** By James E. Smith
Daniel By Paul T. Butler		**Hosea - Joel - Amos Obadiah - Jonah** By Paul T. Butler	**Micah - Nahum - Habakkuk Zephaniah - Haggai - Zechariah Malachi** — By Clinton Gill

SPECIAL STUDIES

The Church In The Bible By Don DeWelt	**The Eternal Spirit** By C. C. Crawford	**World & Literature of the Old Testament** Ed. By John Willis	**Survey Course In Christian Doctrine** Two Bks. of Four Vols. By C. C. Crawford
New Testament History — Acts By Gareth Reese		**Learning From Jesus** By Seth Wilson	**You Can Understand The Bible** By Grayson H. Ensign

WHAT THE BIBLE SAYS SERIES

WHAT THE
BIBLE SAYS
ABOUT

SEXUAL IDENTITY

By

Eleanor Daniel

College Press Publishing Company, Joplin, Missouri

Library of Congress Catalog Card Number: 81-71836
International Standard Book Number: 0-89900-085-1

Scripture quotations, unless otherwise noted, are from the New International Version, New York International Bible Society, 1978.

Table of Contents

TABLE OF CONTENTS

FOREWORD

None of us can envision ourselves without some kind of sexual identity. At the same time, some of us are uncomfortable with that identity, especially in a society where most of the traditions about sex roles have fallen into question. Yet, we are who we are—a man or a woman—called by God to be what He wants.

I have lived my entire lifetime as a single, an unmarried woman seeking to exist in a predominantly male profession. It hasn't always been easy to balance my views of femininity with the demands of my job. Yet, I am a woman, albeit single, who has no desire to be anything other than a woman. That is why I eagerly seized the opportunity to do this book —to take a long look at the Biblical material that examines sexual identity—its purpose, uses/misuses, and proper expression.

It has been a challenging, fulfilling, journey. I trust that the material calls forth your appreciation of your sexual nature and identity as it has mine. If it does, the work has been well worthwhile.

This book is dedicated to Altice, a special friend, who by word and example has taught me more than she shall ever know about being a woman of God.

Part I

A BIBLICAL VIEW OF SEX

We live in a sex-saturated society. Nowhere can we escape it. Advertising appeals to sexuality and sexual desires. Television programs and movies flaunt sexual behavior of all kinds. A new public openness toward sexual matters provides access to a plethora of information about sexual beliefs and behaviors.

To the casual participant in life, the mores of the day suggest that "anything goes" in terms of sexuality. To deny oneself the sensual pleasures is nothing short of stupid, according to the modern ethic. And to the Christian, affected in part by a puritanical interpretation of sexuality, the blatant sensationalism of sex too often calls for suppression of any recognition or discussion of sexuality as a God-accepted and God-ordained life force. But neither the libertine nor the puritan are correct in their understanding of man's sexual identity and behavior.

The place to begin in a study of human sexual identity is with the Bible. The Scriptures are amazingly straightforward and frank in treatment of this fundamental aspect of human personality, much to the surprise of those puritans who would suppress it. Yet it is equally clear as to *where* sexuality fits into life and *how* it is to be expressed, to the chagrin of those who would call for free expression of the sexual appetite. The first section of this book examines sex from a Biblical perspective, examining the nature of sexuality, how it develops, and guidelines for its God-ordained expression.

1

Part I — A Biblical View of Sex

Chapter One

GOD MADE THEM: MALE AND FEMALE

God made man and woman. At the dawn of creation, before He expressed final satisfaction with the world He had fashioned, God created woman to go with man. "It is not good for the man to be alone. I will make a helper suitable for him," God determined (Genesis 2:19), and He made woman from the side of man. That creation, as all of the rest of God's creative work, bore the stamp of quality workmanship: "God saw all that he had made and it was very good" (Genesis 1:31). All previous creative efforts had been judged good, but now with the addition of man and woman to the creative panorama, it was *very good*.

The Biblical account, although concise in its treatment of the creation of man and woman, lays the foundation by which man is to understand himself. It establishes the basis for responsible sexual identity and activity.

Made in the Image of God

God made man in His own image (Genesis 1:27, 5:1). The Psalmist states that man is the crown of all creation (Psalm 8), a little lower than God Himself. Obviously, man's image-bearing personality is not found in his physical make-up, but he shares the image, or reflection, of God in at least five significant ways: rationality, emotionality, volitionality morality, and immortality of spirit.

Rationality. Man was created a rational creature, sharing in God's intelligence. This is most clearly demonstrated in

2

the creation account in Genesis 1:28-30 when God committed nature to man's management. Psalm 8:6-8 restates the same charge. A commitment to management implies a thinking manager, one capable of handling creation as God would. The Bible assumes man to be a thinking, reasoning individual, capable, as it turned out after the Fall, of great good or indescribable sin. But in the Garden of Eden, his rational sense was still pure, in the exact image of God. Those who are redeemed by Christ are redeemed not only for salvation of the soul, but also for renewal of the thought processes (Philippians 4:8).

Emotionality. It is God's emotional attributes that permit Him to relate to His creation. The Old Testament is filled with references to God's love (Psalm 91:14, Isaiah 61:8, Jeremiah 44:4, Zechariah 8:17), His tenderness (Psalm 119:77, 156; 145:9), and His anger (Numbers 22:22, Deuteronomy 6:15, Joshua 7:1, Judges 2:12, Psalm 6:1, and Jeremiah 3:5).

Man shares God's emotional nature. Man, too, is made for relationships, to experience the full gamut of emotions, to love and be loved, to feel, to respond. The essence of the Bible is the call to man to love the Lord God with all his mind and heart and will and to love his neighbor as himself (Mark 12:30-31). He is instructed to be angry yet not sin (Ephesians 4:26), to love (Ephesians 5:2), to relate to others (Galatians 6:2). In short, man reflects the nature of God in his ability to feel and to respond.

Volitionality. God chose to make man (Genesis 1:26), to give him freedom to respond as he chooses (Genesis 2:15-16), and to remake man (Ephesians 1:4-6, 11-12). Man shares in that ability to make choices. He was made for fellowship with God, yet God gave him the privilege of choosing whether to obey Him or not (Genesis 2:15-16), a freedom that he grossly misused (Genesis 3:1-6). Even so, God continued to offer man choices, the supreme one the opportunity to experience transformation of life through Jesus Christ (Ephesians 2:1-10). Every time an individual makes a choice, it is a reminder that he is made in the image of God.

Morality. God is righteous (Psalm 11:7, 116:5; II Timothy 4:8), and He makes no mistakes in judgment and relationships (Revelation 16:5-7). At the moment of creation, man shared that nature, only to lose it when he shook his puny fist at God in disobedience. Even so, God designed a plan by which man, the unrighteous one (Romans 3:10), could be restored to righteousness (Romans 5:7, 19). Once again, man has the potential for perfection (Matthew 5:48). Every noble act of man, every splendid deed, each magnificent choice is testimony that man, imperfect as he is, bears the image of God.

Immortal spirit. God is Spirit (John 4:24), with no beginning and no end (John 1:1, I Timothy1:17, Revelation 21:6, 22:13). Man, though mortal in body, possesses an immortal spirit, one that shall never die (I Corinthians 15:53-54, John 3:16). The choice of where the spirit of man shall reside in eternity is man's to make (Revelation 21:6-8). The fact that man is even concerned about what comes after death is but another indication of his reflection of God's image.

Man was made in the image of God, an image tarnished by sin, but nevertheless a reflection of the nature of God the Creator. He was made for a unique purpose, distinctly different than the animals that preceded him in creation (Genesis 1:28-30). The fact that he reflects God Himself in some measure is evidence of the quality of man's existence. He is

4

more than a biological entity: the principles of experimental biology and psychology are inadequate to explain him or his actions in their totality. He was made answerable to God in his total being, something said of none of the rest of God's creation.

Made Male and Female

Not only was man created in the image of God, but He was also created a biological creature. Man is composed of flesh and blood, a creature made of the dust of the earth, but breathed with Godlike qualities. Man as we know him is not understandable apart from his body.

The Genesis account further reveals that God made man flesh, but biologically differentiated that flesh. "Male and female he created them," the Scriptures state (Genesis 1:27). Man and woman were made for each other (Genesis 2:24). Both were made in the image of God. Their sexual distinction is assumed, not explained, in the Bible.

Genesis 1:27 indicates that sexuality was an intended part of human creation. It was intended as an aspect of human existence. It is fundamental to what it means to be a person. God made Adam and Eve man and woman, wrapping up in a male or female body intelligence, emotions, morality, and spirit reminiscent of Him. But whatever the final purpose of the body, this vehicle for the expression of human personality, it is still a body, made with the capacity for sexual function.

If sexual identity were merely a matter of genital stimulation and intercourse, man would be little different than the animals. But his sexuality is more than a matter of mere biology. He is born with a male or female body, but with no sense of established identity. That remains to be learned

5

during the socialization process that occurs from the time of birth. By the time a child reaches adolescence, he has begun to see himself as a man or a woman, not just a person with a male or female body. Self-image takes bodily form![1]

Essentially, then, man was made a creature with sexual identity. To deny one's sexuality is to refuse the order of creation. But to assume that man is nothing more than a sexual creature is to deny his uniqueness. Man is a total being: physical, emotional, moral. None exists by itself alone to the exclusion of the others. All are answerable to God.

We may conclude that sexuality is an expression of the total person. Overt sexual acts are acts of self-expression, indicators of personal identity.

A person of either sex grows into the wholeness of self-hood by fulfilling his own gender identity as male/female because wholeness is independent of sexual union.

Failure to accept this leads to three fundamental errors: (1) segregation of the sexes into higher and lower orders; (2) preoccupation with physical sex, i.e., intercourse; and/ or (3) feeling that sexuality is an extra, something apart from the total personality.

Ruel Howe correctly observed:

> One of the causes of our difficulties is that we have sought to find the meaning of sex through a limited conception of its nature. We have commonly thought of sex as a function among other functions that one could accept or reject, use or misuse without other than ethical, legal, and communal consequences. Though it is true that sex is a function, one among many, its true role is not to be found until we realize that as a function it does not have its full meaning in itself but

---

1. Chapter 5 develops this theme in greater detail.

6

in its relation to the *being* of which it is a part and expression. Sex as a function cannot be separated from the person of whom it is a part without destructive results.[2]

The fact that sexuality is an expression of the total person is what makes its physical expression beautiful for two people fully committed to each other, yet so devastating when expressed promiscuously. Sexual intercourse is more than mere stimulation of the genitals; it is affective as well as genital in nature. In the Bible, sexuality is always linked to fellowship and love (Genesis 1:28, 8:17, 9:1; Mark 10:7; Matthew 19:5; I Corinthians 6:16; Ephesians 5:31).

Man and woman were designed to complement each other (Genesis 2:18-24). Adam viewed the animals, taking the time to name them, but he found nothing to complement his basic nature. Search as he would, his social void could not be filled. Concluding that it was not good for man to be by himself as he was, God made woman, neither inferior nor superior to him, but to fulfill his needs. Dwight Small said, "Man had an appointed deficit. He was designed for community."[3]

Man and woman complement each other in four ways. The first is in the mutual awareness of their sexuality. "She shall be called woman," Adam exclaimed when he saw Eve (Genesis 2:23). The differences between man and woman were readily apparent. Yet those differences extend beyond genital sex to include everything two people become physically and emotionally.

---

2. Reul Howe, "A Pastoral Theology of Sex and Marriage," *Sex and Religion*, ed. Simon Doniger (New York: Association Press, 1953), p. 98.

3. Dwight Hervey Small, *Christian, Celebrate Your Sexuality*, (Old Tappan, New Jersey: FLeming H. Revell, 1974), p. 15.

Man and woman also complement each other in the personal partnership of marriage (Genesis 2:18, I Peter 3:7). Eve was created to be a helper for Adam. Today, the term "helper" often implies an inferior relating to a superior, but it had no such connotation in the Biblical record. To be a helper was to be a partner, a term that implies equality of personhood.

Man and woman further complement each other in sexual union (Genesis 2:24, I Corinthians 7:3-5). To become "one flesh" was to have sexual intercourse, consummating the marriage (Genesis 24:67). Sexual union is the most appropriate way of demonstrating physical complementarity.

Finally, man and woman complement each other in emotional intimacy (Genesis 2:24, Matthew 19:5-6). This intimacy is implied in the meaning of "one flesh." "Flesh," as we have seen, is more than mere uniting of bodies—it is the symbol of the whole person. Intimacy may not be defined merely in sexual terms. Rather, it includes the sharing of personalities.

God made man and woman individuals, yet with the need for community. "People who need people" was the beginning of a once-popular song. God knew that at the outset. People do need people, and He made man and woman to make up that social deficit. It is as true for celibates as it is for those who marry—the expression merely comes in different ways. The two sexes exist together for cooperation, friendship, teamwork, and/or marriage. Otto Piper observed:

> The limitation of mutual activities to members of one's own sex leads, in the long run, to the destruction of one's personality. The old maid, the old bachelor, the bachelor club, are types of crippled human existence. The reason they live so

joylessly and are so unproductive from the human point of view is not that they are unmarried, but rather that their manhood or womanhod is divorced from every relation to the other sex. This is proved by the fact that there are celibates who remain fully human in their old age because they are quite open and receptive towards the other sex.[4]

God gave both man and woman dominion over his creation (Genesis 1:27-28). Both were directly accountable to God (Genesis 5:1-2). Partnership implies equality—not necessarily of function (that is at least partially defined biologically), but of worth and dignity and responsibility. Both were made to relate to God and to each other.

Purposes Of Sexuality

God made man a sexual being. What, then, did He define as the purposes of sex?

The Bible identifies one purpose of sexuality as the formation of one flesh (Genesis 2:24). Sexual union is the irrevocable unity of two personalities. The Hebrew language contains no word for sex. Rather, it speaks of a man "knowing" his wife. Sapp observes: "Sexuality provides the opportunity for the most complete, most accurate, and most fulfilling knowledge of one another available to humans."[5] Through sexual intercourse one discovers the meaning of his own existence and of the meaning of being male and female.

Sex is a gift to marriage. It is an expression of who we

---

4. Otto Piper, *The Christian Interpretation of Sex* (London: Nisbet and Company, 1942), p. 96.

5. Stephen Sapp, *Sexuality, the Bible, and Science* (Philadelphia: Fortress Press, 1977), p. 21.

are. It is an affirmation of commitment and fidelity. It is symbolic of the total oneness that should occur in marriage. Sexual expression in marriage should carry with it the ecstasy of caring and sharing with one another as each partner plumbs the depths of the other's personality.

Sex also has a procreative purpose, even though that is by no means its sole, or even major, function (Genesis 1:28). (It was not until Augustine that sex was given a merely procreative context, an error that has been propagated by some religious groups through the years.)

Practically speaking, sexuality is a means by which the race may be continued. Through the sexual act and the process of reproduction, man is permitted to create new life. When that creative act is reasoned and expressed in love and caring with both partners accepting the responsibility inherent in it, it is a participation in the creative nature of God.

Conclusion

Sexual identity is intrinsically a part of an individual's self-understanding. Sexual identity cannot develop except in relation to its sexual opposite. Sexual interdependency is essential for that identity to grow.

The entire attitude of a person to his body is affected by his attitude toward his sexuality. It also affects his relationships with other persons. Greater or less confidence and frankness, mistrust, anxiety, all are affected by sexual attitudes. When sexual attitudes are transformed, then life is transformed.

Sigmund Freud developed a school of psychology around the thesis that sex is the basic life force. On the other hand, Erich Fromm, another imminent psychologist, insisted that it is no more than a physical need. But the Bible defies both

10

explanations by insisting that human sexuality cuts across all lines. It is physical—a matter of hormones and gonads. It is emotional, carrying with it feelings and felt needs. And it is spiritual, for two people fully committed to each other and to God use it to God's glory.

What, then, are the responsibilities of him who would accept his sexual identity and use it to God's glory?

1. Accept his personal worth as being made in the image of God.
2. Accept himself as a sexual creature, made so by God.
3. Preserve sexual integrity. Accept it as a gift.
4. Accept sexual partnership, that is, relational interdependence, whether married or not.
5. Maintain chastity, that virtue that integrates sexuality into one's life as a Christian, that is, using sexual identity rationally and responsibly, as a means to bring glory to God.

Summary Statements

1. God made man in His image.
2. God made man and woman.
3. God made man and woman sexual creatures to meet each others' needs.
4. God made man and woman sexual creatures to bring glory to Him.

FOR DISCUSSION

1. How does one's view of being made in God's image affect his sexual attitudes and conduct?
2. In what ways are a person's behavior affected by the knowledge that sex is a part of one's identity?
3. Do you agree or disagree with Ruel Howe's statement on pages 6 and 7? Why?

4. Why is it important for singles to accept their sexual identity for what it is?
5. Is the Biblical view of sexuality like or unlike what you have been taught? How?

REFERENCES

1. DeJong, Peter, and Wilson, Donald R. *Husband and Wife*. Grand Rapids: Zondervan, 1979.
2. Green, Zelma Bell. *Christian Male/Female Relationships*. Grand Rapids: Baker Book House, 1967.
3. Goergen, Donald, *The Sexual Celibate*. New York: Seabury Press, 1953.
4. Howe, Reul. "A Pastoral Theology of Sex and Marriage." *Sex and Religion*. Ed. Simon Doniger. New York: Association Press, 1953.
5. Howell, John. *Equality and Submission in Marriage*. Nashville: Broadman, 1979.
6. Jewett, Paul K. *Man as Male and Female*. Grand Rapids: Wm. B. Eerdmans, 1975.
7. Piper, Otto. *The Christian Interpretation of Sex*. London: Nisbet and Company, 1942.
8. Sapp, Stephen. *Sexuality, the Bible, and Science*. Philadelphia: Fortress Press, 1977.
9. Scanzoni, Letha, and Hardesty, Nancy. *All We're Meant to Be*. Waco, Texas: Word, 1974.
10. Small, Dwight Hervey. *Christian, Celebrate Your Sexuality*. Old Tappan, New Jersey: Fleming H. Revell, 1974.
11. White, Ernest, *Marriage and the Bible*. Nashville: Broadman, 1965.
12. Wood, Frederic C., Jr. *Sex and the New Morality*. New York: Association Press, 1968.

Chapter Two

MARRIAGE UNITED THEM: ONE FLESH

Marriage was made in heaven. It was conceived in the mind of God for divine purpose and with unique responsibilities. Yet, marriage is consummated and worked out on earth. Man and woman, both sinful creatures, are left with the arduous task of achieving their divine mutual purpose, as difficult as that proves to be at times. But even then, God has not left man without guidance. The Bible is replete with examples of and teachings about that most intimate of human relationships—marriage.

The Nature Of Christian Marriage

God-Ordained

The Bible begins with the creation account, an integral part of which was the establishment of the institution of marriage. It is clearly evident that God intended special purpose for the mutual relationship between Adam and Eve. He had a particular mission in mind for them. Marriage, then and now, functions best when it is governed by God.

The Genesis account makes it clear that God instituted marriage as a unique means of companionship (Genesis 2:18). After God had completed His creative work, Adam was yet without companionship. He was lonely. Yet, in looking over all of the creative panorama of God, he found nothing to satisfy his need. Nature nor cats nor dogs nor any other creature was adequate, for what he saw were but inanimate objects or animals who could not share with Adam in thinking or reasoning or feeling.

God, who created man for His companionship, sensed Adam's need, and He knew that only He could satisfy it. The Scripture says that God caused a deep sleep to come

13

over Adam after which He took one of Adam's ribs and made a woman (Genesis 2:21-22). That single creative act made another creature like Adam in feeling, thinking, and reasoning, yet wholly complementary to him biologically.

Biblically speaking, then, marriage is the blending and fusing of two persons (male and female) into a sharing, working unit that meets each other's mental, emotional, and physical needs. "For this reason a man will leave his father and mother and be united to his wife, and they will become one flesh," God declared in Genesis 2:24.

Social Contract

Christian marriage is a social contract. To enter into a contract is to assume legal responsibility and accountability for an agreement between two or more persons.

But marriage is also a social reality. It is a contract between families. Genesis 24:1-67 is a record of marriage as a link between families. Because of his own advanced age, Abraham sent his oldest, most trusted servant, Eliezer, to Mesopotamia to choose a wife for Isaac. Eliezer did as he was bid and negotiated a contract with Rebekah's father, Bethuel, and her brother, Laban. When the contract was made, Rebekah was free to go to Isaac (Genesis 24:51) and Bethuel received extravagant gifts in return (Genesis 24:53).

Such practices sound oddly old-fashioned in modern society where many individuals choose their mates with less discrimination than buying a new car, and often without parental involvement. Even so, Christians must recognize that they marry not only a person, but his family, even if the parents do not live nearby.

A person marries his partner's family whether he realizes it or not, for an individual's understanding of marriage—

its relationships and its permanence—has been shaped largely by his parents' understanding of marriage. His manner of relating to others is modeled to a large extent by his family.

I have a friend who has two sons-in-law whose parental families are not Christian. Nor are their values the same as those in my friends' home. For example, birthdays are major events in her home. But neither son-in-law had ever had a birthday party until after he was a part of his new family. Like it or not, my friend's daughters and their husbands married each other's families, and each couple had to forge a new family out of the values and forces that had shaped their lives.

I have another friend whose daughter married a young man from a rigid, if not legalistic, religious background that does not permit anyone outside its fellowship to participate in the Lord's Supper, and that insists that a person from another church group be immersed again to be a member. The young man's parents taught him that and practice it themselves. The young husband and wife thought it made no difference when they married, but it has, for in a real sense, they married each other's families.

It is inescapable: marriage, even in this day and age, is a contract between families. Most studies of divorce show that people of all ages who eventually dissolve their marriages are likely to be those who rejected the advice of parents and/or families not to marry a particular person.

But marriage is also a contract between persons. Through participation in a legal marriage ceremony, the Christian couple affirm their willingness to uphold the social good of the community of which they are a part. It is likewise a statement of their acceptance of legal, economic, and emotional responsibility for each other and for children born into that relationship. Marriage provides the framework of commitment within which two people confront life. Without that contract, it is easy for a person to resort to selfishness and self-protection.

Spiritual Covenant

But Christian marriage is more than a mere contract—it is also a spiritual covenant.

In the Bible, a covenant is a relationship of blessing based upon mutual responsibilities. For example, God would bless Israel, if she would obey Him. A covenant implies love and response. Marriage is indeed a covenant where there is mutual love and shared response.

Malachi 2:10-16 likens the marriage relationship to the relationship between man and God. He thundered God's judgment against a people who would not continue to respond to him in love.

In the Old Testament, God gave specific instructions to the Israelites regarding their marriages. These instructions were not to be taken lightly. They emphasize the fact that even in marriage, one demonstrates his covenant with God.

Israelites were to marry Israelites. Mixed marriages were not blessed, not so much because God was concerned about the mixture of the races, but because He insisted that a covenant person have nothing to distract him from his supreme purpose of being God's person. God, who made man in the first place, knew better than man himself that a faithless partner or a partner not in agreement spiritually is perhaps one's greatest hindrance to maintaining his own unwavering fidelity to his God-given life purposes.

This principle was demonstrated first when Abraham sent his servant back to Mesopotamia to find a wife for Isaac

(Genesis 24). The concern was that Isaac should have a wife who would, with him, serve Jehovah. The same principle is demonstrated in Genesis 28:1 when Isaac insisted that Jacob should not marry a Canaanite wife whose heart would surely be turned to the Canaanite gods. It was an issue once again when Nehemiah returned to Jerusalem (Nehemiah 13:23, 27), and when Ezra sought priestly reform in post-exilic Jerusalem (Ezra 10:1-15). God has always known that a man cannot serve God as effectively as he otherwise might if he has a divided allegiance.

God's concern for a couple united in serving Him did not diminish in the New Testament era. Paul, writing in II Corinthians 6:14, said, "Do not be mismated with unbelievers. For what partnership have righteousness and iniquity?" Earlier, he had instructed widows, "If the husband dies, she is free to be married to whom she wishes, only in the Lord" (I Corinthians 7:39).

Christians in this era need once again to re-examine the covenant nature of marriage. They need to enter into marriage with those who share their level of commitment to the Christian faith and who view Christian commitment and lifestyle similarly to them. To have a common faith is to provide a common perspective by which to view the victories and defeats, joys and disappointments of life. It is an integrating force to life. And, because they see their marriage as a microcosm of the relationship of God with His church, they continue to respond to each other in love, even when the journey becomes treacherous.

Commitment

Marriage is founded on commitment. Genesis 2:18, 24 demonstrates the commitment that is implicit in marriage.

17

A man is to leave his parents and cleave to his wife. He is to transfer his emotional interdependence from parents and be cemented to his wife. Howell suggests at least three commitments that are implicit in marriage.[1]

1. Marriage is a commitment to mutual need fulfillment. We receive in a marriage, but we are also under obligation to give. We must learn to communicate our needs, and we must seek ways to fulfill our partner's needs.
2. Marriage is a commitment to a continuing relationship. Marriage is to last, regardless of what the modern ethic or the divorce statistics say. Jesus was unequivocal in His assertion in Matthew 19 and Mark 10 that marriage is to last a lifetime. Perhaps not every marriage can survive, but far more could survive than do if both partners were fully committed to maintaining the relationship. It is only commitment that makes it possible to transcend quarreling, arguing, and other human imperfections to achieve God's purposes in life.
3. Marriage is a commitment to fulfilling role relationships. The notion of role in marriage involves the behavioral expectations that men and women have of themselves and of each other. These ideas are shaped by family, culture, and peer group. Such expectations must be eventually worked out and practiced by both partners.

Marriage Meets Needs

A Christian marriage is designed by God to meet specific needs. It is as those needs shape two people's responses toward each other and that two people constructively use their sexuality, that a marriage becomes in fact Christian.

Marriage is intended for *completion.* Genesis 2:18, 24 quotes God as saying, "It is not good for the man to be alone;

---

1. John Howell, *Equality and Submission in Marriage* (Nashville: Broadman Press, 1979).

I will make a helper suitable for him . . . For this reason a man will leave his father and mother and be united to his wife, and they will become one flesh." Marriage was designed for man and woman to complement (complete) each other in genuine fellowship of spirit resulting in incomparable, unparalleled intimacy.

Remember, however, that the key word is *completion*, not competition. Completion implies fellowship, companionship friendship. It suggests dependability, support, safety, trust.

A second need fulfilled in marriage is *consolation*. Genesis 2:18 states, "I will make a helper suitable for him." Consolation (helper) is used in the Bible not to suggest an inferior assisting a superior, but in the sense of encouragement and support. Each is to encourage and support the other.

The nature of any relationship is such that one person may be the recipient of encouragement at one time, but the giver at another point in time. No person is equally emotionally competent at every point in his life span. Sometimes he needs encouragement, but he can give it at other times. Much of the time, he may live on a reasonably even plane, allowing him to both give and take. Marriage is much the same. A married individual has the opportunity to lend and/or receive support in a natural relationship with his partner.

Marriage is also intended for *coition*, or sexual fulfillment. Sexuality is a gift to marriage, for it is through sexual intercourse that an inner union between the two persons can be forged. It is the expression of "one flesh" of Genesis 2:24.

When sexual union is described in Hebrew, the word used means "to know," suggesting that in sexual intercourse one discovers the depths of meaning of the other person. It is an act of the whole self which affects the whole self. It is this fact that makes unfaithfulness so devastating.

This union of "one flesh," described in Genesis 2:24 and pictured by sexual intercourse, by no means suggestss that a man loses his maleness nor a woman her femaleness, but it does express a new union. This union is reaffirmed with every repetition of intercourse. Therefore, union in "one flesh" is both established by intercourse and nourished by it, another powerful argument against extramarital sex.

The Bible speaks of the pleasures of sex as well as its procreative power. Proverbs 5:18-19 states, "Let your fountain be blessed, and rejoice in the wife of your youth, a lovely hind, a graceful doe. Let her affection fill you at all times with delight, be infatuated always with her love." The Song of Solomon further develops the idea that sexual activity brings supreme physical and emotional pleasure when it is expressed appropriately.

Indeed, coition does have a procreative function as well. Genesis 1:28 clarifies mankind's purpose: "Be fruitful and multiply, and fill the earth and subdue it . . ." Through the procreative function man shares in God's creative nature. But nowhere does the Bible ever suggest that sexual intercourse is *only* for, or even primarily for, procreation.

Paul expresses a strong negative notion about marriage in I Corinthians 7, due primarily to the crises of the time. In verse 2, he warns, "Because of the temptation to immorality, each man should have his own wife and each woman her own husband." The implication is that a person's sexuality is such a strong facet of his personality that it can easily usurp a man's will in order to get its own way. Later, in verse 5, Paul adds, to couples, "Do not refuse one another except perhaps by agreement for a season, that you may devote yourselves to prayer, but then may come together again, lest Satan tempt you through lack of self control."

There are two equally insidious errors in regard to sex that are perpetrated in contemporary society. One is to expect too little of it, that is, to see man as no more than an animal. But a second error is equally heretical—to expect too much from sex. Sex cannot bring total satisfaction by itself. Nor can it alone fully express mutual love. Mutual love comes in a genuine sharing of ourselves with our partner, only one facet of which is sex.

Marriage also meets man's need to *give* and *receive love*. But what kind of love?

Eros love is need love, love that seeks sensual expression. Most couples begin marriage with a maximum of eros and a minimum of other kinds of love. But after marriage eros attraction begins to diminish. No marriage can be sustained by eros love alone. Studies show that for most couples intense passion lasts from six to thirty months. If love is to last, then, it must move beyond eros to the level of friendship, or communication.

If, when eros recedes, friendship love remains at a low level, many couples ask, "Why did I marry? I'm not sure I ever loved him/her in the first place." But friendship love enhances eros love. It provides a basis for continuing the relationship.

Beyond friendship love stands the epitome of love—agape, love born of the will that seeks the highest good for its recipient. Only agape can keep a marriage going when eros and friendship are low, as they surely will be at times. It enriches both eros and friendship. But it is not a feeling that happens to you—it is something that is made to happen.

21

It is an act of commitment to the other. It is the kind of love that God desired for a marriage (see Ephesians 5:21-33). It is not love that sustains the marriage so much as it is the marriage that sustains love.

Marriage Requires Mutual Submission

Perhaps the most debated question among contemporaries revolves around the issue of roles and functions in marriage. Interestingly enough, it is the aspect of marriage about which the least is said in the Bible. But what is said is essential.

Ephesians 5:21-33 gives the clearest insight into the roles of marriage. Three principles are presented, one directed to the husband, one to the wife, and one to both husband and wife.

The first principle is a call to both husband and wife *to submit to each other because of their common love for Christ* (5:21). The word "submit" can be translated as "being subjected or being subordinate to a person or persons in authority." In Ephesians 5:21, this is a voluntary yielding in love, a perfectly appropriate translation. It is submission by one person to another because of loving relationships.

The demand for mutual self-giving was a revolutionary idea in social relationships in the first century. Women, slaves, and children were expected to be subordinate to superiors. But to expect men and women to accept each other on equal terms was a concept almost too radical to be believable. The idea extended further than marriage to parent-child, employer-employee, and friend-friend relationships.

The second principle in the passage is directed to the wife. She is to *voluntarily yield to her husband* (5:22-24,

22

Colossians 3:18, Titus 2:4-5). To voluntarily yield to his leadership suggests three responses:

1. She is to respect him as a responsible person. Notice that she is to give respect; he is not commanded to earn it.
2. She is to accept his Christian personhood. She responds in love and respect for who he is.
3. She is to love him. The word used for love is agape, the love of the will.

Then Paul directs his attention to the husband (Ephesians 5:25-31, Colossians 3:19, I Peter 3:7). He is *to love his wife as unselfishly as Christ did the church.* He is the leader in the marriage as Christ is the leader of the church. That leadership has to do with leading in obedience to the law of Christ. It has nothing to do with being boss. Nor does it designate superiority/inferiority. Such leadership is an impossibility without surrendering an autocratic spirit of domination over the wife. It requires active expression.

The husband must accept his wife's Christian personhood and encourage her to express her strength. In short, he expresses caring love (Ephesians 5:28-30). It is understanding love (I Peter 3:7).

How is all of this to affect marriage? Are not there some roles distinctly masculine and feminine? The Bible doesn't seem to indicate any distinctions beyond the biological which, of course, clearly delineates motherhood and fatherhood. It would appear that each couple is free to pursue its own style of mutual interdependence, influenced by parental models, personality and temperament characteristics, and personal experience. In Christ, couples are free to work out role relationships to meet their needs as long as the general principles of Ephesians are recognized and observed.

The implications for Christian marriage are profound:

1. Each person in a marriage is responsible to Christ in faith and personal responsibility in a way that cannot be mediated by the other.
2. Role distinctions can be and are made on the basis of male/female roles that the couple work out for themselves within the parameters established by Ephesians 5:21-31.
3. Decision-making is accomplished through mutual discussion (I Corinthians 13:5). However, in the case of an impasse, the husband is clearly the leader.
4. There is a possibility for conflict since role relationships are worked out in love for each other.

Conclusion

God instituted marriage, but He left it up to a man and a woman to complete that marriage successfully. Both a man and a woman bring everything they are in total sexual identity to the marriage. Together they share love and sex and joys and disappointments, becoming fused together as "one flesh," not just in the oneness of sexual intercourse, but the oneness of purpose and perspective, as well. Together they seek to serve their God who made them man and woman, so different biologically, so diverse emotionally and temperamentally, yet alike in their needs, both physical and emotional, and in their purpose for living. It is no wonder, then, that marriage is described by some as such sheer delight, yet by others as an incredibly difficult burden. In fact, it is at times both, as two people share in the journey of life together, remembering that "male and female God made them" to complete each other, to console one another, to sexually please each other, to give to and receive love from one another, and together to gorify God who made them male and female in the first place.

Summary Statements

1. God instituted marriage.
2. Marriage is a contract between persons and families.
3. Marriage is a covenant with God and between persons.
4. Marriage requires commitment for a lifetime.
5. Marriage is designed to meet man's needs for completion, consolation, coltion, and love.
6. Marriage is based upon the principle of mutual submission.
7. Sexuality is a gift to marriage.

FOR DISCUSSION

1. What difference does it make to a couple whether or not marriage is God-ordained?
2. Do you agree or disagree with the implications on page 14 of the fact that marriage is a contract? Why?
3. How important is agreement about Christian commitment to a marriage? What differences will its presence or absence make in decision-making and life-style?
4. Why is a proper understanding of one's sexuality, as described in Chapter 1, essential to a person's ability to give and/or receive sexually in marriage?
5. How does the principle of mutual submission affect decision-making in a marriage?

REFERENCES

1. DeJong, Peter and Wilson, Donald R. *Husband and Wife*. Grand Rapids: Zondervan, 1979.
2. Engelsma, David. *Marriage: The Mystery of Christ and the Church*. Grand Rapids: Reformed Free Publishing Association, 1975.
3. Howell, John C. *Equality and Submission in Marriage*. Nashville: Broadman Press, 1979.
4. Olthius, James H. *I Pledge You My Troth*. New York: Harper and Row, 1975.
5. Piper, Otto A. *The Christian Interpretation of Sex*. London: Nisbet and Company, 1942.
6. Small, Dwight Hervey. *Design for a Christian Marriage*. Old Tappan, New Jersey: Fleming H. Revell Company, 1974.
7. Sutherland, Joseph. "Coming to Terms," *The Lookout*. (October 5, 1980).
8. White, Ernest. *Marriage and the Bible*. Nashville: Broadman Press, 1965.
9. Wright, H. Norman. *The Pillars of Marriage*. Glendale, California: Regal Books, 1979.

Chapter Three

MARRIAGE: A PICTURE OF THE CHURCH

Marriage was made in heaven. The truth of that statement was validated in the last chapter. Marriage was made for two sexual creatures to be joined to each other in a new relationship. But marriage has a far more profound purpose than that—it was created to provide a day-by-day view of the nature of the church. It is indeed a mystery to believe that God has invested in marriage—our marriages—the symbolism of His relationship with His bride, the church. Nowhere is that so clearly demonstrated as in Ephesians 5:21-33. To understand the principle of the family as a microcosm of the church is to take on new meaning and purpose in our own lives.

The Goal—Unity

The theme of Ephesians is the unity of the church. Paul establishes the fact that the church, to be the church, must be at one with God:

Consequently, you are no longer foreigners and aliens, but fellow citizens with God's people and members of God's household, built on the foundation of the apostles and prophets, with Christ Jesus himself as the chief cornerstone. In Him the whole building is joined together and rises to become a holy temple in the Lord. And in him you too are being built together to become a dwelling in which God lives by his Spirit (Ephesians 2:19-22).

He concludes the first half of the letter by saying:

For this reason I kneel before the Father, from whom his whole family in heaven and on earth derives its name. I pray that out of his glorious riches he may strengthen you with power through his Spirit in your inner being, so that Christ my dwell in your hearts through faith. And I pray that you,

27

being rooted and established in love, may have power, together with all the saints, to grasp how wide and long and high and deep is the love of Christ, and to know the love that surpasses knowledge—that you may be filled to the measure of the fullness of God.

Now to him who is able to do immeasurably more than all we ask or imagine, according to his power that is at work within us, to him be glory in the church and in Christ Jesus throughout all generations, for ever and ever! Amen (Ephesians 3:14-21).

Paul then turns his attention to the practical implications of that unity. He insists that if the church is, in fact, in union with God, unity must be demonstrated in the practical affairs of life. The church is to practice unity (4:1-16). Individual Christians are to demonstrate their unity with God by their behavior (4:17—5:20). "Live as children of light," Paul urged (5:8). A marriage is also to demonstrate that same spirit of unity (5:22-33). So are family (6:14) and work relationships (6:5-9). It is essential to understand marriage in this context.

A Principle for Unity

Just as the church is to be unified under one leader, so is a marriage. The church, to be the church, must take its directions from one source—Jesus Christ. For a marriage to be a Christian marriage, it too must find two partners united under one leader—Jesus. At the same time, for the marriage to function practically, certain guidelines must be followed for it to proceed in the direction God intends.

The basic principle for unity is stated in Ephesians 5:21: "Submit to one another out of reverence for Christ." It applies to a person's interpersonal relationships both within and outside of marriage.

The word used in the original language (*hupotasso*) means literally "to place under." The word in Ephesians 5:21 is a middle voice participle, indicating that 5:21 is a connective, linking the foregoing section with what is to follow. The middle voice should be translated "place yourself under," implying an action done *by* a person, not *to* him.

The picture in the phrase "be subject to one another" is that of a soldier who is no longer an individual, but a part of a whole. A man in the military forfeits *his rights*. The Christian is to view his life in the same way: he ceases to think primarily of his right.

A wife is to place herself under the authority of her husband; the husband is to place himself under the authority of his wife. That is, both are to be committed to each other to meet each other's needs and to share together in demonstrating the unity of the church through their mutual relationship.

Individually, then, we are to place ourselves at the disposal of Christ not to do what we want, but to do what glorifies Him. That then must clearly affect *who* we marry—not just a good person, but one whose absolute commitment is to emulate Christ in every detail. In marriage we place ourselves at the disposal of each other to provide for the needs of the other while together we place ourselves at Christ's bidding to bring glory to Him through our marriage.

Ephesians 5:21 is written to people who are agreed about doctrine. Paul assumes that submission is based on doctrinal unity. He assumes that a Christian marriage occurs only when both people agree doctrinally and submit mutually. Anything other is a marriage, but not an accurate microcosm of the church.

The principle of mutual submission is not at all easy to live out. It is most demanding. It means that to marry should motivate us to choose to commit ourselves to a person who is as intent as we are to place ourselves under Christ's leadership. Although we are never excused from observing the principle, whatever the circumstances of our marriage, it is to make the task immeasurably more difficult if we select a partner whose highest motivation does not reach to the point of full submission to Christ. A person whose every facet of life is not committed to honoring God finds it impossible to measure up to the task of placing himself in submission to the needs of another.

An individual who has placed himself under Christ's leadership has learned to deny self for the benefit of Christ. He can interrupt his schedule, give up comfort or money or prestige, and endure a few hardships for the purpose of bringing glory to God. Similarly, two people committed to each other can tolerate inadequacies and inconveniences in order to bring glory to God through their marriage. Their example must be that of Christ described by Paul in Philippians 2:5-8.

> Your attitude should be the same as that of Christ Jesus: who, being in very nature God, did not consider equality with God something to be grasped, but made himself nothing, taking the very nature of a servant, being made in human likeness. And being found in appearance as a man, he humbled himself and became obedient to death—even death on a cross (Philippians 2:5-8).

Two people—one male, the other female—both equal in God's sight choose to commit themselves to each other because they are committed to Christ. But in spite of their individual equality, they choose to take the nature of a servant to each other.

Short of this underlying principle, marriage is bound to fail. Apart from it, neither husband nor wife can possibly fully carry out the roles assigned to them by God Himself. The remainder of Ephesians 5 shows how to enflesh this principle.

The reason that a Christian assumes a lifestyle of placing himself under the authority of others is stated in 5:21: "out of reverence for Christ." He does it because Christ taught him to do so. He does it to show his gratitude to God. He does it to avoid disappointing Him who loved us. He does it to avoid the judgment that is certain to come.

Roles In Marriage

Roles of a Wife

Once Paul has firmly established the principle of mutual submission, he proceeds to identify the roles of wives and husbands. His attention is directed first to wives when he tersely directs:

> Wives, submit to your husbands as to the Lord. For the husband is the head of the wife as Christ is the head of the church his body, of which he is the Savior. Now as the church submits to Christ, so also wives should submit to their husbands in everything (Ephesians 5:22-23).

That role of submission is a fighting word in contemporary society. Feminists rebel at the idea of being in submission to anyone. But they, and others like them, fail to recognize the meaning or purpose of the principle, for the word submit here, as in verse 21, means to put oneself voluntarily under the leadership of another.

In no way does submission suggest inferiority or slavery. Nor should the Scripture be made to read, "Wives, submit

31

yourselves unto your own husbands in exactly the same way you submit yourselves to the Lord." Rather, it could read, "Wives, submit yourselves unto your own husbands because it is an expression of your submission to the Lord."

Paul makes it clear that the wife's attitude is a picture of the church. As the church is to place itself under the authority of Christ, so she is to repeat that picture in the home by placing herself under the authority of her husband. (That is one reason why a Christian woman should never marry a man who cannot emulate Christ's relationships with the church in his relationships with her.)

What practical results does this principle call forth? In what areas does a woman put herself under her husband's authority?

The first practical result is that *she respects him as a man*. To respect him is to turn to him for physical, mental, spiritual, and emotional protection and guidance. That is not to suggest that she can have no other friends or sources of counsel, but it is to insist that *no man* except Christ be more important to her than her husband. That includes Bible teachers, both men and women, relatives, particularly parents, and friends. More than one marriage has failed to meet the Biblical standard because a woman listened more carefully to her father or a friend than to her husband.

To respect a man is to make oneself financially interdependent with him. A too-common fallacy is for a woman to regard her income as hers to do with what she chooses. (That is a mistake for either partner.) Instead, it is "our" money, not "mine" and "his."

To respect a man is to support his decisions. If, after discussion and mutual consideration of a decision that must be made, he decides differently than what she would have, she still has the responsibility to support and encourage him in it. Never can she bide her time just waiting for a bad outcome so she can say, "I told you soñ" Neither is she to review past failures in an effort to build her own position. She is to wisely appeal for her own opinion or desired action, then give him room to fail. It is all part of demonstrating the unity of the church.

The second practical result is that a wife *will accept her husband as her leader.* To do so is never to act independently of him nor to act before him. It is to voice confidence that God is working through him. It is to be loyal to him even when mistakes are made and pressures increase. It is to be patient during times of stress and to show enthusiasm for his achievements. It is to listen when he talks. It is to accept and please him.

The most practical outcome is to *make a home for him.* A person's home is a symbol of protection and security. This is not to say that a husband cannot share in the ongoing responsibilities of homemaking, especially if she works too, but it is to say that she is responsible for making a home a pleasant place to be. Her spirit sets the atmosphere of the home.

A wife must also *be a person of whom her husband can be proud.* Although she need not be a fashion queen nor a beauty model, she must be aware of her appearance. A woman's appearance reflects her real feelings about herself. Few, if any, men will be proud of a slovenly woman whose body, hair, and clothes reek of an "I don't care about me" message.

But a woman is also to make her husband proud of her through her character and attitudes. The writer of Proverbs states the principle from a negative perspective: "A quarrelsome wife is like a constant dripping" (Proverbs 19:13b). Peter instructed:

Your beauty should not come from outward adornment, such as braided hair and the wearing of gold jewelry and fine clothes. Instead, it should be that of your inner self, the unfading beauty of a gentle and quiet spirit, which is of great worth in God's sight (I Peter 3:3-4).

A meek and gentle spirit is one under control for use for the right purposes. It surely does not imply passivity, but it is a spirit that conquers fear and worry. She is to communicate acceptance, encouragement, kindness, understanding, and gratitude. Such character traits can overcome a husband's resistance and inconsideration. But under any circumstance they designate a woman who is seeking to make her marriage what God would have it to be.

One last question remains: How is a wife to interpret "in everything"? (Eph. 5:24). Two guidelines temper the "in everything" imperative. First, a woman is not to act against her conscience. (Conscience must be distinguished from opinion, however.) Neither is "in everything" to interfere with her relationship to Christ. The directives to the Roman Christians in Romans 14:13, 19, 22-23 apply to the marriage relationship as well.

A woman who fulfills these roles effectively is indeed one who can be called blessed by her husband and family. The secret of real femininity is found in these guidelines.

Roles of a Husband

The role of a husband is clearly defined: he is to love his wife as Christ loved the church (Ephesians 5:25, Colossians 3:18). No man can fulfill this role short of being a Christian and fulfilling the guideline set forth in Ephesians 5:21 to learn the art of mutual submission. For a man to fully emulate Christ, he must learn to set aside his rights in order to do the will of God. He must see his leadership role in the marriage as Christ saw His in the church when Philippians 2:7 states that He "made himself nothing, taking the very nature of a servant . . ."

How is a man to love as Christ did? First, he must love *realistically*. That demands more than mere romantic sentiment. Ephesians 2:1-10 describes man's alienation from God, his disobedience, his sure doom. In no way was man sentimentally desirable. But Christ loved men anyway— enough to die on their behalf. A husband is to love his wife in precisely the same manner: he is to look beyond her deficiencies to her potential.

A husband loves *sacrificially* (5:25-27), just as Christ loved the church. Jesus sacrificed the glories of heaven to be among men. He gave himself willingly (John 3:16). A man loves his wife in the same way. He is willing to sacrifice personal desires, economic resources, time, and/or personal interests for *her*.

A man is also to love his wife *purposefully*. Christ loved the church in that way (Ephesians 5:26-27). His purpose was to set the church apart, to cleanse her, to present her to God. A man must purposefully love his wife—for the same reasons and in the same way that Christ loved the church.

A Christian husband must realize that his wife is part of himself (5:28). He is to see his wife as a partner—and more. All of his thinking must include her. His goals must consider her. His routine activities must take her into account. In short, what a man's body is to his personality, his wife should be to him as well. She is not to be abused, neglected, or taken for granted, but loved, cherished, and protected.

What are the practical consequences of a man loving his wife in the same way Christ loved the church? How will

35

these principles affect a man's behavior?

A husband is to *provide a spiritual example to his wife and family.* It is his responsibility to emulate Christ and provide Christ's example in family functioning. (Some women are forced to assume this role because their husbands have abdicated it.) This is never tyrannical leadership nor spiritual dictatorship. But it is to seek the Lord and His ways so fervently that she be motivated to follow.

A man is to *make his wife feel special.* Telling her that she is cherished is inadequate; she must see it in demonstration. The tendency of a man is to seek and demonstrate success, but fail to be transparent in weaknesses and areas of need. A wife must know that only she is able to meet his deepest physical, emotional, and spiritual needs and can share in his finest successes.

To cherish a wife is to see so great a value in her as a person that a husband wants to protect her and praise her to others. This is important to her. She needs to hear her husband recite the character qualities and personality traits that attracted him to her in the first place.

A man is also to *protect his wife.* A woman's emotional security is based on the assurance that she is valued and protected. That protection extends to a man's observance of schedules and standards in the home. Any emergency departure must be temporary. He should protect her dignity. She should never be "cut down" before others nor ridiculed in the presence of outsiders. He must encourage her to develop her own unique gifts.

A Christian husband must *plan and provide for intimate conversation with his wife.* She needs to talk, especially if she is at home with children all day, every day. Half listening or hurried listening will never suffice. A man must make it easy for a woman to share her deepest needs and emotions. She remembers his attentiveness before marriage and longs for the same attention now.

A man's greatest manliness is demonstrated when he becomes a man walking in the steps of Christ and demonstrating the mind of Christ in his relationship with his wife.

The Unequally Yoked

The Biblical teaching regarding marriage, a picture of the church, is clearly delineated. But to apply that teaching is difficult for a sizable segment of population, for they are unequally yoked. They are married to partners who are unbelievers, weak spiritually, or at odds doctrinally. What are their roles in such a case?

To be permanently unequally yoked is the plight of many Christians. More than a few are burdened with spiritual responsibility in a union with a mate who shares neither their joy of salvation nor their goals for life. These unequal yokes may occur in one of four ways:[2]

1. Two unbelievers marry and one of them later becomes a Christian. There is no disobedience involved.
2. A Christian marries an unbeliever, thinking the mate is a believer when, in fact, he is not. Many go to church, even read the Bible, yet are unconverted. The Christian must accept responsibility for failing to probe the deeper issues of his mate's personal relationship to Christ.
3. Ignorance of Biblical principles. Some people have not been taught not to marry someone who does not live by faith in Jesus Christ.

---

2. Jo Berry, "Does Your Husband Need Jesus?," *Christianity Today* (February 20, 1981), pp. 28-31.

4. Willful disobedience of II Corinthians 6:14: "Do not be yoked together with unbelievers." There is no escaping the fact that sin is involved, although, of course, it can be forgiven.

It is a heartbreaking position for either a man or a woman to be a committed follower of Jesus without his partner's cooperative sharing in the joy of salvation or the pleasure of service. Unequally yoked people are limited in freedom of time and movement. They and their partners may differ radically in lifestyle, causing added pressures to the marriage. They often carry guilt for unwise choices and extreme care for their partner's spiritual condition.

Women married to unbelievers or weak Christians have to assume spiritual leadership by default. Many of these men are good husbands, of course, but never can they genuinely cherish and nourish their wives as Christ did the church (Ephesians 5:29). It is a significant dilemma for a Christian woman.

But it is no less a dilemma for a man with an unbelieving or spiritually weak wife. He can set an example, but he cannot make his wife follow. The dilemma is particularly critical in the area of parenting: parenting, with no spiritual support from the wife, is most difficult. The mother is a motivator and planner and sets the emotional climate of the home. The children frequently reflect her attitudes.

Regardless of the difficulties, the Christian is called to act out the principles for marriage in the best way he can. Spiritual insensitivity is no basis for severing a marriage. Paul wrote:

> If any man has a wife who is not a believer and she is willing to live with him, he must not divorce her. And if a woman

has a husband who is not a believer and he is willing to live with her, she must not divorce him . . . But if the unbeliever leaves, let him do so. A believing man or woman is not bound in such circumstances; God has called us to live in peace. How do you know, wife, whether you will save your husband? Or, how do you know husband, whether you will save your wife? (I Corinthians 7:12-13, 15-16).

Peter gave the same advice:

Wives, in the same way be submissive to your husbands so that, if any of them do not believe the word, they may be won over without talk by the behavior of their wives, when they see the purity and reverence of your lives (I Peter 3:1-2).

A Christian woman is surely outside God's will when she nags, acts independently, delivers ultimatums, deceives, even if her partner is a non-Christian or weaker than she spiritually. She still must respect her husband as an individual, treating him with kindness and consideration. Neither is a Christian husband to lord it over his non-Christian or spiritually weak wife. Rather, he is to maintain a powerful silent witness.

It is indeed a hard task for a Christian to be unequally yoked. He should not have made the decision in the first place. But even so, it is the Christian's responsibility to do everything humanly possible to fulfill the roles God assigned to him. Then, when it is humanly impossible, he turns to God whose grace is sufficient to empower him.

Conclusion

Marriage for Christians *is not* the same as it is for everyone else. Certainly, it resembles that of non-Christians in that it is the union of a man and a woman. Both Christians and non-Christians enjoy sexual expression. Both experience the ups and downs of a human relationship. Both find emotional satisfaction. But marriage for the Christian is more than that. Christians have an ideal to reach—they are to act out the very nature of the church as they fulfill their roles. Their ultimate purpose is to demonstrate God's relationship with the church and to bring glory to God.

Summary Statements

1. The goal of Christians is to glorify God.
2. The goal of Christian marriage is to glorify God.
3. Marriage is an indissolvable covenant, an exclusive fellowship between two persons.
4. The basic principle for unity in the Christian life, including marriage, is stated in Ephesians 5:21: "Submit to one another out of reverence for Christ."
5. The basic role of a wife is to place herself under the leadership of her husband.
6. The basic role of a husband is to love his wife as Christ loved the church.
7. The Christian married to an unbeliever is responsible to embody the principles of marriage outlined in Ephesians 5, even though that is a difficult task.

FOR DISCUSSION

1. How does understanding the theme of Ephesians clarify our understanding of the importance of the roles of husband and wife in marriage?
2. What are the practical results in a marriage if Ephesians 5:21 is observed by both husband and wife?

3. What motivates a Christian to take on the lifestyle described in Ephesians 5:21-33?
4. What are the roles of a wife in a marriage? How can these be practically applied?
6. What advice can be given to a person who is unequally yoked?

REFERENCES

1. Berry, Jo, "Does Your Husband Need Jesus?," *Christianity Today* (February 20, 1981).
2. Lloyd-Jones, D.M. *Life in the Spirit*, Grand Rapids: Baker Book House, 1973.
3. Staton, Julia, *What the Bible Says About Women*. Joplin, Missouri: College Press, 1980.
4. White, Ernest, *Marriage and the Bible*, Nashville: Broadman Press, 1965.

Chapter Four

SIN DIVIDED THEM: MAN VS. WOMAN

Man's idyllic existence was not to last. Man and woman, husband and wife, dwelled in Eden reveling in the presence of each other, each exploring the uniqueness of the other, sharing in community, enjoying themselves as sexual creatures in fellowship with each other and with God. Their perfect bliss might have lasted forever—but man's stubborn will interrupted. Insistent that they knew more than God and that their way was *the* way to live, Adam and Eve shook their puny fists at God and demanded their way. At that very moment when Adam and Eve believed Satan instead of God, they gave in to their misdirected pride—and sin became a reality.

Response to Sin

Sin—the belief and action that man is superior to God's judgment—totally disrupted the serenity and idyllism of a perfect creation. Never again on this earth—not until the new heaven and earth—would the puzzle be put back together in its totality. Certainly redemption in Jesus Christ restores man's potential for perfection (maturity), but that will not be completed this side of heaven.

The results of the intrusion of sin into the world were indeed devastating, evident from the very moment of the beginning of sin. Even before God pronounced the outcomes of their disobedient behavior, Adam and Eve demonstrated guilt. And that guilt was evident in their response to their sexuality.

Before sin, Adam and Eve lived in Eden, evidently existing there in nakedness. But they were perfect and nakedness was nothing to hide, for sexuality was used for its intended purpose. But Genesis 3:7 records: "Then the eyes of both of them were opened, and they realized that they were naked, so they sewed fig leaves together and made coverings for themselves." Shame was now a part of man's nature—it continues to be to this day.

Adam and Eve further expressed their guilt and shame as it related to their sexuality. Genesis 3:8-11 records:

> Then the man and his wife heard the sound of the Lord God as he was walking in the garden in the cool of the day, and they hid from the Lord God among the trees of the garden. But, the Lord God called to the man, "Where are you?"
>
> He answered, "I heard you in the garden, and I was afraid because I was naked, so I hid myself."
>
> And He said, "Who told you that you were naked? Have you eaten from the tree that I commanded you not to eat from?"

Adam's response to God's question is a clear declaration of the newborn enmity between persons, especially between men and women. Rather than Adam and Eve's previous sense of community and common goals and working together, both now engaged in a game of scapegoating and one-upmanship. Although God's original design for marriage was still the same, never again would it be perfect, for Adam said: "The woman you put here with me—she gave me some fruit from the tree, and I ate" (Genesis 3:12). Nor would woman assume responsibility either. She too passed the buck: "The serpent deceived me, and I ate" (Genesis 3:13). The so-called battle of the sexes was on!

Consequences of Sin

The consequences of sin were quickly pronounced by God. Scapegoating could not deter a just God from declaring the results with which man had to cope. Those consequences disrupted four relationships.

Alienation from God

Adam and Eve experienced alienation from God, even before He pronounced it, for they refused to face God when He came to them in the garden (3:8). Even when God called to them, Adam and Eve acknowledged their shame (3:11) and refused to take personal responsibility when they were questioned by God (3:12-13). But that alienation was sealed when God, fearing that man would eat from the tree of life and live forever as a sinful being, cast them out of Eden, allowing them no possibility to return and permitting the reality of physical death (3:22-24).

To this day, man carries the marks of sin. Every man is a sinner (Romans 3:21-23), totally separated from God, having no means of his own to bridge the gap.

But God, being God, was not to leave man defenseless in his newly hostile world. Even in Eden, He set into motion a means for the chasm to be spanned. In His condemnation of the serpent (Satan), He gave a hint to the future when He said, "I will put enmity between you and the woman, and between your offspring and hers; He will bruise you on the head, and you will strike his heel" (Genesis 3:15). The whole of the Old Testament is a witness to the redeeming activity of God. That one who crushed Satan's head was Jesus Christ (Romans 5:12-19).

Alienation from Nature

Not only was man separated from God, he was also alienated from nature. No longer was it a perfect world. God announced to Adam:

> Cursed is the ground because of you; through painful toil
> you will eat of it all the days of your life. It will produce thorns
> and thistles for you; and you will eat the plants of the field.
> By the sweat of your brow you will eat your food until you
> return to the ground, since from it you were taken; for dust
> you are and to dust you will return (Genesis 3:17-19).

No longer was nature man's ally; it was to be hostile to
him. Only through toil was man to subdue nature. Only by
hard labor could man till and keep the earth, as God had
directed him from the beginning of creation. Never again,
until the new heaven and earth, would man find nature
cooperative.

Many of the Old Testament prophets pictured the New
Jerusalem in terms of the reconciliation of man and nature.
For example, Isaiah declared:

> Behold, I will create new heavens and a new earth. The
> former things will not be remembered, nor will they come to
> mind. I will rejoice over Jerusalem, and take delight in My
> people; and the sound of weeping and the sound of crying
> will be heard in it no more. Never again will there be in it
> an infant that lives but a few days, or an old man who does
> not live out his years . . . The wolf and the lamb will feed
> together, and the lion will eat straw like the ox; but dust will
> be the serpent's food (Isaiah 65:17, 19-20, 25).

Alienation from Self

Man also became alienated from himself. Without God,
life degenerates into a purposeless trek to nowhere. He was
no longer able to accept personal responsibility for his actions.
He began to scapegoat, attributing his behavior to something
or someone outside himself. "The woman you put here to
be with me," Adam insisted. "The serpent deceived me,"

the woman lamented. Neither person was willing to say, "It was my fault."

From that day to this, man has been plagued by guilt and fear, by psychological game playing, by projection of responsibility to others, by inability to consistently handle his desires and emotions. Psychological disintegration became —and remains—a reality.

Only when a person finds maturity in Jesus Christ will he overcome the psychological disintegration set loose in Eden. He must admit his personal guilt for sin and depend upon Jesus Christ (Romans 10:8-13). He will be prepared to live in the New Jerusalem where he will abide in absolute harmony with self and with God (Revelation 22:3-5, 14).

Alienation from Others
Man's disharmony with himself resulted in a serious disruption of his relationship with others. Although after Eden the disharmony extended to man's relationships with both men and women, the interesting aspect for our study is the chasm created between man and woman. It began with Adam's blaming Eve and was completed by God's pronouncement to Eve.

Adam began to project blame to Eve, even though he was as clearly guilty as she. From that day to this, men and woman tend to absolve themselves of responsibility and blame someone else. This is infinitely more so in man's relationship with woman than in nearly any other relationship, perhaps because it is such an intimate union. Husband and wife, who can know each other more intimately than they can know any other, find their relationship marred by sinful responses.

God's announcement to Eve clearly affected her sexuality. "I will greatly increase your pains in childbearing; with pain

46

you will give birth to children," He instructed her (Genesis 3:16). Her womanness was definitely affected.

Note, however, that God did not alter Eve's function: at the beginning she had been instructed to populate the earth. That she was still to do. But that function was to carry with it a real reminder of the reality of sin, for childbirth, as much as she still desired it and planned for it, was to be completed in pain, a pain that would not have been had sin not affected her sexuality.

But sexuality was affected in another way. In spite of the pain experienced in childbirth, a woman would experience desire for her husband. Sexuality, originally intended to express and demonstrate unity, lost its original form. Thielicke observes,

> "Whereas originally its purpose, in conformity with the common origin of both man and woman, was to maintain its original unity and make them 'one flesh' (Genesis 1:24), now it is promised that the sexes will be 'against' each other and the question is who shall triumph and who shall be subjugated."[1]

The result was that structure now had to be imposed upon the husband-wife relationship, for no longer could it be assumed that both were seeking common goals. That is why God announced, "He will rule over you" (Genesis 3:16). Again Thielicke observes, "In this context (16-19) the fact that one shall 'rule' over the other is not an imperative order of creation, but rather the element of disorder that disturbs the original peace of creation . . ."[2] Some means of ordering the marriage relationship was essential.

---

1. Helmut Thielicke, *The Ethics of Sex* (New York: Harper and Row, 1964), p. 8.
2. *Ibid.*

Judaism, although the repository of God's dealings with man, still demonstrated the disrupted relationships between men and women. Isolated statements praise women, but the general attitude presented a picture of a disturbed order. It was Judaism that banned man from conversing with a woman, that proclaimed blessings to those whose children were male and woe to those whose offspring were female, that described women as greedy eaters, indolent, jealous, and frivolous. It was a Jewish man who would pray, thanking God that he was created neither a Gentile nor a woman.

Jesus' attitude toward women was revolutionary then, for He dared to talk to a woman (John 4:1-7), healed women (Matthew 15:21, 8:14, e.g.), appeared to women when he had been resurrected (Matthew 28:1ff., Mark 16:1ff., Luke 24:10, John 20:1ff.), and dealt mercifully with an adulteress (John 8:1-11). He treated women as equals, looking beyond the Fall and recalling God's original intentions.

Paul is often accused of male chauvinism because of his statements in I Corinthians 11:1-15. In 11:3, he describes man as the head of the woman. He proceeds to argue that in worship man should have his head uncovered and a woman should cover hers.

What does Paul mean by 'nature' in 11:14? Is it an order of creation? Or could it be social custom? Most likely, he meant social custom, not an order of creation. Social differences between men and women exist in every culture, but these differences do not imply theological differences of personal responsibility before God. Thielicke observes:

> In summary we may say that here Paul is not making a conservative judgment sociologically but a revolutionary judgment theologically, for certainly the equal status of the sexes before God was in contradiction to the social customs of the

times. The double intention which he here pursues is directed against the fanatical, "eschatologistic" leveling of the sexes as well as the orthodox Jewish differentiation of the sexes.[3]

Thielicke further observes in regard to headship in Ephesians 5:21:

The statement that the man is the head of the woman—which has reference only to the *married* woman and therefore contains no sociological statement concerning the status of women—is inserted in a more general framework, namely, in the commandment to 'be subject to one another,' and to be so 'in the fear of Christ.'[4]

Conclusion

Sexuality was inevitably affected by sin as we have seen. Relationships, once perfect, were disrupted. But in the order of redemption men are called back to the original design of creation. Both man and woman stand equally before God. In Christ there is no male and female (Galatians 3:27-28). Even so, there is a structure given to male-female relationships in marriage: he is 'head,' she is follower, but now to show forth the very nature of the church. And the basic facts of the Fall remain with us: she does experience pain in childbirth, yet she does desire her husband. He sometimes misuses his headship. And together they must strive for a new order in Christ.

Sin totally and catastrophically upset the perfection of Eden. No part of man's existence was to be spared. Adam and Eve were separated from God. They were set at odds

---

3. *Ibid.*, p. 11.
4. *Ibid,* p. 12.

with nature. They experienced personal disintegration. To these disrupted relationships was added the alteration of man-woman relationships, a result that affected the structure of marriage and the sexuality of those involved in that marriage. From Eden to now, man's sexuality has been clearly affected by these four troubled relationships. From now until redemption is completed in heaven, his sexuality will continue to be affected. Then when he is completed in Christ Jesus, he will take on a new heavenly body which will be neither male nor female, and he will take his place worshiping God forever and ever, as he was intended to do from the beginning.

Summary Statements

1. Sin affected sexuality.
2. The consequences of sin are fourfold: alienation from God, alienation from nature, alienation from self, and alientation from others.
3. Enmity between persons affected the relationship be-between a man and a woman in a marriage.

FOR DISCUSSION

1. How did Adam and Eve's first actions after the Fall demonstrate that their sexuality was affected?
2. Considering the four disrupted relationships resulting from the intrusion of sin, give specific examples of how each is demonstrated in man's subsequent sexuality.
3. How would your sexual identity differ had it not been for sin?

4. How should your sexual identity be affected if you are experiencing new life in Jesus Christ?

REFERENCES

1. Scanzoni, Letha and Nancy Hardesty. *All We're Meant To Be*. Waco, Texas: Word, 1974.
2. Schaeffer, Francis. *Genesis in Space and Time*. Downer's Grove, Illinois: InterVarsity Press, 1972.
3. Small, Dwight. *Christian, Celebrate Your Sexuality*. Old Tappan, New Jersey: Fleming H. Revell, 1974.
4. Thielicke, Helmut. *The Ethics of Sex*. New York: Harper and Row, 1964.

Chapter Five

HOW SEXUAL IDENTITY DEVELOPS

"Boys will be boys." We are accustomed to that saying and would probably also agree with the other side of the coin: girls will be girls. But the question that either statement raises is this: How do boys learn to be boys and how do girls learn to be girls?

It is this question to which this chapter is addressed. Although the Bible does not deal specifically with the answer, it does contain some hints to assist parents in childrearing.

Components of Sexual Identity

Psychological literature and developmental research have spent considerable time and money to get a picture of how a person develops sexually. The Bible, on the other hand, says little, although not surprisingly, for the Bible is not a detailed scientific explanation, but a book describing the activity of God. Then what are the components of sexual identity? How is it learned? Psychological literature speaks of at least four components that make up the totality of one's sexuality.

Gender

A person's biological morphology is genetically determined. Therefore, much of a person's development can be explained biologically. Yet almost every developmental text asserts that being born a male or a female in no way comprises everything that society identifies as masculine or feminine. Even so, a couple eagerly awaits the arrival of its offspring, often referring to the baby as "It" until the newborn takes on a male or female gender. Very soon afterwards, baby is dubbed with a name appropriate for the gender. (Those

52

children whose names are inappropriate for their gender often experience unbearable teasing.) And right away, mother and father set out treating this tiny person as male or female, as the case may be, in keeping with the expectations of their effective culture.

Gender Identity

Children become aware of their gender identity quite early, perhaps as early as two years of age. This is to say that they know that there are anatomical differences between boys and girls and they have acquired a stereotyped set of male/female behaviors. Gender identity continues to develop throughout the childhood years and seems to be reasonably well set by adolescence.

Sex Role

A third component of sexuality is an individual's sex role. It is a behavioral concomitant of gender identity. An individual becomes aware of sexual differences and sex-appropriate behaviors. Then he must develop his own sex-appropriate behaviors. That is a tall order, far easier to write about than to do.

Sex role acquisition begins early in life. As early as two or three years of age, children begin to identify with the behaviors of those with the same gender identity as they. Little boys begin to imitate their fathers' behaviors; girls, their mothers.

Lamb insists that the father is the key to sex role development, either masculine or feminine.[1] This assertion comes close to the several Biblical references to the father's influence

---

1. Michael E. Lamb (ed.), *The Role of the Father in Child Development* (New York: John Wiley and Sons, 1976), pp. 122-44.

in transmitting values.[2] It is not at all difficult to believe that fathers are essential to the sex role identification process since the Bible makes it clear that fathers are to be the spiritual leaders of a home.[3]

Sexual Orientation

A fourth component of sexual development is sexual orientation. The roots are planted in early childhood, but the final step toward sexual orientation occurs in the adolescent and adult years when an individual works out his personal pattern of relating to the sexes. The normal procedure is for males and females to relate to each other sexually, although that pattern sometimes goes awry.

How Sexual Identity Develops

The components of a person's sexuality are relatively simple to understand. But the situation is far more complex when it comes to explaining *how* this development occurs. Far too many questions remain unanswered. However, current findings lend some insights to Christian parents.

A child is born male or female. All things proceeding equally, the baby will grow to maturity able to function sexually as a man or a woman, as the case may be. But by no means is the infant yet a man or a woman, psychologically or biologically.

As soon as parents greet a newborn, they also begin to treat him as a boy or a girl. Boys are given balls and cars and baseball gloves. Girls are dressed in frills and ribbons. The socialization process is interjected with directives like:

2. See Deuteronomy 6:4-9, Ephesians 6:4, and Colossians 3:21.
3. See Ephesians 5:23, Deuteronomy 6:4-9, and Ephesians 6:4.

"Be Daddy's little man," "Boys don't cry," "Girls must be courteous," and other culturally-laden expectations for appropriate sex role behavior.[4]

As has been previously noted, a child becomes aware of his sexual gender by age two or three. At the same time, be begins to generalize as to what boys do and what girls do. He begins to select and imitate those behaviors in keeping with his gender identity. Watson and Lindgren suggest that children first develop sex-stereotyped behavior, that is, determine what girls and boys do, and then imitate the same sex models.[5]

But how a girl knows to identify with women and a boy with men remains unexplained. Sigmund Freud developed an entire school of psychology around the concept of sexual identity. He saw most of the work (he called it conflict) occurring in the first five years of life. His explanation is complex in nature. Even though one cannot indiscriminately accept his notions, he did a great service in helping society to recognize the importance of the early years in psychosexual development.

Social learning theorists, accepting Freud's view of the importance of the early years for healthy psychosexual development, have examined nearly every facet of such development. Robert Sears and his associates observed that children of both sexes initially adopt feminine-maternal ways of behaving. Girls keep that up, generally speaking,

---

4. These are identified as culturally-laden because the Bible no place makes explicit statements about items such as those mentioned. As a matter of fact, the Bible spends little time making sex role definitions. What the New Testament does do is to list Christlike behaviors for both men and women. Even those characteristics outlined for elders, who are clearly men, are mentioned in other contexts as characteristics of all Christians, both male and female.

5. Robert Watson and Henry Clay Lindgren, *Psychology of the Child and Adolescent*, 4th ed. (New York: Macmillan, 1979), p. 339.

but boys soon express masculine-paternal bahavior (those culturally defined). They concluded that during the first three years or so the boy makes a cognitive map of the male role and shapes behavior toward it. (This is done more readily if a male model is available.) This is where imitation becomes critically important.

Study as long as we will concerning Freud's, Sears', or anyone else's views about sexual development, we will not find a concise explanation of the *how* of sexual development. It is sufficient to say that it is somehow within the created nature of a person to know how and when to look to the correct sources in order to complete sexual development. The problem is that too often the models are inadequate or non-existent, leaving the individual with insufficient input to complete the task successfully.

With that observation out of the way, we are free to look at some salient points made by psychologists.

Stages of Sexual Growth

Most psychologists, from whatever school of psychology they represent, agree that people develop sexually, roughly, in three stages.

Autosexual stage (2-7). This stage is akin to the egocentric thinking period that occurs at the same time. The child is aware of himself and how he differs from others and believes that the world revolves around him. This is frequently demonstrated by how a child thinks and reasons in areas quite apart from sexual functioning.

This stage is marked by curiosity and experimentation. Preschool children learn that touching is pleasurable. Most touching is motivated by curiosity, by a desire to compare his bodily apparatus with that of someone else. In the process, he learns that touching is pleasurable.

For most children, autosexual activity passes with time *if* it is not coupled with extreme reactions by parents who observe the behavior and associate it with adult masturbatory activity. Parents must, of course, teach their children appropriate social behavior, but it is the emotional tone of their reactions that affect how the child identifies the behavior and how he handles his eventual sexual identification.

Homosexual stage (7-13). This is not to be understood as homosexual in the sense of adult homosexuality. But it is to be seen as a time when boys prefer to be with boys and girls with girls. Freud called this the latent stage of sexuality.

There continues to be some experimentation and curiosity seeking. But the stage is generally transitory, a lull before the strong sexual impulses of adolescence. Once again this seems to be dependent on the presence and quality of models and the nature of adult reactions to seeking deviations.

Heterosexual stage (13 --). With the arrival of puberty, new intense sexual feelings begin to emerge in both males and females. Even though both continue to have friends of the same sex, they usually become most attracted to those of the opposite sex, and a new stage of sexuality emerges. But an adolescent also brings with him all of his previous experiences with sex, all of his conclusions about sexuality (both conscious and unconscious), his newly acquired personal sexual functioning, and his own responsibility for making choices to form the totality of his own sexuality and sexual lifestyle. It has been a precarious journey.

Influences on Sexual Development

Lamb's book, *The Role of the Father in Child Development*, cited earlier in this chapter, devotes an entire chapter to the role of the father in sexual and personality development. It provides key insights.

Looking first at the role of the father in masculine develop-ment, the general conclusion is that the quality of a father's relationship with his son is a more important influence on the boy's development than the actual amount of time the father spends at home. Imitation of the father (something the boys will do because of inborn design) directly enhances the father's masculine behavior in the presence of his son. When the father is active in family interactions and decision-making, the son is likely to develop a satisfactory masculine role. If not, he is likely to be low in masculinity.

It is not enough, then, for father to be masculine outside the home. He must also demonstrate it actively within the home. A boy will never learn masculinity from a father who, although very masculine in the workaday world, abdicates the family leadership role. A boy learns little from a passive father who leaves his masculinity at work and comes home to hide behind the newspaper or to sleep on the sofa.

There is an exception to this. Everything that has been said seems to be negated by a domineering father who lords it over his wife and children. Boys who have undemon-strative, frustrating, critical fathers seem to reject them as models. But when the father is warm, affectionate, and supportive, boys take them as models.

The effect of father absence has not been clearly deter-mined, although the evidence seems to suggest that father absence before the age of four or five appears to have a retarding effect on masculine development. The key seems to be the presence of a male model which can, of course, be provided by grandfathers, uncles, or stepfathers.

The conclusion is this: fathers (or male models) are essen-tial for healthy masculine development. Paternal deprivation often results in difficult development and difficulty in form-ing lasting heterosexual relationships.

The evidence is equally as compelling when one looks at the father's influence on the feminine development of girls. A girl's feminine development is intensely influenced by how the father differentiates his "masculine" role from her "feminine" role. When the father is not involved in the family a daughter is likely to have problems in achieving a suitable sex role. Girls from mother-dominant homes have difficulty relating to males.

A female's ability to have a successful marriage is increased when she has experienced a warm, affectionate relationship with her father who encouraged positive feminine development. An interesting bit of research indicates that low-orgasmic women lack meaningful relationships with their fathers.

All in all, the conclusion is the same as that for boys: fathers (or substitute fathers) are essential for healthy feminine development. Low father availability and inadequate fathering are clearly associated with female sex-role conflicts and female homosexuality.

Further evidence indicates that a great hazard for the appropriate identification of either sex lies in lack of harmony between their mothers and fathers. If the father is unreasonable, domineering, and inconsiderate, the girl interprets womanhood as an inferior sexual position and resents it, while the boy rejects the model. If the mother is a whiner and complainer, girls often fear the role of womanhood and feel uncomfortable as females.[6]

Perhaps it would be fair to summarize the research this way: when a man and a woman relate to each other in marriage as God intended, each assuming his God-given role

---

6. Harold W. Bernard, *Human Development in Western Culture*, 4th ed. (Boston: Allen and Bacon, 1975), p. 252.

in the marriage, offspring from that marriage grow to maturity with a healthy view of sexuality and personal sexual identification. But to deviate from God's pattern is to invite deviant results. God knew what He was doing when He created marriage as He did.

How Psychological Data Relates to Biblical Principles

The Bible is not a psychological textbook nor a scientific treatise. But Biblical principles are often validated by psychological data. That is certainly the case as it relates to sexual development.

The Bible makes no statement about sexual development, but it does set forth some essential principles for a healthy home. When these are practiced, the result is not only spiritually sensitive adults, but also adults who have a healthy self-concept and sexual identification.

The Biblical teaching about marriage in Ephesians 5 is the starting point. Men who take their God-given role, not lording it over their wives and children, but actively involving themselves in the family situation while showing respect for the personalities of others, lead healthy families and produce wholesome children. Someone observed that the best sex education a child can receive is to watch two parents in a healthy marital relationship.

What God told Israel about transmitting religious values to their children applies to other values as well, including sexual behavior. Deuteronomy 6:4-9 states:

Hear, O Israel: The Lord our God, the Lord is one. Love the Lord your God with all your heart and with all your soul and with all your strength. These commandments that I give you today are to be upon your hearts. Impress them on your children. Talk about them when you sit at home and when you walk along the road, when you lie down and when you get up. Tie them as symbols on your hands and bind them on your foreheads. Write them on the doorframes of your houses and on your gates.

In the same way, parents are to realize that they as men and women are constantly on display before their children's eyes. What they are rubs off on their children. When a child interacts with loving parents who both show and tell how to be a man and a woman, the child receives a rich heritage indeed.

The psychological data also verifies the validity of God's instructions in regard to discipline. Ephesians 6:4 puts it this way: "Fathers, do not exasperate your children; instead, bring them up in the training and instruction of the Lord." Colossians 3:21 sums it up in these words: "Fathers, do not embitter your children, or they will become discouraged." This is a guiding principle to avoid domineering, rejection, and criticism. How definite this is in insisting that discipline involves parental interaction, patient teaching, and genuine caring. It is not only essential for general behavioral change, but apparently also for effective sexual development, if we are to believe contemporary literature.

Conclusion

It is nothing short of astounding that God provided from the very outset that homes should contain the components for proper sexual development. According to contemporary research, sexual development is comprised of gender, gender identity, sex role identification, and sexual orientation. These occur best when a child develops in a home where two parents relate to each other and to their children in an interactive atmosphere, each valuing the other. According to the Bible, this occurs in a home where father and mother relate to each other and their children in the way God defined in Ephesians 5 and Colossians 3.

Perhaps it is inaccurate then to say, "boys will be boys" or "girls will be girls." Boys will learn to be boys and girls will learn to be girls when they are blessed with a father and a mother (or substitute mother) who show, as well as tell, them how to be men and women.

Summary Statements

1. Sexual identity is composed of gender, gender identity, sex role, and sexual orientation.
2. The role of the father is critical for the development of sexual identity, either masculine or feminine.

FOR DISCUSSION

1. How important are a mother and father, respectively, for healthy sexual development?
2. Is it more important for a parent to be or to do in modeling sexual behavior for his children? Why?
3. How are God's principles for the home and discipline related to current findings on psychological development?
4. If you could devise a program of sex education for your congregation, what would you suggest? Why?

REFERENCES

1. Bernard, Harold W. *Human Development in Western Culture.* 4th ed. Boston: Allyn and Bacon, 1975.

2. Biehler, Robert F. *Child Development and Introduction.* 2nd ed. Dallas: Houghton Mifflin, 1981.
3. Evans, Ellis D., and McCandless, Boyd R. *Children and Youth: Psychosocial Development.* 2nd ed. New York: Holt, Rinehart and Winston, 1977.
4. Macoby, Eleanor Emmons, and Jacklin, Carol Nagy. *The Psychology of Sex Differences.* Stanford University Press, 1974.
5. Lamb, Michael E. (ed.). *The Role of the Father in Child Development.* New York: John Wiley and Sons, 1976.

Chapter Six

GOD'S IDEAL WOMAN

God made man and woman in His image to be His companions and to glorify Him. But sin intervened, and man and woman became alienated from their Creator and from each other. Since that day in Eden, the sin factor has clouded the minds of men and women when they have sought to be like God. That confusion is perhaps most evident in the contemporary issue of determing proper male and female roles.

A Feminine Dilemma

Women in American society are in a dilemma of no small magnitude. From every direction come pronouncements of what it means to be feminine, many of them conflicting. Even those who purport to give Christian advice differ as to what are feminine characteristics.

Women's liberation has shaken the very foundations of what has been historically accepted as feminine behavior. The more radical liberationists have insisted on a "unisex" motif that would obliterate all differences, except biological ones, between the sexes.

Feminine Mystique

The liberation movement was given impetus in 1963 when Betty Friedan published *The Feminine Mystique.* She claimed that women had lost basic identity because society had reduced them solely to wife and mother roles, largely as a result of Freudian psychology. Friedan defined the problem as a stunting or evasion of growth because culture does not permit women to be anything but wives and mothers.[1]

---

1. For further development of this idea, see Betty Friedan, *The Feminine Mystique,* (New York: Dell Publishing Company, 1963).

Fascinating Womanhood

But those who appeal to the Bible also present conflicting advice. For example, Helen Andelin, in her book *Fascinating Womanhood* suggests that women's roles are no more than wives and mothers. At best, it provides manipulative advice. According to Andelin, a man lives in constant insecurity and needs a woman who makes him feel secure. His desires, according to her, are for a mother to protect him and a child whom he can dominate. A woman who is feminine will make him 'feel' like a man, yet at the same time lead him to think that he dominates her. Andelin says that the ideal woman should demonstrate dependency because she was created to be that way.[2]

A woman is to observe how children dress and act and then emulate them. Andelin insists that, a woman should never show competence, strength, or ability. She is to be totally dependent upon a man to take care of her.

Total Woman

Basic to Marabel Morgan's *The Total Woman* is the thesis that women need to be loved while men need to be admired.[3] A total woman is defined as one who is a warm, loving homemaker, a sizzling lover, one who inspires.[4] She is responsible first to God, then to her husband, then to her children, and finally to profession and public. In other words, the total woman finds fulfillment only as a wife and mother.

---

2. See Helen Andelin, *Fascinating Womanhood* (Santa Barbara, California: Pacific Press, 1965).

3. Marabel Morgan, *The Total Woman* (New York: Pocket Books, 1975), p. 19.

4. *Ibid.*, p. 244.

The Christian Family

Larry Christenson orders a family according to headship. Thus, a woman lives under the authority of her husband. Since women are vulnerable physically, emotionally, psychologically, and spiritually, they need a man's authority and protection. Christenson takes Genesis 3, the statement that "man shall rule over you," as a divine mandate for the position of men and women.[5]

All We're Meant to Be

Letha Scanzoni and Nancy Hardesty respond to women's liberation by offering a Biblical approach in *All We're Meant to Be*. Theirs is an insightful examination. However, according to them, the roles of male and female are totally determined by culture. They suggest that women do have a choice about what they will do with their lives, just as men are given choices.[6]

Summary

Some questions emerge from the midst of the dilemma:
1. Is women's role God-ordained to be only that of wife and mother? If so, what are single and professional women to do?
2. Must women be liberated from wife/mother roles to find their own identity?
3. Are female roles only culturally determined? If so, why were we created male and female to begin with?

The only possible resolution of these questions is to look at the Bible itself.

---

5. For further information, see Larry Christenson, *The Christian Family* (Minneapolis: Bethany Fellowship, 1970).

6. See Letha Scanzoni and Nancy Hardesty, *All We're Meant to Be* (Waco, Texas: Word 1974) for a full development.

Women in the Bible

Since the Bible nowhere makes a clearly definitive statement regarding feminity, perhaps the only way to determine what is accepted as feminine is to look at several examples of Bible women to learn what they were like that elicited commendation either directly or implicitly.

Old Testament

Eve. Our introduction to Eve comes at the dawn of creation. She was formed from Adam's side and placed in the Garden of Eden to share with Adam the responsibility to populate the earth, subdue creation, and manage creation (Genesis 1:29-30). Apparently she was to share equally with Adam in the maintenance of Eden.

After sin became a reality, woman's feminity was affected. She experienced pain in the reproductive process, yet she gave birth to children—Cain, Abel, and Seth, among others. Little else is described of Eve's activity—Adam's either—probably because the Bible was written to establish a record of God's activity among men, not to give a detailed anthropological study.

Sarai. Our first introduction to Sarai comes in Genesis 12:5 when she is identified as Abraham's wife who followed him to a land promised by God. She is described as beautiful in Genesis 12:11. She was to be the mother of Abraham's promised son (Genesis 17:15ff), a promise she unwisely attempted to resolve in her own way since she was childless (Genesis 16). She gave her handmaiden Hagar to Abraham to bear a son, but that resulted in enmity between Hagar and Sarai. (The jealousy resulting from Hagar's pregnancy by Abraham verifies the validity that God's original design was for one man married to one woman.)

Rebekah. Rebekah's first mention in the Bible was in Genesis 22:23. An expanded introduction occurs in Genesis 24 where she was described as a beautiful virgin (24:16) who was carrying water for the family. She was hospitable (24:17-21) and a woman of faith (24:57-60). The mother of Jacob and Esau, she deviously sought the patriarchal blessing for Jacob, then sent Jacob to her homeland for protection and to find a wife (Genesis 27).

Rachel. Rachel's name first appears in the Biblical record in Genesis 29 where she is identified as a shepherdess (29:9). Jacob loved her, a beautiful woman, so much that he worked for his father-in-law for fourteen years to be able to have her for a wife. Her barrenness became a source of irritation between her and Jacob (Genesis 30). She resorted to selling Jacob's sexual services to her sister Leah (Genesis 30:14-16). She was finally privileged to have children (Genesis 30:22-24). A negative commentary regarding her was when she took Laban's household gods (Genesis 31:19), keeping it a secret from Jacob (Genesis 31:32). She died giving birth to Benjamin (Genesis 35:16).

Leah. Not as attractive as her sister (Genesis 29:16), Leah was pawned off on Jacob, much to his dismay (Genesis 29:22-30). Always the unloved wife, she gave birth to six sons and one daughter (Genesis 29:32-35, 30:17-21).

Miriam. The Bible first mentions Miriam when she guarded her little brother Moses who had been hidden in the bulrushes to protect his life (Exodus 2:4-10). She is not mentioned again until after the miraculous crossing of the Red Sea at which time she is identified as a prophetess who led the women in a time of praise to God (Exodus 15:20-21).

Miriam apparently was influential among the Israelites, for Numbers 12:1ff records how she and Aaron began to oppose Moses because of his foreign wife. It was a situation serious enough for God to speak to them directly (Numbers 12:4-9). Miriam became leprous until Moses interceded with God on her behalf (Numbers 12:10-15).

Zelophehed's Daughters. Mahlah, Noah, Hoglah, Milcah, and Tirzah appealed to Moses for consideration for land rights (Numbers 27:1-3). Their father had died in the desert, leaving no male heirs. "Why," they asked, "should our father's name disappear from his clan because he had no son? Give us property among our father's relatives" (Numbers 27:4). Their appeal was granted (Numbers 27:5-7).

Deborah. Judges 4-5 describes the activities of the only woman judge of Israel. She was married, a prophetess who held court in the hill country of Ephraim (4:4-5). She is said to have settled many disputes (4:5). It was she who encouraged Berak to go to war against the Canaanites (4:6). He agreed to do it if she would accompany him (4:8-10), and the Canaanites were soundly defeated (4:14-24). When the victory was complete, she and Barak sang a song of praise to God for deliverance (Judges 5).

Ruth. The book of Ruth describes Ruth as a widow who was deeply devoted to her mother-in-law, Naomi. She accompanied her back to Bethlehem where a beautiful love story developed. She gleaned grain in the fields of Boaz where she attracted his attention and finally his love and companionship. She is also described as a woman of noble character (3:11), perhaps the reason God chose her, a Moabite woman, a foreigner, to be a part of the royal bloodline from which would come Jesus of Nazareth.

Hannah. Hannah is identified as a devoted woman of God who bore a heavy burden because she could not conceive a child (I Samuel 1). But her prayers for a child were answered, and she gave birth to Samuel (I Samuel 1:20) whom she dedicated to the Lord (I Samuel 1:21—2:11).

Abigail. Abigail is said to be intelligent and beautiful (I Samuel 25:3). She was a hospitable woman in spite of her husband Nabal's churlishness, riding over rough countryside to take victuals to David (25:14-31). After Nabal's death, she became David's wife (25:39-42).

Esther. The queen of Persia, this Jewess, Esther, stepped beyond the definite limits of propriety for a queen and appealed personally to Xerxes to save the Jews from an evil plot to kill them. Her courage saved her people and is acclaimed in the book.

The Wife of Noble Character. The writer in Proverbs 31 devotes the concluding verses of his collection of advice to describe a woman of noble character (Proverbs 31:10-31). The section begins by touting her value, "She is worth more than rubies." Then her characteristics are noted:

1. Trustworthy (11).
2. A helping partnership with her husband (12).
3. Industrious to get clothing and food (13-15).
4. Good business sense (16, 24).
5. Hard worker (17, 19).
6. Bargain hunter (18).
7. Compassionate (20).
8. Planner (21).
9. Attractively clothed (22).
10. Supports husband (23).
11. Dignified (25).
12. Wise teacher (26).
13. Efficient (27).
14. Loved by her husband and children (28).
15. Fears the Lord (30).
16. Worthy of praise (31).

New Testament

Anna. Luke called Anna a prophetess, an old widow of the tribe of Asher, who resided continually at the Temple to await the Messiah. When she saw Jesus, she gave thanks to God (Luke 2:36-38).

Mary and Martha. Jesus frequented the home of Mary, Martha, and Lazarus at Bethany. Theirs was a special friendship. Neither woman is identified as being married. Even so, Martha was the efficient homemaker, while Mary was more of a learner who preferred to sit at Jesus' feet to listen to Him (Luke 10:38-42). Both demonstrated perceptive faith when they asked Jesus to raise their brother Lazarus from the dead (John 11). Mary later anointed Jesus' feet, an act He commended (John 12:1-11).

Dorcas. Mentioned only briefly in Acts 9:36-39, Dorcas was one who did good and helped the poor, especially by sewing.

Lydia. When Paul and Silas went to Europe, they found Lydia in Philippi. She was a businesswoman who worshiped Jehovah. She turned out to be the first European convert and exercised gracious hospitality (Acts 16:13-15, 40).

Priscilla. Fully a partner with her husband Aquila, Priscilla is first mentioned in Acts 18. They were co-workers with Paul in Corinth. After Paul left, they continued their witness for the Lord, particularly when they instructed Apollos more fully in the way of the Lord (Acts 18:23-26). They are mentioned again in I Corinthians 16:14 and II Timothy 4:19.

Daughters of Philip. In Acts 21:7-9, the text mentions that Philip the evangelist, one of the original deacons, had four virgin daughters who had the gift of prophecy.

Phoebe. Romans 16:1-2 identifies Phoebe as a servant, whatever that term meant in the first century. Paul here officially endorsed her work.

71

Women in I Corinthians. In I Corinthians 11:2-16, Paul dealt first with what was probably a cross-cultural position that women in public are to be veiled. Paul's conclusion was this: Don't throw off all the customs of society just to prove that you are free. Even so, women were to be participants in the worship (11:5) and express their spiritual gifts (12-14). But their attire is to be proper (culturally determined). Paul further qualified when they could speak in 14:33-36 when he insisted that they are not to disrupt the congregation when they do participate.

Euodia and Syntyche. In Philippians 4:2-3, Paul urged Euodia and Syntyche to come to a reconciliation. Nothing else was said about them, but it is the opinion of this writer that they were in positions of leadership of a magnitude that their disagreement could affect the unity of the church. Paul called them true yokefellows, denoting a sharing in the ministry of the gospel.

Women in Timothy. In I Timothy 2:11-15, Paul said women are not to teach or to have authority over men. The word translated "allow" in the English is a present active indicative in the original language. That means that it could readily have been translated, "I am not permitting a woman to teach or have authority over a man . . ." "Authority" means "to domineer." To the liberationists of the first century, Paul was urging caution. To the conservatives who would have banned women from instruction Paul insisted that they be permitted to learn. His arguments parallel I Corinthians 11:2-16 when he said woman are to learn, not to domineer. In the Timothy passage, four positive feminine characteristics are identified: faith, love, holiness, and propriety.

Some believe that I Timothy 3:11 is addressed to women

deacons. Others think it is to the wives of deacons. Which-
ever is the case, the proper characteristics of these women
were to be: (1) respected, (2) in control of the tongue, (3)
temperate, and (4) trustworthy.

In I Timothy 5:3-16, Paul addressed the problem of caring
for widows. Most of the characteristics of a widow worthy
to be cared for by the church seem to be feminine qualities
to be emulated by all women. Those were identified as:

1. Wife of one husband.
2. Doer of good deeds which included raising her family,
   showing hospitality, serving others ("washing the feet
   of saints"), demonstrating humility, and caring for the
   afflicted.

Women in Titus. In Titus 2:3-5, Paul again identified the
desirable characteristics of older women. They were:

1. Role models of a godly life.
2. Evidencing their inner devotion by their outward behavior (reverence).
3. In control of their desires such as the tongue and desire
   for drink.
4. Faithful sexually (chaste).
5. Caring for their households.
6. Placing themselves under their husband's leading.

Women in Peter. In I Peter 3:1-6, Peter suggested the
following characteristics:

1. Purity (chastity).
2. Evidencing inner devotion by outward behavior (reverence).
3. Gentleness.
4. Following husband's leading.

Conclusion

This brief survey of the Bible shows women who pursued

various kinds of work. Some were homemakers and mothers, but others, like Deborah and Lydia, were mentioned in the context of their work. Women were wives, mothers, judges, prophetesses, businesswomen, and teachers. Some were subdued while others, like Zelophehed's daughters and Esther, were courageous and assertive. Abigail was described as intelligent. The woman of Proverbs 31 was a "working wife." It would seem, then, that women can do a variety of kinds of work and still be God's women. At the same time, some common characteristics do seem to be feminine characteristics: reverence, doer of good deeds, exercising self-control, purity, gentleness, and following her husband's leading, if she is married. Paul nowhere denies cultural sexual roles.

So Who is an "Ideal Woman"?

God's ideal woman is to find her identity in Jesus Christ (Romans 6:4 and 13:4, II Corinthians 5:17, and Galatians 3:27-28). That exhortation is the same for both men and women. It is an identity that transcends this world.

It is clear, however, that the Bible never advocates a unisexual nor a homosexual model for the relationship between men and women. Paul especially makes it clear that we are to live equally before God with each other while recognizing biological and cultural differences.

The Bible does seem to emphasize six predominately feminine characteristics that a woman should demonstrate.

Reverent

I Timothy 3:11 states, "In the same way, wives are to be women worthy of respect." It could easily be translated,

74

"They are to be venerated for their character." Married or not, a woman is to be an honorable person. The whole tone of this exhortation is that a woman is to be dignified. Self-respect is not pride; it is the basis for effective Christian living (Leviticus 19:18). God's woman must live in a way that produces positive expressions from others.

Another aspect of reverence is trustworthiness. Women are to be trustworthy in everything (I Timothy 3:11). It is the ability to protect some information, yet to pass on other information accurately.

Reverence may well be one of the most important characteristics for a twentieth-century woman to pursue. It is lacking in all too many women today.

Self-Control

A woman is to exercise self-control. The first area for self-control is in the use of the tongue. Gossip is an insidious disease that seems to plague women more than it does men. But God's woman is to use her tongue for good (I Timothy 3:11, Titus 2:3). How a woman uses her tongue is a measure of her maturity.

A woman may use her tongue for gossip—that sharing of information that, either maliciously or "innocently," tears people down. It is all too easy to lose control of one's tongue and create a furor. It is impossible to estimate how many people have been hurt by gossip or how many churches have been split or rendered unproductive by wagging tongues.

A woman must also exercise control of the tongue in her relationships with her children. Inferiority feelings and low self-esteem often have their origins from a mother who criticized and nagged her children, exasperating them to anger. Most mothers would do well to act more and talk less in relationship to disciplining their children.

75

A woman's self-control must extend to her appetites. When I Timothy 3:11 said, "In the same way their wives are to be . . . temperate," Paul was probably cautioning them in the area of drinking wine. But he could as well have meant eating, using tobacco, buying clothing, watching television, or spending money.

Self-control also means to accurately assess ourselves and then proceed to use what God has given us for His glory—without pride and calling attention to self. That extends to dress as well (I Timothy 2:3).

Pure

Purity refers to sexual conduct. The word Paul used in Titus 2:3-5 means to be chaste, to be free of carnality. Women are to realize their responsibility in maintaining chaste relationships with men. They are to recognize themselves as sexual creatures who have power over men. Those powers are to be used exclusively within marriage. Otherwise, her behavior is to be discreet. Purity must be maintained in a society where seemingly "anything goes." In an effort to free themselves from the Victorian ethic of a previous age, women in this day and age are in mortal danger of ignoring discretion and leaving themselves open to grievous temptations. Paul's advice for women is still accurate: be pure.

Do Good

A woman is to do good. Doing good is variously described in Scripture as "showing hospitality" (Romans 12:13, I Peter 4:9) and helping those in trouble, which could mean almost any kind of assistance. It can be words as well as deeds. A woman is to be one who is sensitive to the needs of others and acts to meet those needs.

Gentle

Today's society says that a woman must be "sexy" and "sensual." But not the Bible. It says that a woman is identified by her inner qualities which can be summed up by the phrase "gentle spirit."

Gentleness is the spirit of keeping oneself in proper perspective. It carries the idea of courtesy—keeping others in proper perspective. It is considerateness, sensitivity to the other person's needs and feelings. It is a submissive spirit. Gentleness is learning to show sentiment, to express tenderness.

There is a special appeal to a gentle woman. She radiates a quality of life, not so much in words as in general decorum. It is a quality to be sought by every woman.

Makes A Home

A woman must take proper responsibility for her home. If she is married, she must voluntarily submit to her husband's leadership. She is to demonstrate loyalty, affection, and commitment to her husband. She is to rear her children in the Lord.

A woman's home is a clear indication of her personality and self-respect. A cluttered home shows lack of self-control both for married and unmarried women. A woman disloyal to her husband contradicts any claim to reverence. Disregard for children is a direct contradiction of God's laws. But an ordered home demonstrates self-control. Loyalty and proper rearing of children brings self-respect as a by-product.

Conclusion

A good look at the Bible for feminine roles and characteristics immediately refutes much of the contemporary advice for women. Nowhere does the Bible restrict a woman solely to the roles of wife and mother. Those are desirable roles, but not exclusive ones. Nor does the Bible support Andelin's advice for women to suppress all demonstrations of competence and ability. Proverbs 31 is anything but a description of a weak, vulnerable woman incapable of action apart from her husband. But neither does the Bible suggest that cultural distinctions are to be obliterated.

Three questions were posed in the midst of the contemporary dilemma. These have been answered:

1. Women are not restricted to the roles of wives and mothers. I Corinthians 7:25 makes that clear enough.
2. To be truly feminine, women do not need to work outside the home. They can achieve identity doing the work of wife and mother.
3. Being feminine is determined in part by culture, but apparently not entirely. The feminine characteristics identified in this chapter are transcultural.

So who is God's ideal woman? She is that woman who seeks to reflect the image of her Creator by a life of reverence, self-control, purity, doing good, and making a happy home.

Summary

1. Women are the recipients of conflicting advice by twentieth-century writers.
2. Bible women performed many different kinds of work, all apparently with God's blessing.
3. Identifiable feminine characteristics in the Bible are: reverence, doer of good deeds, self-control, purity, gentleness, and making a happy home.

FOR DISCUSSION

1. Is woman's role God-ordained to be only that of wife and mother? Why?
2. Must women be liberated from wife/mother roles to find their own identity? Why?
3. Are female roles culturally determined? Why? Give examples.
4. What characteristics are identified as feminine in the Bible?
5. How can these feminine characteristics be applied in contemporary culture? Cite specific applications.

REFERENCES

1. Andelin, Helen. *Fascinating Womanhood*. Santa Barbara, California: Pacific Press, 1965.
2. Christenson, Larry. *The Christian Family*. Minneapolis: Bethany Fellowship, 1970.
3. Drakeford, Robina and John Drakeford. *In Praise of Women*. San Francisco: Harper and Row, 1980.
4. Friedan, Betty. *The Feminine Mystique*. New York: Dell Publishing Company, 1974.
5. Getz, Gene. *The Measure of a Woman*. Glendale, California: Regal, 1977.
6. Hunt, Donald. *Pondering the Proverbs*. Joplin, Missouri: College Press, 1974.
7. Scanzoni, Letha, and Nancy Hardesty. *All We're Meant to Be*. Waco, Texas: Word, 1974.
8. Williams, Don. *The Apostle Paul and Women in the Church*. Glendale, California: Regal, 1977.

Chapter Seven

GOD'S IDEAL MAN

Who is a real man? It is a matter of intense concern for males in a society whose traditional foundations are challenged on every hand. What is manliness? Even men are confused today with the onslaught of the equal rights movement that seems to question the historical values this society has taken for granted.

Check it out with some people and you will find that they have a clearcut definition of manliness. He is a male who is assertive, forceful, goal-oriented, and inclined toward outdoor and athletic activities and interests. He is not to demonstrate tenderness nor emotion, nor to be overly concerned about the needs of others. But at the same time, others insist that men are to be no different than women. A unisexual society would suit them very well.

But the question is not what society says. It is this: who is a man of God? How is a man of God to be identified? This is the crucial issue, for a Christian man is not to be totally defined nor shaped by his culture except as it is attuned to the Word of God. For men, as much as for women, it is essential to turn to the Bible to find out God's guidelines for manliness.

A study of the Bible indicates four clusters of personality traits and behaviors that mark a man of God. Perhaps the best source of that information is in the letters to Timothy and Titus where Paul outlines the characteristics of those men who are spiritually mature enough to be leaders in the church. Such men are surely the ideal man that God desires.

Flawless Reputation

The man of God's choosing is a man who has developed, and carefully protects, a flawless reputation. The writer of

80

Proverbs states it this way: "Thus you will walk in the ways of good men and keep to the paths of the righteous" (Proverbs 2:20). Paul said it similarly, "The overseer must be above reproach" (I Timothy 3:2), and "The elder must be blameless" (Titus 1:7).

Paul was not the first to believe that Christian men should be men with good reputations. In the early days of the church, when the problem of providing food for the widows surfaced and the Greeks complained that their widows had been neglected, the apostles decided to appoint seven deacons to assist with the serving. One of the criteria for the selection of the men was that they be "of good reputation" (Acts 6:3).

Paul suggests several traits that would affect what the public says about another person. There are some things that a man cannot hide from others, regardless of how he tries. These are tests of Christian manliness.

A Christian man is respectable. Respectability is developed by responsible behavior and orderliness. The word in the original language, *kosmios,* means orderly. That orderliness extends to a man's appearance, obedience to those in authority, giving an honest day's work for a day's pay, honesty in relationships with people, and living in such a way that his lifestyle adorns the teachings of the Bible. The writer of Proverbs summarized it in this fashion, "Do not plot harm against your neighbor who lives trustfully near you. Do not accuse a man for no reason when he has done you no harm" (Proverbs 3:30-31). It is no mark of commendation for a man to be known as discourteous to authority, dishonest in personal and community relationships, or professing one thing while living out another. A real man is respectable.

Neither is a Christian man a drunkard. In his instructions to Timothy and Titus, Paul said that an elder is "not given

81

to much wine" (I Timothy 3:3 and Titus 1:7). The word, *paroinos*, means a man who sits too long at his wine; he overdrinks and consequently loses control of himself.

The writer of Proverbs describes the man who is addicted to wine:

> Who has woe? Who has sorrow? Who has strife? Who has complaints? Who has needless bruises? Who has bloodshot eyes? Those who linger over wine, who go to sample bowls of mixed wine. Do not gaze at wine when it is red, when it sparkles in the cup, when it goes down smoothly! In the end it bites like a snake and poisons like a viper. Your eyes will see strange sights and your mind imagine confusing things. You will be like one sleeping on the high seas, lying on top of the rigging. "They hit me," you will say, "but I'm not hurt! They beat me, but I don't feel it! When will I wake up so I can find another drink" (Proverbs 23:29-35).

It is not a pretty picture—surely not behavior worthy of a genuine man.

Again, the writer of Proverbs said:

> Listen, my son, and be wise, and keep your heart on the right path. Do not join those who drink too much wine or gorge themselves on meat, for drunkards become poor, and drowsiness clothes them in rags (Proverbs 23:19-21).

The principle of appetite control really extends to self-control of every physical desire whether that is food, alcohol, tobacco, sex, or recreation. Nothing brings greater disrepute than to be a man with unrestrained appetites.

A man of good reputation is not quick tempered (Titus 1:7). He does not easily 'fly off the handle.' He is in control of his spirit. The writer of Proverbs said: "Do not make friends with a hot-tempered man, or you may learn his ways and get yourself ensnared" (Proverbs 22:24-25). A temperamental man falls far short of what God wants a man to be.

Nor is a real man pugnacious (Titus 1:7). Pugnaciousness is anger that is out of control, both physically and verbally. It was perhaps best illustrated by Cain whose jealousy of his brother Abel resulted in anger that culminated in murder (Genesis 4:1-15), and Cain was plagued the rest of his days for his evil deed. It was further demonstrated by Moses who in a fit of anger slew an Egyptian. It was also Moses who threw the tablets of stone to the ground and shattered them to pieces when he saw the people involved in idolatrous worship (Exodus 32:19). But a mature man of God is in control of his spirit, even when he is angry with proper motives.

Another aspect of a man's reputation is his attitude and behavior in relationship to money. The mature man of God is free from the love of money (I Timothy 3:2-3). Note that the directive is to *be free from the love of money, not free from money.* It is quite possible for a man to have money, much of it, yet not to love it. It is a matter of priorities. The writer of Proverbs said, "Honor the Lord with your wealth, with the first fruits of all your crops" (Proverbs 13:9).

Leroy Trulock, vice president at Lincoln (Illinois) Christian College, is an example of the way a man and his money should be related. Mr. Trulock has been an eminently successful businessman, making much more money than most people. But his money does not manage him; he manages his money. When this writer taught at Lincoln, she—and others—got her paycheck more than once because of Mr. Trulock's generosity with the college. No one but he could estimate the dollars he has shared with others. Earl Hargrove, chancellor at Lincoln, said one time that despite the large widely acclaimed gifts given to that college, not one person had given as much as the Trulocks have over the years.

But Mr. Trulock gives his funds quietly where it is needed and insists that no publicity be given. It is no wonder that so many see him as a man among men.

Materialism is a status symbol in modern American culture —and more than one man has given everything he is and has—health, energy, family, friends—to gain status through money. What a tragic trade when God is looking for manly men who handle money well.

A reputable man is also just (*dikaios*), that is, he possesses practical righteousness. A mature man of God lives a godly life, judged so by his daily behavior. It calls for both spiritual and psychological maturity. A man is known by his fruits. A genuine man, then, has a flawless reputation. Those in the community know him to be what he professes. When it comes to respectability, control of appetites, control of temper and anger, use of money, and practical lifestyle, no word of complaint can be found.

Peerless Character

A genuine man of God is a male whose character is faultless. What the community believes him to be is synonymous with what he is. A character of this kind is marked by specific characteristics that set a man apart as a man of God.

One mark of superlative character is temperance. A man of God should be temperate (I Timothy 3:2). What Paul meant here is a man who has a clear perspective on life and a proper spiritual orientation. Thayer defines the word as a state untouched by any beclouding influence. The temperate man is a man who remains stable and steadfast at all times, keeping his reasoning clear.

A temperate man is a man of faith and action, for he knows *who* controls life and eternity. In Hebrews 11, the writer states that by faith Abel *offered* a better sacrifice (11:4); by faith, Noah *prepared* an ark (11:7); by faith, Abraham *obeyed by going out* (11:8); by faith, Abraham *offered* up Isaac (11:17); by faith, Isaac *blessed* Jacob (11:20); and by faith, Moses *left* Egypt (11:23). A temperate man today, like those of old, *believes* God and *acts* on His promises.

A temperate man keeps himself in the proper perspective. He is not unduly proud of himself apart from the grace of God. He heeds the advice of Proverbs 3:5-7:

> Trust in the Lord with all your heart and lean not on your own understanding; in all your ways acknowledge him, and he will make your paths straight. Do not be wise in your own eyes, fear the Lord and shun evil.

A man's character should also be marked by prudence (I Timothy 3:2, Titus 1:8). The word *sophron* could be translated sober, sensible, of sound mind and judgment, or prudent. It is a proper view of oneself in relationship to God and others. It is a characteristic to value, for the writer of Proverbs said: "My son, preserve sound judgment and discernment, do not let them out of your sight; they will be life for you, an ornament to grace your neck" (Proverbs 3:21-22).

A prudent man is keenly aware that all he has is from God. Yet the man is no weakling nor a coward, for he has the confidence of being what God wants him to be.

Furthermore, a man of flawless character is a man who is not self-willed (Titus 1:7). He does not always have to have his own way at home, at work, and in the church. An overindulgent male who demands pampering and petting is known for his selfish behavior. But the man of God can control his preferences in order to seek what is best for his family, business, and church.

A man of superb character is uncontentious (I Timothy 3:2-3). Some men are good men when they are the center of decision-making, when they "call the shots," yet are difficult to deal with when they are one among equals. The Greek word for contentious is *amachos* and could be translated "quarrelsome." A contentious person struggles against others, competes, debates, and is generally unwilling to bend.

But rather than a quarrelsome man, God wants a man who is intent on demonstrating unity in the congregation and home. "Blessed are the peacemakers," Jesus said, "for they shall be called sons of God" (Matthew 6:9). He wants men who refuse to use authority as a club to beat people into submission, but who love and demonstrate to their families, employees, and congregations how to live as God wants.

Akin to a peacemaking spirit is a gentle heart. A man of God is to be gentle (I Timothy 3:2-3). A gentle man is mild-mannered, forbearing, kind, and in control of himself. Gentleness is tenderness, a quality all too often believed to be an exclusively feminine characteristic. But Paul identified himself in that light when he wrote to the Thessalonians, "But we proved to be gentle among you, as a nursing mother tenderly cares for her children (I Thessalonians 2:7).

A man of character also loves what is good (Titus 1:8). There should be no doubt about what and whom he loves. To "love what is good" means to *do* good. The "good" is best summed up by Philippians 4:8: "Finally, brothers, what ever is true, whatever is noble. Whatever is right, whatever is pure, whatever is lovely, whatever is admirable—if anything is excellent or praiseworthy—think about such things."

A man who loves what is good must be a man who loves God, for God is good. He must seek to copy his life after the Good Teacher—Jesus. He must pursue with fervor the Word of God that teaches him what he is to do if he does good.

This cluster of traits that reflect a man's inner character are alien to contemporary culture. But alien to culture or not, these traits mark a real man—the one who is God's man.

Christlike at Home

Contrary to the modern business ethic that pushes a man to produce despite what it means to family life, Paul says that a man gives attention to his home. It is manly to be concerned about wife and children.

A man must first of all be intimately related to one woman. A man's sexual behavior is of utmost concern to God. It is not a mark of manhood for a male to see how many women he can conquer. It is a distinction of a Christian man to faithfully love, protect, and nurture one woman.

The writer of Proverbs is explicit in his instructions to young men. Two extended passages emphasize the value, the commendation, the manliness, of remaining faithful to one woman:

> My son, pay attention to my wisdom, listen well to my words of insight, that you may maintain discretion and your lips may preserve knowledge. For the lips of an adulteress drip honey, and her speech is smoother than oil; but in the end she is bitter as gall, sharp as a double-edged sword. Her feet go down to death; her steps lead straight to the grave. She gives no thought to the ways of life; her paths are crooked, but she knows it not.
>
> Now then, my sons, listen to me; do not turn aside from what I say. Keep to a path far from her, do not go near the

door of her house, lest you give your best strength to others
and your years to one who is cruel, lest strangers feast on
your wealth and your toil enrich another man's house. At
the end of life you will groan, when your flesh and body are
spent. You will say, "How I hated discipline! How my heart
spurned correction! I would not obey my teachers or listen
to my instructors. I have come to the brink of utter ruin in
the midst of the whole assembly."

Drink water from your own cistern, running water from
your own well. Should your springs overflow in the streets,
your streams of water in the public squares? Let them keep
yours alone, never to be shared with strangers. May your
fountain be blessed, and may you rejoice in the wife of your
youth. A loving doe, a graceful deer—may her breasts satisfy
you always, may you ever be captivated by her love. Why
be captivated, my son, by an adulteress? Why embrace the
bosom of another man's wife?

For a man's ways are in full view of the Lord, and he examines all his paths. The evil deeds of a wicked man ensnare
him, the cords of his sin hold him fast. he will die for lack of
discipline, led astray by his own great folly (Proverbs 5, NIV).

My son, keep your father's commands and do not forsake
your mother's teaching. Bind them upon your heart forever;
fasten them around your neck. When you walk, they will
guide you; when you sleep, they will watch over you; when
you awake, they will speak to you. For these commands are a
lamp, this teaching is a light, and the corrections of discipline
are the way to life, keeping you from the immoral woman,
from the smooth tongue of the wayward wife. Do not lust in
your heart after her beauty or let her captivate you with her
eyes, for the prostitute reduces you to a loaf of bread, and
the adulteress preys upon your very life. Can a man scoop
fire into his lap without his clothes being burned? Can a man
walk on hot coals without his feet being scorched? So is he

who sleeps with another man's wife; no one who touches her will go unpunished.

Men do not despise a thief if he steals to satisfy his hunger when he is starving. Yet if he is caught, he must repay seven-fold, though it costs him all the wealth of his house. But a man who commits adultery lacks judgment; whoever does so destroys himself. Blows and disgrace are his lot; and his shame will never be wiped away; for jealousy arouses a husband's fury, and he will show no mercy when he takes revenge. He will not accept any compensation; he will refuse the bribe, however great it is (Proverbs 6:20-35).

But faithfulness extends beyond physical intercourse. Jesus taught, "You have heard that it was said, 'Do not commit adultery.' But I tell you that anyone who looks at a woman lustfully has already committed adultery with her in his heart" (Matthew 5:27-28).

"To lust" means to desire intensely a sexual, physical relationship. To be tempted is not to sin. But for a man to secretly and deliberately enjoy an illegitimate sexual union with a woman in his mind is the lust to which Jesus referred.

A man in today's society faces provocative temptations, and he must determine a plan of action if he is to maintain moral purity. He must protect himself against deliberately exposing himself to literature, movies, television programs, and provocative women who by design illegimately stimulate his sexual nature.

When a man takes seriously his responsibility to his wife, then he is ready to manage his household (I Timothy 3:2-4). But a man who cannot manage himself finds it most diffi-cult to lead a home. Management of a man's home reflects the quality of every other personality trait. Not every man is married or has children, of course, but if he is married and if he does have children, his maturity is marked by how his children behave.

An Old Testament man whose manliness was less than what God desired was Eli. Neither of his sons knew the Lord. Both were immoral and worthless (II Samuel 2:12, 17). And God judged *both* Eli and his sons (II Samuel 2:13).

Yet a man of God need not have a perfect family. There is no such thing. But it does mean that it is a family where the father is modeling for his family how to grow in Jesus Christ. A man is a failure as a man if he is too busy with his business to involve himself with his wife and children.

A man is to use his home to practice hospitality (I Timothy 3:2, Titus 1:8). In first century Israel hospitality was an essential art, for travel was arduous and accommodations were sparse. In twentieth-century America, it is no less an essential art, for the world teems with lonely, needy people who need a word of encouragement from a brother.

This writer watched this mark of hospitality operate on the campus where she taught last year. A student in his mid-thirties, divorced and unable to see his child with any degree of regularity, became despondent and frustrated. A co-student sensed his need and practiced hospitality, inviting the lonely fellow to share time with him and his family. It was a dose of medicine, for the hospitality extended the necessary encouragement. A Christian man is hospitable.

A genuine man is a man whose inner life, home, and public life are lived in tune with God's Word.

Faithful Devotion

The fourth cluster of manly traits relates to a man's faith. It is not "sissy" for a man to serve God. As a matter of fact, the writer of Proverbs said:

My son, if you accept my words and store up my commands within you, turning your ear to wisdom and applying your heart to understanding, and if you call out for insight and cry aloud for understanding, and if you look for it as for silver and search for it as for hidden treasure, then you will understand the fear of the Lord and find the knowledge of God. Thus you will walk in the ways of good men and keep to the paths of the righteous (Proverbs 2:1-5, 20).

Let love and faithfulness never leave you; bind them around your neck, write them on the tablet of your heart. Then you will win favor and a good name in the sight of God and man. Trust in the Lord with all your heart and lean not on your own understanding; in all your ways acknowledge him, and he will make your paths straight (Proverbs 3:3-6).

Paul said that a man is to be devout (Titus 1:8). The word devout, *hosios* in the original language, refers to practical holiness. It is an attitude of holiness that is acted out in observable human behavior.

Paul himself sets this example of masculinity. He wrote: "You are witnesses, and so is God, of how holy, righteous and blameless we were among you who believed" (I Thessalonians 2:10). It was observable behavior. Today's man must do the same.

A real man must develop a quality of life that accurately communicates God's will to others (I Timothy 3:2, Titus 1:9). Such a man is sensitive to God's will, but he must be able to communicate with others in a non-threatening, objective manner. Paul told Timothy, "And the Lord's servant must not quarrel; instead, he must be kind to everyone, able to teach, not resentful. Those who oppose him he must gently instruct . . ." (II Timothy 2:24-25). He further added, "He must hold firmly to the trustworthy message as it has been taught, so that he can encourage others by sound doctrine and refute those who oppose it" (Titus 1:8).

91

The man who is God's man must:
1. *Learn* more and more of God's Word (II Timothy 2:2).
2. *Believe* more and more of God's Word (Titus 1:9).
3. *Live* more and more of God's Word (II Timothy 2:24-25).[1]

He has a faith and he can communicate it.

Conclusion

The Bible is a practical book with practical guidelines for Christian men. Much of what American culture insists is masculine is not even mentioned in Scripture. Many qualities, such as gentleness and uncontentiousness, that are believed to be unbecoming to a "real man" are a part of God's prescriptions for successful manhood.

What are we to conclude then? For men, as it was for women, there are masculine characteristics that are culturally determined. There seems to be no reason to feel compelled to reject them so long as they are not direct violations of God's prescriptions for manhood. At the same time, males must keep their eyes on Biblical definitions and practice those regardless of the prevailing cultural ethic. Flawless in reputation, peerless in character, Christlike at home, and faithfully devoted to God—that is genuine masculinity!

Summary Statements

A Christian man is marked by four distinctive qualities:
1. Flawless reputation.
2. Peerless character.
3. Christlike at home.
4. Faithful devotion.

---

1. Gene Getz, *The Measure of a Man* (Glendale, California: Regal, 1974), p. 78.

FOR DISCUSSION

1. What does the Bible define as genuinely masculine characteristics?
2. How can these masculine characteristics be applied in contemporary society?
3. In what ways do the Bible and contemporary culture differ as to what are genuine masculine characteristics? In what ways are they alike?

REFERENCES

1. Barclay, William. *The Letters to Timothy, Titus, and Philemon.* Philadelphia: Westminster, 1976.
2. Getz, Gene A. *The Measure of A Man.* Glendale, California: Regal, 1974.
3. Mounce, Robert. *Pass It On.* Glendale, California: Regal, 1979.

Chapter Eight

LAWS REGARDING SEXUAL CONDUCT

Covenant people are different than their neighbors. Nowhere is this more clearly seen than in the area of sexual attitudes and practices. The Bible is explicit when it comes to man's sexual nature and conduct, making clear a major difference between God's people and her pagan neighbors.

Because personality is inextricably bound up in a person's sexuality, God provided man with guidelines for dealing with this powerful human force that colors so much of his conduct and intention. Sexuality is frankly recognized and accepted in the Bible, yet is kept in its proper perspective in the totality of life.

Covenant People are Distinctive

To understand the Biblical directives in regard to sexual conduct, one must first understand the religions of Israel's neighbors whose practices were in stark contrast to Hebrew monotheism. Those peoples who surrounded Israel practiced religions that were essentially nature cults. Religious ritual was often erotic, sensual, bound to and celebrating the rhythms of the seasons.

Pagan neighbors had become farmers, people of the land who were aware of a certain degree of dependability in their environment. Polytheistic religions sprang up to adapt to the forces of nature and to insure dependability in seasonal cycles. Generally speaking, each god in the pantheon had his sphere of influence and power, and he also had a goddess with a complementary task. They begat children who joined in the pantheon.

In pagan religions there was constant conflict between opposing forces of nature. For example, according to one

94

myth, the goddess of fertility was carried off to dwell captive in the underworld each fall and winter, but in the spring she would escape her captor and spring would come once again.

The gods were rooted in nature. Man's problem, then, was to integrate his own existence into the cosmic rhythm. His life was a reflection of the life of the gods. All of this had profound implications for the relationship between sex and religion.

Egyptians

In Egypt, the Nile and the sky were the greatest of the gods. Anything born was the result of intercourse between the sky god Sibu and the earth goddess Muit. The greatest of the sky gods was Ra, the sun god, whose function was fertilization of the earth. Plants, birds, reptiles, and animals, especially the goat and the bull, were at various times symbols of sexual power. Osiris, the god of popular religion, was thought to dwell in the bull and the ram, and he was depicted with large sexual organs to signal his tremendous power to fertilize the Nile. Many temple reliefs showed gods with large, erect sex organs.

Osiris' wife and sister was Isis, the Great Mother. It was she who, it was believed, fertilized the rich, black earth, bringing forth grain and vegetation.

Egyptian belief had several consequences. First, it gave rise to temple prostitution, although not practiced on as wide a scale as some of the other fertility religions. Secondly, Egypt was a matriarchial society where women occupied a high status. For example, estates were handed down through the female line. Finally, there was the practice of incest. The Pharaoh married his own sister as did others of nobility.

95

However, during the Hyksos period, perhaps 1800-1600 B.C., a more patriarchal society emerged.[1]

Babylonians

The gods of Babylon numbered sixty-five thousand. Each township or village had its own gods or goddesses whose appetites were large—for food, for drink, for sex. Gradually, these gods and goddesses were organized into a pantheon with Marduk as the chief deity. Side by side with him sat Ishta, the goddess of fertility, who had jurisdiction over love and war, motherhood and prostitution, masculinity and femininity. She was sometimes pictured as a nude female with inviting breasts offered for suck to her devotees. Her love affairs were numerous and colorful.

A popular Babylonian myth had Ishtar as the central character. Her lover-brother-son, Tammuz, was killed by a wild boar and traveled to the underworld which was ruled over by Ishtar's sister, Ereshkigal. Ishtar, weeping for her lover, journeyed to Aralu (the Babylonian name for the realm of the dead) to restore him to life. While Ishtar was in the underworld, the world lost its fertility and all life languished. That alarmed the deities who demanded Tammuz' release. That accomplished, Ishtar and Tammuz returned to the earth where fertility was revived.

The religion of Babylon had little connection with morality. In fact, Babylon was synonomous with immorality and unbridled license. Herodotus reports one custom:

> Every native woman is required, once in her life, to sit in the temple of Venus, and have intercourse with some stranger

---

1. Much of the data for this section was taken from William Graham Cole, *Sex and Love in the Bible* (New York: Association Press, 1959), pp. 166-171.

. . . Passages marked out in a straight line lead in every direction through the women, along which strangers pass and make their choice. When a woman has once seated herself, she must not return home until some stranger has thrown a piece of silver into her lap, and lain with her outside the temple . . . The woman follows the first man that throws, and refuses no one. But when she has had intercourse and has absolved herself from the obligation to the goddess, she returns home, and after that time however great a sum you may give her you will not gain possession of her.[2]

These women described by Herodotus were not prostitutes proper, although temple prostitutes were common. The worship of the principle of fertility logically included the sexual act, and both male and female concubines were common.

A large amount of freedom was permitted in premarital relationships in Babylon, but marriages were strictly monogamous. Trial marriages were permissible.[3]

Canaanites

The Canaanites worshiped a variety of deities designated by the generic term *baal*. The pantheon also included goddesses such as Asherah, Astarte, and Anak. They, too, were goddesses of fertility. One of the Canaanite myths describes Baal as being killed every spring by Mot who then dominated the climate from April to October. But Baal overcame death in the fall and was restored to life. Virility then returned to the land in early spring when Baal mated with one of the fertility goddesses.

---

2. Herodotus, *Book I*, p. 199.
3. Cole, *op cit.*, pp. 166-172.

The Canaanites were a pastoral people. Emerging from their chief concerns of life, their worship assumed an identical concern: to insure the fertility of the land, flocks, and the human populace. It was considered an act of worship to assist in the fertility rites, so much so that sacred prostitution was common. A characteristic feature was sexual intercourse by priests and priestesses and others to emulate and stimulate the deities who bestowed fertility. Orgies involving the use of intoxicants and indiscriminate sexual activity were not at all uncommon. There was also a recognized homosexual guild in the Canaanite temples.[4]

Israelites

In the religions of her neighbors, Israel saw sex elevated to the realm of the divine. The inexperience of the nomadic Hebrews in the agricultural arena would leave them particularly vulnerable to the local baals who promised good harvests. The exotic mystic cult, with sensual pleasures encouraged in worship, would hold an attraction, especially if the Hebrews were not clearly instructed in appropriate sexual conduct.

The worship of God was not a fertility cult. Never did God want it to be confused with any of the sexual practices of pagan religions. God would act in the experience of human history, not in the heavens or the seasonal cycles. There was no consort, no divine family, no sexual activity. Contrary to the practices of other nations, God was alert, awake, watching, deeply involved in the concerns of life. That was why the Old Testament opposed the sexual behaviors of the fertility cults.

---

4. *Ibid.*, pp. 177-181.

Hebrews were not prudes, however. It was not sexuality to which God objected (it was He who had made man a sexual creature), but it was to the uses to which sexuality was put, the quality of relationships involved, and their consequences.

Sexuality and personality belonged together, subject to God who cherished and sanctified human existence. To use one's sexuality to manipulate another or for purely sensual use was to divorce it from personality. Persons are never to be treated as things. But Israel's neighbors disregarded responsibility, respect, and reverence. Temple prostitutes were used and left. Fertility cult orgies tore sexuality away from personality.

The teachings regarding sexual behavior in Leviticus 15 and 18 were a distinct contrast to all those cultures with whom Israel interacted. They called for a disciplined life and clearly repudiated the idea of magic or sexuality as an influence in a man's relationship to God. One source suggests:

> In Canaan prostitution and fertility rites were all mixed up in worship. In Israel, by sharp contrast, anything suggesting the sexual is strictly banned from the worship of God . . . The intention was not to write off this side of life as "dirty" . . . The purpose is to ensure its separation from the worship of God.[5]

Provision For Sexual Hygiene

Hygienic considerations prevail in Leviticus 15: "The role of strict cleanliness in all sexual matters was a positive safeguard to health."[6]

---

5. David and Pat Alexander (ed.), *Eerdmans' Handbook of the Bible* (Grand Rapids: William B. Eerdmans Publishing Company, 1973), p. 176.
   6. *Ibid.*

Male Discharges

The Lord said to Moses and Aaron, "Speak to the Israelites and say to them, 'When any man has a bodily discharge, the discharge is unclean. This is how his discharge will bring about uncleanness: Any bed the man with a discharge lies on will be unclean, and anything he sits on will be unclean. Anyone who touches his bed must wash his clothes and bathe with water, and he will be unclean till evening. Whoever sits on anything that the man with a discharge sat on must wash his clothes and bathe with water, and he will be unclean till evening. Whoever touches the man who had a discharge must wash his clothes and bathe with water, and he will be unclean till evening. If the man with the discharge spits on someone who is clean, that person must wash his clothes and bathe with water, and he will be unclean till evening. Everything the man sits on when riding will be unclean, and whoever touches any of the things that were under him will be unclean till evening; whoever picks up those things must wash his clothes and bathe with water, and he will be unclean till evening. Anyone the man with a discharge touches without rinsing his hands with water must wash his clothes and bathe with water, and he will be unclean till evening. A clay pot that the man touches must be broken, and any wooden article is to be rinsed with water. When a man is cleansed from his discharge, he is to count off seven days for his ceremonial cleansing, he must wash his clothes and bathe himself with fresh water, and he will be clean. On the eighth day he must take two doves or two young pigeons and come before the Lord to the entrance of the Tent of Meeting and give them to the priest. The priest is to sacrifice them, the one for a sin offering and the other for a burnt offering. In this way he will make atonement before the Lord for the man because of his discharge'" (Leviticus 15:1-15).

100

This seems to refer to a secretion from the sexual organ. It would appear to be a diseased flow of semen, or perhaps a urethal problem. One commentator suggests that it could refer to a venereal disease.[7]

Whatever the cause of the discharge, the directive seems to be an hygienic precaution designed to protect the nation from disease. The procedure was to wash the clothes and bathe, then bathe ceremonially after seven days. On the eighth day, he was to make a burnt offering to signify his cleansing.

> When a man has an emission of semen, he must bathe his whole body with water, and he will be unclean until evening. Any clothing or leather that has semen on it must be washed with water, and it will be unclean until evening. When a man lies with a woman and there is an emission of semen, both must bathe with water, and they will be unclean till evening (Leviticus 15:16-18).

The text is unclear at this point. This could be a spontaneous, involuntary emission, the so-called "wet dream," or it could be premature ejaculation, or possibly *coitus interruptus*. No definitive word can be given, for there is no other Biblical source to aid in interpreting this one. It seems clear that it does *not* refer to normal sexual intercourse. At any rate, whatever the action, which must have been understood by the Israelites, the cleansing was merely bathing.

Female Discharges

> When a woman has her regular flow of blood, the purity of her monthly period will last seven days, and anyone who

---

7. R. K. Harrison, *Leviticus* (Downers Grove, Illinois: InterVarsity Press, 1980), p. 161.

touches her will be unclean till evening. Anything she lies on during her period will be unclean, and anything she sits on will be unclean. Whoever touches her bed must wash his clothes and bathe with water, and he will be unclean till evening. If a man lies with her and her monthly flow touches him, he will be unclean for seven days; any bed he lies on will be unclean (Leviticus 15:19-24).

Do not approach a woman to have sexual relations during the uncleanness of her monthly period (Leviticus 18:19).

If a man lies with a woman during her monthly period and has sexual relations with her, he has exposed the source of her flow, and she has also uncovered it. Both of them must be cut off from their people (Leviticus 20:18).

Two reasons could provide motivation for this directive. The first was to give a woman respite from sexual activity during her time of discomfort. Such a reason gives woman's needs equal consideration to those of men.

However, the second reason could well have to do with Israel's distinctiveness. The Hebrews regarded blood as the source of life: ". . . the life of every creature is its blood" (Leviticus 17:14a). Some of Israel's neighbors who practiced fertility rites ate raw flesh and drank blood as a part of their orgiastic rituals. It could well be that God wanted to totally divorce Israel's worship and sexual practices from that of her neighbors. After seven days, however, a woman would be ceremonially cleansed, after which she would make an offering of pigeons or doves.

When a woman has a discharge of blood for many days at a time other than her monthly period or has a discharge that continues beyond her period, she will be unclean as long as she has the discharge, just as in the days of her period. Any bed she lies on while her discharge continues will be unclean, as is her bed during her monthly period. Whoever touches them will be unclean; he must wash his clothes and bathe with water, and he will be unclean till evning. When she is cleansed from her discharge, she must count off seven days, and after that she will be ceremonially clean. On the eighth day she must take two doves or young pigeons and bring them to the priest at the entrance to the Tent of Meeting. The priest is to sacrifice one for a sin offering and the other for a burnt offering. In this way he will make atonement for her before the Lord for the uncleanness of her discharge (Leviticus 15:25-30).

This was a vaginal discharge apart from the regular menstrual flow. After the flow ceased, she was to wait seven days for ceremonial cleansing and the offerings.

Regulations Regarding Childbirth

The Lord said to Moses, "Say to the Israelites: 'A woman who becomes pregnant and gives birth to a son will be ceremonially unclean for seven days, just as she is unclean during her monthly period. On the eighth day the boy is to be circumcised. Then the woman must wait thirty-three days to be purified from her bleeding. She must not touch anything sacred or go to the sanctuary until the days of her purification are over. If she gives birth to a daughter, for two weeks the woman will be unclean, as in her period. Then she must wait sixty-six days to be purified from her bleeding. When the days of her purification for a son or daughter are over, she is to bring to the priest at the entrance to the Tent of Meeting a year-old lamb for a burnt offering. He shall offer them before the Lord to make atonement for her, and then she will be ceremonially clean from her flow of blood. These are the regulations for the woman who gives birth to a boy or a girl. If she cannot afford a lamb, she is to bring two doves or two young pigeons, one for a burnt offering and the other for a sin offering. In this way the priest will make atonement for her, and she will be clean'" (Leviticus 12:1-8).

The laws of purification following childbirth are straightforward. If the child was male, a thirty-three day purification period was to be observed, double that for a girl. The mother was ceremonially unclean for seven days, just as during her monthly period. There was to be restraint from intercourse during that time. On the eighth day the boy was to be circumcised, a covenant rite. Then she was to wait thirty-three days for complete cleansing of discharge, after which she presented her purification offerings. Every period of time was doubled for a girl, perhaps because in antiquity it was commonly believed that bleeding and watery discharge continued longer after the birth of a girl.[8]

Regulations Concerning Sexual Relationships

Leviticus 18:6 states the general principle for sexual relationships:

> The Lord said to Moses, "Speak to the Israelites and say to them: 'I am the Lord your God. You must not do as they do in Egypt, where you went to live, and you must not do as they do in the Land of Canaan, where I am bringing you. Do not follow their practices. You must obey my laws and be careful to follow my decrees. I am the Lord your God. Keep my decrees and laws, for the man who obeys them will live by them. I am the Lord. *No one is to approach any close relative to have sexual relations. I am the Lord God.'"*

---

8. C. F. Keil and F. Delitzsch, *Biblical Commentary on the Old Testament,* Vol. 2. *The Pentateuch* (Grand Rapids, William B. Eerdmans Publishing Company, 1971), p. 376.

This entire section is a distinct contrast to the practices of Egypt, Babylon, or Canaan, outlined earlier in this section. The remainder of the chapter explicitly instructs them of those persons with whom they are *not* to engage in sexual intercourse:

1. *Mother:* "Do not dishonor your father by having sexual relations with your mother. She is your mother; do not have relations with her" (Leviticus 18:7).
2. *Stepmother:* "Do not have sexual relations with your father's wife; that would dishonor your father" (Leviticus 18:8).
3. *Sister or Stepsister:* "Do not have sexual relations with your sister, either your father's daughter or your mother's daughter, whether she was born in the same home or elsewhere. Do not have sexual relations with the daughter of your father's wife, born to your father; she is your sister" (Leviticus 18:9, 11).
4. *Grandchild:* "Do not have sexual relations with your son's daughter or your daughter's daughter; that would dishonor you" (Leviticus 18:10).
5. *Aunt:* "Do not have sexual relations with your father's sister; she is your father's close relative. Do not have sexual relations with your mother's sister, because she is your mother's close relative. Do not dishonor your father's brother by approaching his wife to have sexual relations; she is your aunt" (Leviticus 18:12-14).
6. *Daughter-in-law:* "Do not have sexual relations with your daughter-in-law. She is your son's wife; do not have relations with her" (Leviticus 18:15).
7. *Sister-in-law:* "Do not have sexual relations with your brother's wife; that would dishonor your brother. Do not take your wife's sister as a rival wife and have

105

sexual relations with her while your wife is living" (Leviticus 18:16, 18).

8. *Relatives:* "Do not have sexual relations with a woman and her daughter. Do not have sexual relations with either her son's daughter or her daughter's daughter; they are her close relatives. That is wickedness" (Leviticus 18:17).

9. *Neighbor:* "Do not have intercourse with your neighbor's wife and defile yourself with her" (Leviticus 18:20).

10. *Same sex:* "Do not lie with a man as one lies with a woman; that is detestable" (Leviticus 18:22).

11. *Animals:* "Do not have sexual relations with an animal and defile yourself with it. A woman must not present herself to an animal to have sexual relations with it; that is a perversion" (Leviticus 18:23).

The results of ignoring God's directives were also clearly delineated:

Do not defile yourselves in any of these ways, because this is how the nations that I am going to drive out before you became defiled. Even the land was defiled, so I punished it for its sin, and the land vomited out its inhabitants. But you must keep my decrees and my laws. The native-born and the aliens living among you must not do any of these detestable things, for all these things were done by the people who lived in the land before you, and the land became defiled. And if you defile the land, it will vomit you out as it vomited out the nations that were before you. Everyone who does any of these detestable things—such persons must be cut off from their people. Keep my requirements and do not follow any of the detestable customs that were practiced before you came and do not defile yourselves with them. I am the Lord your God (Leviticus 18:24-30).

God meant for His people to reflect His character, not that of their neighbors.

Conclusion

God's regulations for sexual conduct take on meaning only as they are viewed against the backdrop of the sensual religious practices of Egypt, Canaan, and Babylon. God knew that a man's conduct reflected his deity. He called for responsible followers whose very lives, to the last intimate detail, reflected His character. In that light, the laws of Leviticus make sense, for they set Israel apart. Never could her worship and her behavior be confused with paganism if she were to heed the guidelines given by God. The same is true of this age as well.

Summary Statements

1. Covenant people are to reflect sexual conduct distinct from pagan religions.
2. Israel's neighbors worshiped in fertility religions where sexual intercourse was an act of worship.
3. God gave Israel explicit guidelines in sexual matters to preserve His worship from confusion with fertility cults.

FOR DISCUSSION

1. How was sexuality interwoven with Egyptian, Canaanite, and Babylonian religious practice?
2. In what ways did God's laws for sexual conduct make Israelites distinctive in worship and conduct.
3. Summarize the laws of sexual conduct given to Israel.
4. How were Hebrew sexual relationships distinctive?

5. In what ways do God's regulations for sexual conduct reflect the personal nature of God and His call for worship?

REFERENCES

1. Albright, William F. *Archaeology and the Religion of Israel*. Baltimore: Johns Hopkins University, 1968.
2. Alexander, David and Pat (ed.). *Eerdmans' Handbook of the Bible*. Grand Rapids: William B. Eerdmans Publishing Company, 1973.
3. Anderson, Bernhard W. *Understanding the Old Testament*. 3rd ed. Englewood Cliffs, New Jersey: Prentice-Hall, 1957.
4. Buttrick, George (ed.) *The Interpreter's Dictionary of the Bible*. New York: Abingdon Press, 1959.
5. Cole, William Graham. *Sex and Love in the Bible*. New York: Association Press, 1959.
6. DeWelt, Don. *Leviticus*. Joplin, Missouri: College Press, 1975.
7. Harrison, R. K. *Introduction to the Old Testament*. Grand Rapids: William B. Eerdmans Publishing Company, 1969.
8. _____. *Leviticus*. Downers Grove, Illinois: Inter-Varsity Press, 1980.
9. Keil, C. F. and Delitzsch. *Biblical Commentary on the Old Testament*. Vol. 2. *The Pentateuch*. Grand Rapids: William B. Eerdmans Publishing Company, 1971.

Part II — Misuses of Sexual Identity

The first section of this book described the grand purposes God designed for sexuality and outlined the blessings realized from its proper use. A beautiful gift, sexuality is sometimes distorted and used for unfortunate ends. Like all the rest of the gifts given to him at the time of creation, sexuality, good by design, has often been grossly misused by man.

Fornication, adultery, divorce, homosexuality, licentiousness, bestiality, rape—all are obscene misuses of man's sexual nature. The second section of this book focuses on the tragic misuses all too often made of sexuality. Just as frankly as the Bible extols the virtues of sexuality properly expressed, it describes the misuses and warns of the consequences of that misuse.

Part II — Misuses of Sexual Identity

Chapter Nine

FORNICATION: FLESH SERVING ITSELF

Man was made for specific purpose: to glorify God. Male and female, Adam and Eve, were made to bring glory to their Creator. Designed as sexual creatures and intended to enjoy their sexuality, they were created to praise God and to achieve God's goals for them, even sexually. Sexuality is a basic component of man's personality, and it, like every other facet of his personality, is to be used as God intended it to be.

To state man's intended purpose is to state a lofty ideal, one marred by the intrusion of sin. One awful distortion of man's ideal is the use of his sexuality in a way that is alien to God's purposes. Fornication is one such distortion.

Fornication Defined

The word translated "fornication" or "sexual immorality" is *porneia* in the original language, a word used several times in the New Testament. Without exception it refers to illicit sexual intercourse, that is, intercourse not within the parameters of God's guidelines for the use of sexuality.

Porneia is a broader term than the one used for adultery, although the two words are equivalent in content. *Porneia* refers to any illicit sexual intercourse while adultery refers specifically to illicit intercourse by married people. In either case, illicit sexual conduct is listed as a vice next to idolatry in the letters of the New Testament.

The New Testament deals with the subject of fornication in far greater detail than does the Old Testament, although explicit instructions are given in Leviticus and Deuteronomy for dealing with fornicators. This may be due, at least in part, to the moral tone of the Greek world with which the early church had to contend.

The early church was established in the midst of Greek culture. In pre-Homeric times, the Greeks had worshiped a great mother goddess who annually took to herself a new main consort whose only function was to be a royal stud. This matriarchal society became a patriarchy only in Hellenic times. Homosexuality flourished in Crete, and both male and female prostitution were common. It is little wonder, then, that the churches in Greek cities—Corinth, Ephesus, Colossae, and Thessalonica—had members who would have been greatly influenced by the culture of the day. Old patterns of thinking were difficult to break.

Greek culture dominated even though the known world was under Roman political domination. But Roman morality was little different than that of her political predecessors, for Romans valued neither morality nor monogamy, and prostitution was prevalent. Roman values were as alien to the faith as were those of Greek culture. There was no doubt about it: it was the church against the world. And God was explicit in defining illicit sex as unacceptable behavior for covenant people.

Fornication Rejected

Old Testament

The Old Testament law clearly established the fact that sexuality, as divinely established as it is, was to be fully expressed only within marriage. Sexual intercourse was seen as a surrender of one's private identity to another for the sake of creating a single corporate identity. Anything else

111

is exploitation. (That is not to say, of course, that sexuality cannot be exploited within marriage—it sometimes is, especially when it is used as an emotional weapon.)

Old Testament law was straightforward and unequivocal.

> If a man seduces a virgin who is not pledged to be married and sleeps with her, he must pay the bride-price, and she shall be his wife. If her father absolutely refuses to give her to him, he must still pay the bride-price for virgins (Exodus 22:16-17).

Fornication was clearly a violation of God's law.

Fornication was also equated with prostitution in the Old Testament:

> Do not degrade your daughter by making her a prostitute, or the land will turn to prostitution and be filled with wickedness (Leviticus 19:29).

> If a priest's daughter defiles herself by becoming a prostitute, she disgraces her father; she must be burned in the fire (Leviticus 21:9).

A person's sexual integrity was thought to be of such importance that the high priest could marry *only* a virgin.

> The high priest, the one among his brothers who has had the anointing oil poured on his head and who has been ordained to wear the priestly garments, must not let his hair become unkempt or tear his clothes. He must not enter a place where is a dead body. He must not make himself unclean, even for his father or mother, nor leave the sanctuary of his God or desecrate it, because he has been dedicated by the anointing oil of his God. I am the Lord.
>
> The woman he marries must be a virgin. He must not marry a widow, a divorced woman, or a woman defiled by prostitution, but only a virgin from his own people, so he will not defile his offspring among his people. I am the Lord, who makes him holy (Leviticus 21:10-15).

112

Likewise, any man had the right to insist that his bride be a virgin. Yet, at the same time, God protected her from whimsical divorce on the grounds that she was not a virgin.

If a man takes a wife and, after lying with her, dislikes her and slanders her and gives her a bad name, saying, "I married this woman, but when I approached her, I did not find proof of her virginity," then the girl's father and mother shall bring proof that she was a virgin to the town elders at the gate. The girl's father will say to the elders, "I gave my daughter in marriage to this man, but he dislikes her. Now he has slandered her and said, 'I did not find your daughter to be a virgin.' But here is the proof of my daughter's virginity." Then her parents shall display the cloth before the elders of the town, and the elders shall take the man and punish him. They shall fine him a hundred shekels of silver and give them to the girl's father, because this man has given an Israelite virgin a bad name. She shall continue to be his wife; he must not divorce her as long as he lives.

If, however, the charge is true and no proof of the girl's virginity can be found, she shall be brought to the door of her father's house and there the men of her town shall stone her to death. She has done a disgraceful thing in Israel by being promiscuous while still in her father's house. You must purge the evil from among you (Deuteronomy 22:13-21).

The law established other conditions of protection for a woman. At the same time, it held her responsible for her sexual conduct.

If a man happens to meet in a town a virgin pledged to be married and he sleeps with her, you shall take both of them to the gate of that town and stone them to death—the girl because she was in a town and did not scream for help, and the man because he violated another man's wife. You must purge the evil from among you.

113

But if out in the country a man happens to meet a girl pledged to be married and rapes her, only the man who has done this shall die. Do nothing to the girl; she has committed no sin deserving death. This case is like that of someone who attacks and murders his neighbor, for the man found the girl out in the country, and though the betrothed girl screamed, there was no one to rescue her.

If a man happens to meet a virgin who is not pledged to be married and rapes her and they are discovered, he shall pay the girl's father fifty shekels of silver. he must marry the girl, for he has violated her. He can never divorce her as long as he lives (Deuteronomy 22:23-29).

There is simply no escaping the fact that pre-marital sex was unacceptable behavior to God. A person was—and is—responsible to use his sexuality for its intended purpose.

New Testament

The issue of sexual ethics recurs in the New Testament. A direct prohibition of fornication is found in Acts 15:20 during the Jerusalem Council. The issue precipitating the call of the council was the demand by some Pharisaical Jews that Gentile believers be circumcised in order to be fully Christians. After lengthy deliberation of the question, the decision was reached to excuse the Gentiles from circumcision since it was distinctly a Jewish covenant rite. But they did instruct the Gentiles to abstain from four practices: (1) eating food offered to idols; (2) eating meat of animals that had been strangled; (3) eating blood; and, (4) sexual immorality. The word used for sexual immorality was *porneia*, including, therefore, illicit sexual intercourse for both married and single people. That directive is reiterated in Acts 15:29 and 21:25.

114

The basic Christian ethic regarding fornication is set forth in I Corinthians 6:12-20:

> "Everything is permissible for me"—but not everything is beneficial. "Everything is permissible for me"—but I will not be mastered by anything. "Food for the stomach and the stomach for food"—but God will destroy them both. The body is not meant for sexual immorality, but for the Lord, and the Lord for the body. By his power God raised the Lord from the dead, and he will raise us also. Do you know that your bodies are members of Christ himself? Shall I then take the members of Christ and unite them with a prostitute? Never! Do you not know that he who unites himself with a prostitute is one with her in body? For it is said, "The two will become one flesh." But he who unites himself with the Lord is one with him in spirit.
>
> Flee from sexual immorality. All other sins a man commits are outside his body, but he who sins sexually sins against his own body. Do you not know that your body is a temple of the Holy Spirit who is in you, whom you have received from God? You are not your own; you were bought at a price. Therefore honor God with your body.

The basic teaching is this: there is a lawful purpose and function for everything created by God. To misuse anything made by God is to pervert it. The passage makes it crystal clear that although sex is good and sexuality is a gift from God, it is to be expressed *with one person within marriage*. As a matter of fact, Paul states it this way in I Corinthians 7:2:

> But since there is so much immorality, each man should have his own wife, and each woman her own husband.

It wasn't that Paul had a low view of marriage, as some have charged. Rather, it is admission of the prominence of sexuality in a person's life, a force that can overwhelm an individual if he isn't on the alert. It is also recognition of the fact that this physical force can—and should—be channeled into proper expression—in marriage.

The letter to the Ephesians also calls for proper sexual behavior:

> But among you there must not be even a hint of sexual immorality, or of any kind of impurity, or of greed, because these are improper for God's holy people.
>
> . . . .
>
> For of this you can be sure: No immoral, impure or greedy person—such a man is an idolator—has any inheritance in the kingdom of Christ and of God (Ephesians 5:3, 5).

Similar instructions were given to the churches at Colossae and Thessalonica:

> Put to death, therefore, whatever belongs to your earthly nature: sexual immorality, impurity, lust, evil desires and greed which is idolatry. Because of these the wrath of God is coming (Colossians 3:5-6).
>
> It is God's will that you should be holy; that you should avoid sexual immorality; that each of you should learn to control his own body in a way that is holy and honorable, not in passionate lust like the heathen, who do not know God; and that in this matter no one should wrong his brother or take advantage of him. The Lord will punish men for all such sins, as we have already told you and warned you. For God did not call us to be impure, but to live a holy life. Therefore, he who rejects this instruction does not reject man but God, who gives you his Holy Spirit (I Thessalonians 4:3-8).

Fornication was also included in the list of sins that would disqualify a person from the kingdom of God:

116

The acts of the sinful nature are obvious: sexual immorality, impurity and debauchery; idolatry and witchcraft; hatred, discord, jealousy, fits of rage, selfish ambition, dissensions, factions and envy; drunkenness, orgies, and the like. I warn you, as I did before, that those who live like this will not inherit the kingdom of God (Galations 5:19-21).

He who overcomes will inherit all this, and I will be his God and he will be my son. But the cowardly, the unbelieving, the vile, the murderers, the sexually immoral, those who practice magic arts, the idolators and all liars—their place will be in the fiery lake of burning sulfur. This is the second death (Revelation 21:7-8).

Why Fornication Is Wrong

The contemporary ethic argues that pre-marital sex is acceptable. Only prudes and killjoys would deny its validity, they contend. This ethic insists that pre-marital sex is perfectly normal and appropriate if two people are committed to each other. Current statistics suggest that pre-marital sexual intercourse is a common practice, making that "average" behavior.

Regardless of the contemporary ethic or the current practice, however, the Bible clearly designates pre-marital sex as fornication and calls it sin. But that designation emerges from more than mere capriciousness on the part of God. Fornication is sin for at least two reasons:

1. It is alien to man's nature (I Corinthians 6:18). The Bible calls it a sin against oneself, perhaps because it is flesh serving itself and its desires.
2. It defeats God's purpose for sexuality (I Corinthians 6:13). A person's sexuality was given to him by God for a specific purpose: to know intimate love in marriage.

But fornication takes a body, made to belong to Christ, and severs it from its holy purpose in relation to Christ, a grievous sin indeed to trade a God-given function for the pleasure of a moment.

Indeed the Biblical evidence is in regarding fornication, and the verdict is that it is a distortion of everything God wants men to be.

Fornication Can Be Forgiven

To all those who have violated God's design for sexual behavior there is good news: forgiveness is yours if you want it. Paul acknowledged that forgiveness when he wrote to the Corinthians:

Do you not know that the wicked will not inherit the kingdom of God? Do not be deceived: Neither the sexually immoral nor idolators nor adulterers nor male prostitutes nor homosexual offenders nor thieves nor the greedy nor drunkards nor slanderers nor swindlers will inherit the kingdom of God. *And that is what some of you were. But you were washed, you were sanctified, you were justified in the name of the Lord Jesus Christ and by the Spirit of our God* (I Corinthians 6:9-11).

He restated it in his letters to the Ephesians and Colossians:

Be imitators of God, therefore, as dearly loved children and live a life of love, just as Christ loved us and gave himself up for us as a fragrant offering and sacrifice to God.

But among you there must not be even a hint of sexual immorality, or of any kind of impurity, or of greed, because these are improper for God's holy people. Nor should there be obscenity, foolish talk or coarse joking, which are out of place, but rather thanksgiving. For of this you can be sure: No immoral, impure or greedy person—such as man is an

118

idolator—has any inheritance in the kingdom of Christ and of God. Let no one deceive you with empty words, for because of such things God's wrath comes on those who are disobedient. Therefore, do not be partners with them.

For you were once darkness, but now you are light in the Lord (for the fruit of the light consists in all goodness, righteousness and truth) and find out what pleases the Lord (Ephesians 5:1-10).

Put to death, therefore, whatever belongs to your earthly nature: sexual immorality, impurity, lust, evil desires and greed, which is idolatry. Because of these, the wrath of God is coming. *You used to walk in these ways, in the life you once lived. But now you must rid yourselves of all such things as these:* anger, rage, malice, slander, and filthy language from your lips. Do not lie to each other, since *you have taken off your old self with its practices and have put on the new self, which is being renewed in knowledge in the image of its Creator* (Colossians 3:5-10).

That message is for today, too.

Conclusion

Man was made with a specific purpose: to use his sexuality, as well as the remaining components of his personality, to glorify God. The Bible clearly teaches that fornication is a direct violation of man's design. Yet, the good news is that sexual sin, like all other sin, can be forgiven through Jesus Christ.

Summary Statements

1. Fornication is any illicit sexual intercourse.
2. The Old Testament prohibits fornication.
3. The New Testament teaches that fornication is a direct

violation of God's design for sexuality.
4. Fornication defeats God's purpose for man because it severs a person's body from intimate relationship with Christ.
5. Fornication is a forgivable sin.

FOR DISCUSSION

1. Summarize the Old Testament teaching about fornication.
2. Summarize the New Testament teaching about fornication.
3. What is the basic teaching about sexuality outlined in I Corinthians 6?
4. How would you explain to a person that pre-marital sex is a violation of God's will?
5. Suppose a person, known to be sexually immoral, talks to you about becoming a Christian. He expresses guilt about his previous sexual conduct and doubt that God could forgive him. How would you respond?

REFERENCES

1. Applebury, T. R. *Studies in I Corinthians.* Joplin, Missouri: College Press, 1963.
2. Cole, William Graham. *Sex and Love in the Bible.* New York: Association Press, 1959.
3. Feucht, Oscar E., Harry G. Coines, Alfred Von Rohr Sauer, and Paul G. Hanson (ed.). *Sex and the Church.* St. Louis: Concordia Press, 1961.
4. Small, Dwight. *Christian, Celebrate Your Sexuality.* Old Tappan, New Jersey: Fleming Revell Company, 1974.
5. White, John. *Eros Defiled.* Downers Grove, Illinois: InterVarsity Press, 1977.

Chapter Ten

ADULTERY: ONE FLESH SEVERED

"Until death do us part" is an accepted—and essential —part of the wedding ceremony. It is affirmation of God's intentions for marriage as a permanent, lifelong commitment between a man and a woman who now become one flesh.

One man married to one woman for a lifetime is positively God's design, as the Bible plainly sets forth. It is not an easy goal to achieve, although it is obviously desirable and possible. To succeed is a supreme victory in realizing God's purpose for a person. But to fail is to distort God's gift of sexuality and to thwart achievement of divine purpose.

The Bible is explicit when it deals with the sin of adultery. One is never left without direction in regard to this use of his sexuality.

Adultery Defined

The word translated "adultery" is *moicheia* in the original language. It literally means "illicit sexual intercourse," the same as *porneia,* discussed in the previous chapter, but with one additional qualifier. It is willful violation of the marriage contract by either of the partners through sexual intercourse with a third party. *Porneia*, then, is the broader term for illicit sexual intercourse, while *moicheia* is the narrower term designating the same behavior as does *porneia*, but behavior in which one person is already married.

It was imperative that God define adultery and warn of its grave consequences, for first the children of Israel and then the church existed in a culture alien to God-given values for marriage. It was not uncommon for a Greek to have a wife plus a courtesan (called *hetaira*). Marriage was not regarded as the establishment of an exclusive sexual relationship. Sexual pleasure was to be taken where one could find it. Demosthenes once said, "We have courtesans for the sake of pleasure; we have concubines for the sake of daily cohabitation; we have wives for the purpose of having children legitimately, and of having a faithful guardian for all our household affairs."

Although the Romans glorified heterosexual love, they valued neither virginity nor monogamy. Cicero said in his speech *In Defense of Caelius,* "If there is anyone who thinks that young men should be absolutely forbidden the love of courtesans, he is indeed extremely severe. I am not able to deny the principle that he states. But he is at variance, not only with the license of his own age, but also from the customs and concessions of our ancestors. When indeed was this not done? When did anyone ever find fault with it? When was permission denied? When was it that that which is now lawful was not lawful?"

The dominant mood of the first century world was easy sex wherever one could find it. Within marriage or outside it made little difference. New believers, especially those Gentile Christians who came to the faith apart from Judaism, took on a totally new lifestyle, one that required new patterns of thinking and conduct.

Adultery Condemned

Old Testament

From the very beginning God had had one design for man's use of his sexuality. One man and one woman, married to each other, were to be committed to each other for

122

a lifetime. Other sexual alliances were unacceptable to Him. (At times, the Israelites practiced polygamy, but that was never said to be a norm for sexual behavior. Some practices existed because of the "hardness of their hearts.")

The sanctity of marriage and the exclusiveness of a marital relationship were presented in the Decalogue. One of the Ten Commandments flatly states: "Thou shalt not commit adultery" (Exodus 20:14). Later, in Leviticus, that principle was expanded and explained. As an introduction to a whole list of illustrative situations, Leviticus 18:1-5 states:

> The Lord said to Moses, "Speak to the Israelites and say to them: 'I am the Lord your God. You must not do as they do in Egypt, where you used to live, and you must not do as they do in the Land of Canaan, where I am bringing you. Do not follow their practices. You must obey my laws and be careful to follow my decrees. I am the Lord your God. Keep my decrees and laws, for the man who obeys them will live by them. I am the Lord.'"

The original penalty for violation of the directive regarding adultery was swift and severe:

> If a man commits adultery with another man's wife—with the wife of his neighbor—both the adulterer and the adulteress must be put to death. If a man sleeps with his father's wife, he has dishonored his father. Both the man and the woman must be put to death; their blood will be on their own heads. If a man sleeps with his daughter-in-law, both of them must be put to death. What they have done is a perversion; their blood will be on their own heads (Leviticus 20:10-12).

There was even a provision for a test of a woman's sexual faithfulness should her husband suspect her of adultery. It is detailed in Numbers 5:11-31. If a man suspected his wife of adultery, he brought her to the priest to undergo a ritual. She was set before the tabernacle with head uncovered and hair loosed. The priest placed some holy water in a clay jar and then stirred in dust from the floor. Curses were written in a book which was dipped into water. Then the woman drank the water. If she had committed adultery, her abdomen would swell. But if she was innocent, there were no ill effects. It not only provided a test of fidelity, but at the same time was a visual symbol to remind the Israelites of the truth: "Thou shalt not commit adultery."

Joseph recognized the exclusiveness of a marital relationship even before the Ten Commandments were formally stated. And he saw fornication and adultery for what they are—sin against God.

> Now Joseph was well-built and handsome, and after a while his master's wife took notice of Joseph and said, "Come to bed with me!" But he refused, "With me in charge," he told her, "my master does not concern himself with anything in the house; everything he owns he has entrusted to my care. No one is greater in this house than I am. My master has withheld nothing from me except you, because you are his wife. How then could I do such a wicked thing and sin against God?" And though she spoke to Joseph day after day, he refused to go to bed with her or even be with her (Genesis 39:6b-10).

Later, when David was king over Israel, II Samuel 11 records the king's adulterous relationship with Bathsheba. Trapped by the knowledge of Bathsheba's pregnancy, David compounded his trouble by arranging for her husband Uriah to be killed in battle. But king or not, he couldn't avoid the judgment of God. The prophet Nathan pronounced that judgment in II Samuel 12, and finally, David, fully convicted of the seriousness of his actions, confessed, "I have sinned against the Lord" (II Samuel 12:13). In his psalm of contrition, he exclaimed, "Against you, you only, have I sinned and done what is evil in your sight" (Psalm 51:4).

Again, warning about the sin of adultery is presented in Proverbs:

> My son, pay attention to my wisdom, listen well to my words of insight, that you may maintain discretion and your lips may preserve knowledge. For the lips of an adulteress drip honey, and her speech is smoother than oil; but in the end she is bitter as gall, sharp as a double-edged sword. Her feet go down to death; her steps lead straight to the grave. She gives no thought to the way of life; her paths are crooked, but she knows it not.
>
> Now, then, my sons, listen to me; do not turn aside from what I say. Keep to a path far from her, do not go near the door of her house, lest you give your best strength to others and your years to one who is cruel, lest strangers feast on your wealth and your toil enrich another man's house. At the end of your life you will groan, when your flesh and body are spent. You will say, "How I hated discipline.' How my heart spurned correction! I would not obey my teachers or listen to my instructors. I have come to the brink of utter ruin in the midst of the whole assembly."
>
> Drink water from your own cistern, running water from your own well. Should your springs overflow in the streets, your streams of water in the public squares? Let them be yours alone, never to be shared with strangers. May your fountain be blessed, and may you rejoice in the wife of your youth. A loving doe, a graceful deer—may her breasts satisfy you always, may you ever be captivated by her love. Why be captivated, my son, by an adulteress? Why embrace the bosom of another man's wife?

For a man's ways are in full view of the Lord, and he examines all his paths. The evil deeds of a wicked man ensnare him; the cords of his sin hold him fast. He will die for lack of discipline, led astray by his own great folly (Proverbs 5:1-23).

For these commands are a lamp, this teaching is a light, and the corrections of discipline are the way to life, keeping you from the immoral woman, from the smooth tongue of the wayward wife. Do not lust in your heart after her beauty or let her captivate you with her eyes, for the prostitute reduces you to a loaf of bread, and the adulteress preys upon your very life. Can a man scoop fire into his lap without his clothes being burned? Can a man walk on hot coals without his feet being scorched? So is he who sleeps with another man's wife; no one who touches her will go unpunished.

. . . .

But a man who commits adultery lacks judgment; whoever does so destroys himself (Proverbs 6:23-29, 32).

New Testament

It is possible for a person never to commit physical adultery, yet be totally unfaithful to his mate in his thought life. Jesus knew that and tightened the principle of marital faithfulness to include thinking as well as overt behavior.

You have heard that it was said, "Do not commit adultery." But I tell you that anyone who looks at a woman lustfully has already committed adultery with her in his heart (Matthew 5:27-28).

Jesus did not mean that one would never have moments of physical attraction, even sexual arousal, to a person of the opposite sex to whom he is not married. But what Jesus was prohibiting was a man's use of his eyes to awaken passion and deliberately stimulate sexual desire.

The I Corinthians 6:12-20 passage, examined in the previous chapter, applies to adultery as well as to fornication. Adultery, like fornication, is using God-given sexuality for a function alien to its intended purpose, thereby severing the body from its intended relationship with Christ.

Judgment for adulterers is certain:

> Do you not know that the wicked will not inherit the kingdom of God? Do not be deceived: neither the sexually immoral nor idolators nor adulterers nor male prostitutes nor homosexual offenders nor thieves nor the greedy nor drunkards nor slanderers nor swindlers will inherit the kingdom of God (I Corinthians 6:9-10).

> Marriage should be honored by all, and the marriage bed kept pure, for God will judge the adulterer and all the sexually immoral (Hebrews 13:4).

> Blessed are those who wash their robes, that they may have the right to the tree of life and may go through the gates into the city. Outside are the dogs, those who practice magic arts, the sexually immoral, the murderers, the idolators and everyone who loves and practices falsehood (Revelation 22:14-15).

Why Adultery is Wrong

Adultery is sin. The Biblical statement is absolute. There are some definite reasons why adultery is so certainly abhorred by God.

Three statements can be safely made about normative patterns for sexuality:[1]

1. The sexuality of every person is meant to be woven into the whole character of that person.

---

1. Lewis B. Smedes, *Sex for Christians* (Grand Rapids: William B. Eerdmans Company, 1976), p. 42.

2. The sexuality of every person is meant to be an urge toward a deep personal relationship with another person.
3. The sexuality of every person is meant to move him toward a heterosexual union of committed love.

Anything contrary to that is a serious violation of God's will.

In the sexual act, the two become one flesh, for it is, after all, surrender of one's private identity to another for the sake of creating a single corporate identity. To do so indiscriminately with whoever happens to be available at the moment is an anomaly. A person cannot become one with more than one person at the same time.

Betrayal of an oath is betrayal of a person. Probably the most devastating result of an adulterous relationship to the wronged partner is the awful feeling of rejection he experiences. The self-esteem of that person plummets to terrible lows to the point where it is often hard for him to learn to trust and be open and honest with a person again. As much as the sexual behavior itself, the lying and cheating make adultery so bad.

Marriage is a picture of the church (Ephesians 5:22-33). A faithful committed relationship between a man and a woman picture the relationship of Christ and the church. Adultery completely distorts that symbolism.

Careful evaluation of Biblical material make the conclusion inescapable: adultery is rejection of God's intentions for a man's use of his sexuality. Adultery is sin.

Adultery Can Be Forgiven

Some in contemporary society act as if adultery were normal behavior. The Biblical evidence presented in this chapter has refuted that argument. But others act as if it is the unforgivable sin. That position is equally erroneous. The good news is that adulterers, like any other sinner, can be forgiven.

Do you not know that the wicked shall not inherit the kingdom of God? Do not be deceived: neither the sexually immoral nor idolators nor adulterers nor male prostitutes nor homosexual offenders nor thieves nor the greedy nor drunkards nor slanderers nor swindlers will inherit the kingdom of God. *And that is what some of your were. But you were washed, you were sanctified, you were justified in the name of the Lord Jesus Christ and by the Spirit of our God* (I Corinthians 6:9-11).

It is no less true today: sexual sin can be forgiven through Jesus Christ.

Conclusion

Adultery is a misuse of sexual identity. The Bible leaves no room for argument about that. It is totally alien to God's design for man. But adultery, like other sin, can be confessed to God and forgiven through Jesus Christ.

Summary Statements

1. Adultery is willful violation of the marriage contract by either of the partners through sexual intercourse with a third party.
2. The Old Testament prohibits adultery and prescribes a severe penalty for it.
3. The New Testament reinforces the Old Testament teaching about the sexual exclusiveness of marriage.
4. Adultery is not only a violation of God's purpose by severing a man's body from Christ, as in the case of fornication, but it is also betrayal of another person.
5. Adultery can be forgiven.

FOR DISCUSSION

1. Summarize the Biblical teaching about adultery.
2. What makes adultery such a serious misuse of sexual identity?
3. Assuming a person came to you for counsel about his unfaithfulness to his wife, how would you explain his sin and the possibility for forgiveness?

REFERENCES

1. Beck, M. N. "The Bed Undefiled." *Christianity Today.* October 10, 1975, pp. 4-6.
2. Howe, Ruel L. "A Pastoral Theology of Sex and Marriage." *Sex and Religion Today.* Ed. Simon Doniger. New York: Association Press, 1953.
3. Pittenger, Norman. *Love and Control in Sexuality.* Philadelphia: Pilgrim Press, 1974.
4. Small, Dwight Hervey. *Christian, Celebrate Your Sexuality.* Old Tappan, New Jersey: Fleming Revell Company, 1974.
5. Smedes, Lewis B. *Sex for Christians.* Grand Rapids: William B. Eerdmans Company, 1976.
6. White, John. *Eros Defiled.* Downers Grove, Illinois. InterVarsity Press, 1977.

Chapter Eleven

SPIRITUAL ADULTERY

Nothing is quite so sad as unrequited love. To watch as a spurned lover seeks to recapture the heart of one who once responded to him in love and joy is to view intense suffering and grief. A somber note is struck when a person sobs, "But I loved him so much. Why has he rejected me?"

Even more somber, however, is to see God as a spurned lover whose deepest desire is for His people to return to Him. It is a sobering moment indeed when one comes to grips with God's steadfast love.

The Old Testament is a record of God's continuous, seeking love for His people. It is a log of their recurring rejection of Him. It provides an historical backdrop by which the very nature of God is to be demonstrated.

Nowhere is God's nature more clearly seen than in the prophecy of Hosea who emphatically holds forth steadfast love that will not let go. This prophecy becomes especially beneficial for inclusion in a study of sexual identity, for God's love and mankind's response are parabolically demonstrated by the prophet's marriage to Gomer. The message of Hosea is primarily an exegesis of God's love, yet secondarily a commentary on marriage and the heinous sin of adultery. A look at the book reveals both.

The Setting

Hosea's prophetic ministry began during the reign of Jeroboam II of Israel, perhaps at the latter part of his reign about 755-750 B.C., and extended until sometime after 725 B.C. However, his work was finished before the fall of Samaria to Assyria in 721 or 722 B.C.

Jeroboam II brought a golden age to the northern kingdom. He was a shrewd trader, restoring the old trade routes and expanding commercial interests. He maintained a lavish military enterprise that was used to extend the borders of Israel to include Gilead, Ammon, and Moab. He refortified Samaria. In short, he led Israel to the height of her glory.

But, in spite of his military and commercial skills, Jeroboam II was a dismal failure, for while wealth increased, the covenant pattern and moral fiber of the people of Israel deteriorated. The worship of Jehovah became a hybrid religion mixed with the sensual practices of the Canaanite fertility cults. Israel was decaying internally, and no one seemed to recognize the inevitable outcome. Off on the eastern horizon, a few black clouds could be seen from Assyria, but nothing imminent. It was a time of luxury, and materialism, not religion, triumphed.

Zechariah succeeded Jeroboam II to the throne, but he reigned only six months until he was murdered by Shallum who, in turn, ruled only a month until he, too, was assassinated by Menahem. Israel was in political anarchy. Meanwhile, back in Assyria, Tiglath-pileser (Pul) had succeeded in settling the nation's domestic problems and set his sights to rule all of the Fertile Crescent as well as Egypt. Israel was merely in the way.

Menahem courted Assyrian favor in order to survive. He surrendered Galilee and paid a heavy tribute to Assyria (II Kings 15:19), an act of deference that temporarily kept Assyria from all-out military action against her. He reigned ten years and was succeeded by his son Pekahiah who ruled only two years before he was murdered by his chief military officer, Pekah.

Pekah was tired of paying tribute, so he approached Rezin of Syria with a plan to combine military forces to defeat

Assyria. Rezin agreed. The two of them approached Jotham of Judah who would have nothing to do with the plan. That motivated Pekah and Rezin to attack Judah in order to force her to cooperate (II Kings 13:37, 16:5-6), a move that proved unsuccessful. Assyria attacked Syria and Israel and carried off some Israelites into bondage (II Kings 15:29).

Pekah was assassinated by Hosea (II Kings 15:30). He was nothing more than a puppet king who was abolished by Shalmaneser when he turned traitor to Egypt (II Kings 17:1-6).

The Assyrian threat from without and the political anarchy within Israel were matched by her inner collapse. Hosea summed it up well:

> Hear the word of the Lord, you Israelites, because the Lord has a charge to bring against you who live in the land: "There is no faithfulness, no love, no acknowledgment of God in the land. There is only cursing, lying and murder, stealing and adultery; they break all bounds, and bloodshed follows bloodshed" (Hosea 4:1-2).

The picture in Israel, politically, morally, and spiritually, was dark indeed. Israel was a nation in need of renewal. To that Hosea spoke.

Hosea's Marriage

Hosea 1-3 describes Hosea's marriage to Gomer and the comparison of that marriage to Israel's faithlessness and God's steadfast love. Hosea's marriage became a living parable for the nation to view.

The biographical material begins in 1:2-3 when, it is recorded, the Lord instructed Hosea to marry a "wife of whoredom" (KJV) or an "adulterous" woman (NIV). That directive

133

has been the subject of considerable debate among scholars. Four possibilities emerge:

1. Hosea was to marry a soliciting prostitute. Some scholars, like Wolff, believe that the language eliminates that option.
2. The story is an allegory: there was no historical marriage of Hosea and Gomer. That is inconsistent with the narrative.
3. Hosea married Gomer in good faith only to later learn of her adulterous behavior. Hosea 1:2 is taken to be a later reflection on what had actually transpired in Hosea's life. That seems unlikely.
4. God did direct Hosea to marry a "wife of whoredom," understood in a different light than a soliciting prostitute. Wolff goes into some detail to explain how this could be possible. He maintains that "wife of whoredom" describes a personal trait recognizable before marriage: a woman with a spirit of a faithless people.

Fertility rites were common in Hosea's day. Canaanite rites, for example, insisted that a woman had to have sexual relations with a stranger *once* (see Chapter 8 in this book). Phoenicians commonly prostituted their daughters before giving them in marriage. Among the Amorites, those who wanted to be married sat at the gate for seven days and engaged in prostitution. Therefore, "wife of whoredom" could refer to a young woman ready for marriage who had submitted to the rather commonly accepted bridal rites of initiation. She whom Hosea was to marry would not, then, be an especially wicked exception, but representative of contemporaries in Israel.[1]

---

1. Hans Walter Wolff, *Hosea*, trans. Gary Stansell (Philadelphia: Fortress Press, 1965), pp. 13-15.

Hosea did marry Gomer, and they were the parents of three children. Each child was given a prophetic name, symbolic of God's dealing with Israel. The first child was a son whose name was Jezreel because, God instructed, "I will soon punish the house of Jehu for the massacre at Jezreel" (Hosea 1:4). The second offspring was a daughter who was named Lo-Ruhamah, for, God said, "I will no longer show love to the house of Israel" (Hosea 1:6). Finally, a third child was born, another son whose name was Lo-Ammi, for "you are not my people, and I am not your God" (Hosea 1:9).

But Gomer was an unfaithful wife, rejecting her husband and seeking new lovers to titillate her. Love her as he would, Hosea was left to view her unfaithfulness. God intervened in Hosea's affairs by insisting that he seek Gomer and reclaim her as his wife in spite of her adulterous ways. "Love her as the Lord loves the Israelites," God insisted (Hosea 3:1). Hosea responded as he was bid: he bought Gomer back for a price (six ounces of silver and ten bushels of barley). Only one condition was imposed upon their relationship: if Hosea was to be her husband, she could have sexual intimacy with no other man.

Indeed, Hosea's marriage is a tragic picture of infidelity and misuse of sexual identity. It is a direct warning of the terrible effects of sexual unfaithfulness. But it is also a picture of steadfast love, the kind of love that sacrifices personal desires for the benefit of another.

God's Love

Hosea likens God's covenant relationship with Israel to that of a marriage. God is the faithful, loving husband, Israel the faithless, adulterous wife.

135

Hosea was profoundly aware of the great heritage that belonged to Israel. The memory of Abram's call, the exodus, the wilderness sojourn, the covenant at Sinai, and the conquest of Canaan were always in mind as he proclaimed his message of God's judgment.

One fact stood out in Israel's history. God chose Israel, which became most clear in Exodus. Hosea compared that to a marriage. But Israel had broken the covenant, just as Gomer had broken her marriage contract. The 'wife' that God had betrothed to himself become a whore, and the people had become estranged from God. Hosea stated it this way: "A spirit of prostitution leads them astray; they are unfaithful to their God" (Hosea 4:12b).

The consequences of Israel's betrayal of the covenant were found in:

1. Regicides
   They delight the king with their wickedness, the princes with their lies. They are all adulterers, burning like an oven whose fire the baker need not stir from the kneading of the dough till it rises. On the day of the festival of our king the princes become inflamed with wine, and he joins hands with the mockers. Their hearts are like an oven; they approach him with intrigue. Their passion smolders all night; in the morning it blazes like a flaming fire. All of them are hot as an oven; they devour their rulers. All their kings fall, and none of them calls on me (Hosea 7:3-7).

2. Conciliatory foreign policy
   Ephraim is like a dove, easily deceived and senseless —now calling to Egypt, now turning to Assyria (Hosea 7:11).

3. Reliance upon arms

Israel has forgotten his Maker and built palaces; Judah has fortified many towns. But I will send fire upon their cities that will consume their fortresses (Hosea 8:14).

She had insisted on being "like the nations" and was now swallowed up by them: "Israel is swallowed up; now she is among the nations like a worthless thing" (Hosea 8:8). Strangers were consuming her strength:

Ephraim mixes with the nations; Ephraim is a flat cake not turned over. Foreigners sap his strength, but he does not realize it. His hair is sprinkled with gray, but he does not notice (Hosea 7:8-9).

This adulterous spirit had led the people of Israel into a false and idolatrous religion. Popular religion, corrupted by the Canaanite fertility cults, was a means of obtaining the good things of nature and tethering God to human interests. The priests and the prophets, exploiting the popularity of "get something" religion, "fed on the sin" of God's people (Hosea 4:7-10).

Israel, then, was like a fickle woman. She lacked *hesed*, a word usually translated as "steadfast love." (The word refers to a loyal love that binds two people together in covenant relationship.) On the other hand, God had *hesed*: constancy, steadfastness, trustworthiness.

Israel's inner flaw was her lack of knowledge of God:

Their deeds do not permit them to return to their God. A spirit of prostitution is in their heart; they do not acknowledge the Lord (Hosea 5:4).

She had always sought her own desires, and now her sinful history had swallowed her up. Only an historical catastrophe could bring Israel to healing. Only when she was disciplined could she be redeemed and a new covenant established.

> Therefore I am now going to allure her; I will lead her into the desert and speak tenderly to her. There I will give her back her vineyards, and will make the Valley of Achor a door of hope. There she will sing as in the days of her youth, as in the day she came up out of Egypt (Hosea 2:14-15).
>
> Return, O Israel, to the Lord your God. Your sins have been your downfall! Take words with you and return to the Lord. Say to him: "Forgive all our sins and receive us graciously, that we may offer the fruit of our lips. Assyria cannot save us; we will not mount war-horses. We will never again say "Our gods" to what our own hands have made, for in you the fatherless find compassion."
>
> "I will heal their waywardness and love them freely, for my anger has turned away from them. I will be like the dew to Israel; he will blossom like a lily. Like a cedar of Lebanon he send down his roots; his young shoots will grow. His splendor will be like an olive tree, his fragrance like a cedar of Lebanon. Men will dwell again in his shade. He will flourish like the grain. He will blossom like a vine, and his fame will be like the wine from Lebanon. O Ephraim, what more have I to do with Idols? I will answer him and care for him. I am like a green pine tree; your fruitfulness comes from me."
>
> Who is wise? He will realize these things. Who is discerning? He will understand them. The ways of the Lord are right; the righteous walk in them, but the rebellious stumble in them (Hosea 14:1-9).

Israel's relationship with God is, like Hosea's marriage, a tragic picture of infidelity. It is a sure warning of the terrible effects of unfaithfulness. But it is also a picture of steadfast love.

138

Lesson For Today

What can be learned from the prophet Hosea, his marriage, and his message? What lessons can be drawn from the text that illustrate or expand the teachings about adultery presented in the previous chapter?

The first lesson is this: God is righteous, and He expects His people to emulate His righteousness. Hosea 4 is a recital of the ways in which Israel had betrayed those expectations. One was adultery: "There is only cursing, lying and murder, stealing and adultery" (Hosea 4:2b). Since the Bible nowhere lifts the prohibition against adultery, it is safe to conclude that God still regards it as a betrayal of righteousness.

Spiritual adultery was a sin against the trust of God (1:2—3:5); physical adultery is a sin against the trust of another partner. God said:

> She has not acknowledged that I was the one who gave her the grain, the new wine and oil, who lavished on her the silver and gold—which they used for Baal (Hosea 2:8).
>
> The Lord said to me, "Go, show your love to your wife though she is loved by another and is an adulteress. Love her as the Lord loves the Israelites, though they turn to other gods and love the sacred raisin-cakes" (Hosea 3:1).

Once trust has been broken in a relationship, it is difficult to restore, especially when that fractured trust relates to sexuality.

Israel's sin was also a sin against truth (4:1—6:11).

> Because you have rejected knowledge, I also reject you as my priests; because you have ignored the law of your God, I will also ignore your children (Hosea 4:6b).
>
> For I desire mercy, not sacrifice, and acknowledgment of God rather than burnt offerings (Hosea 6:6).

Physical adultery is almost always accompanied by lying and misrepresentation of truth, no less a sin when committed

139

against one's marriage partner as it is when committed against God. Sin against truth further erodes trust.

Furthermore, adultery—physical or spiritual—is a sin against troth (7:1—13:6). Troth is a covenant, an agreement between two people. To violate that commitment is to break it, to render it void, for in a covenant, each party must keep his end of the bargain.

> Woe to them, because they have strayed from me! Destruction to them, because they have rebelled against me! I long to redeem them but they speak lies against me! (Hosea 7:13).
>
> When I found Israel, it was like finding grapes in the desert; when I saw your fathers, it was like seeing the early fruit on the fig tree. But when they came to Baal Peor, they consecrated themselves to that shamful idol and became as vile as the thing they loved (Hosea 9:10).
>
> When Israel was a child, I loved him, and out of Egypt I called my son. But the more I called Israel, the further they went from me. They sacrificed to the Baals and they burned incense to images (Hosea 11:1-2).

Physical adultery is a blatant disregard for a person's previous promise to love, honor, and be faithful to his partner until death severs the relationship.

Finally, Hosea's message proclaims the kind of love that is necessary to nurture a marriage. It is *hesed*, enduring, suffering, forever love that balances judgment with mercy. It is God's kind of love.

> How can I give up, Ephraim? How can I hand you over, Israel? How can I treat you like Admah? How can I make you like Zeboiim? My heart is changed within me; all my compassion is aroused. I will not carry out my fierce anger, nor devastate Ephraim again. For I am God, and not man—the Holy One among you. I will not come in wrath (Hosea 11:8-9).

140

God's love is the model for marriage (see Ephesians 5:22-33). A spiritual relationship built on anything less than God's love is inadequate. A physical relationship built on nothing more than sexual attraction will fail.

Conclusion

The prophet Hosea, by action and word, presents a powerful argument against spiritual unfaithfulness which was illustrated by marital infidelity. It is a strong argument for lifelong commitment to God. It is an equally strong call for marital commitment and faithfulness. The example of Gomer's unfaithfulness to Hosea verifies God's earlier demand for sexual exclusiveness in marriage.

Summary Statements

1. The prophet Hosea teaches two important lessons: (a) a person of God is called to lifelong commitment; and, (b) in a marriage both people are called to lifelong commitment.
2. Unfaithfulness to God is pictured by unfaithfulness in a marriage.
3. God expects His people to emulate His righteousness.
4. Adultery—spiritual or physical—is a sin against trust, truth, and troth.
5. God calls us to love with steadfast love in our relationships with Him and with others.

FOR DISCUSSION

1. How can a marriage relationship and a relationship with God be compared?
2. Describe how Gomer's relationship with Hosea pictured Israel's response to God.

141

3. What does the message of Hosea teach about adultery?
4. If we were to love as God does, how would that affect our marriage relationship?

REFERENCES

1. Anderson, Bernhard W. *Understanding the Old Testament.* Englewood Cliffs, New Jersey: Prentice-Hall, Inc., 1975.
2. Cole, William Graham. *Sex and Love in the Bible.* New York: Association Press, 1959.
3. Hubbard, David Allen. *With Bonds of Love.* Grand Rapids: William B. Eerdmans Publishing Company, 1968.
4. Scott, Jack B. *The Book of Hosea.* Grand Rapids: Baker Book House, 1971.
5. Wolff, Hans Walter. *Hosea.* Trans. Gary Stansell. Philadelphia: Fortress Press, 1965.
6. Yates, Kyle M. *Preaching from the Prophets.* Nashville: Broadman Press, 1942.

Chapter Twelve

DIVORCE: ONE FLESH DISSOLVED

The American family is in transition. Only one family in four now conforms to the traditional image of bread-winning Dad, homemaking Mom, and dependent children. Working mothers, intentionally childless couples, working teenagers, all are deviations from the stereotype. But by far the most serious threat is the rising incidence of divorce.

Hardly anyone in this day and age has been immune from divorce touching them in some way. If the person himself is not divorced, then he probably has encountered it with his parents or grandparents, a brother or a sister, or a close friend. Statistics reveal that 96% of all American adults will marry. Thirty-eight percent of those marriages will end in divorce. However, 79% of those divorced will marry again, and 44% of those remarried will divorce again. What is even more sobering is that many of these people are Christians.

It is in this milieu that a Christian must live. Armed with Biblical information, yet challenged and tested by the surrounding culture, he is confronted with God's ideal for marriage and must balance that against the reality of a sinful world. What does the Bible say about divorce? Can the divorced person fit into the church? Must Biblical principles for marriage be sacrificed in order to minister effectively to those whose marriages have failed?

This chapter examines the Biblical material to determine God's mind about divorce and how that relates to sexuality. Yet it is a call for ministry to a group of folk who, having failed, need to experience redemption.

Divorce Defined

Two words are used in the New Testament to describe divorce. It is helpful to examine both in order to reach a

143

definition for the word 'divorce.'

The first word is *apoluo*. It is a commonly used word in the New Testament, often translated as 'put away.' But it was also a term that signified the absolute dissolution of a marriage. A review of the major lexicons reveals that the word signifies 'to set free,' 'to loose,' 'to radically dissolve,' 'to undo a bond,' 'to sever,' 'to cause all obligation and responsibility to cease.'

The primary meaning of *apoluo* is 'to set free.' An example is found in Mark 15:6-15 when Barabbas lay bound in a prison, but was *released (apelusen)* by Pilate. He was freed. The same idea is present when a person is released from the marriage law. He is free from it.

A second word is *chorizo*. It is used in I Corinthians 7:10-11 and is translated as 'leave.' Some say that since Paul used this word instead of *apoluo*, he meant for couples to remain separate, not to divorce. However, Thayer, Arndt-Gingrich, Liddel and Scott, and other readily accepted lexicons say that the word means 'to divorce.'

The words used for divorce in the New Testament clarify the meaning of the action. Biblically speaking, then, to divorce is to totally dissolve a marriage contract; it is to declare the marriage null, void, and dead.

What the Bible Teaches About Divorce

It is one thing to define divorce, quite another to determine when a divorce is acceptable to God. But the Bible makes that clear as well.

Old Testament

Earlier chapters in this book have examined God's original design for marriage. Genesis 2:24 presents that design:

marriage is to be a lifelong partnership in love and in sexual faithfulness. Two become one flesh. God's original intention for a marriage was for it to last until severed by death.

But the intrusion of sin marred God's original purpose for His creation. It altered sexuality. It affected the marriage relationship. God's original plan continued, but now He began to deal with failure.

One failure that God had to deal with was the misuse of sexuality, especially as it related to a marriage. For that reason the Bible does deal with the issue of divorce: under what circumstances it was permitted and procedures for it (designed particularly to protect the defenseless woman).

The Old Testament presents two allowable exceptions for dissolvement of a marriage. The first was when one of the partners was put to death by execution for sexual unfaithfulness:

> If a man commits adultery with another man's wife—with his wife of his neighbor—both the adulterer and the adulteress must be put to death. If a man sleeps with his father's wife, he has dishonored his father. Both the man and the woman must be put to death; their blood will be on their own heads. If a man sleeps with his daughter-in-law, both of them must be put to death. What they have done is a perversion; their blood will be on their own heads (Leviticus 20:10-12).
>
> If a man is found sleeping with another man's wife, both the man who slept with her and the woman must die. You must purge the evil from Israel (Deuteronomy 22:22).

That same principle is further expanded in the case of a man marrying a woman, thought to be a virgin, who in fact had engaged in sexual intercourse (Deuteronomy 22: 13-21).

145

Another allowable exception for dissolvement of a marriage was mentioned, this time the dissolution to be a divorce. It is mentioned in Deuteronomy 24:1-4 in a section presenting procedures for divorce. The grounds for divorce were "indecency." In this case, divorce was not commanded, but it was permitted.

If a man marries a woman who becomes displeasing to him because he finds something indecent about her, and he writes her a certificate of divorce, gives it to her and sends her from his house, and if after she leaves his house she becomes the wife of another man, and her second husband dislikes her and writes her a certificate of divorce, gives it to her and sends her from his house, or if he dies, then her first husband, who divorced her, is not allowed to marry her again after she has been defiled. That would be detestable in the eyes of the Lord (Deuteronomy 24:1-4).

What was 'indecency'? Two Jewish schools of thought gave interpretation to the word.

1. The school of Shammai held out for the sanctity of marriage and insisted that indecency was equivalent to adultery. Therefore, sexual unfaithfulness was the only permissible reason for divorce.
2. The school of Hillel took a far more liberal approach to the issue. Indecency, by their interpretation, was anything the husband did not like. It could be for her burning his food, talking with a man in public, having long hair over her shoulders, laughing in the street, talking so loudly that the neighbors could hear, saying something bad about her in-laws, having an unsatisfactory appearance, or some other similar action. This was obviously the school of thought that was most popular by Jesus' time.

146

Neither Hillel nor Shammai could have been entirely correct in their views, however. 'Indecency' certainly must have involved something other than adultery, for the law was already explicit about what to do in that case. But surely 'indecency' was not to be so loosely interpreted as Hillel would have it, for his view reduced marriage to little more than a whim. Indeed, the Hebrew word for 'indecency' meant exposure of self to another short of intercourse, nakedness, and/or sexual perversion.

Note that Deuteronomy 24:1-4 is not a command for divorce. Divorce is permitted, not commanded. However, there is a command involved: if divorce became the chosen route of action, then a bill of divorcement must be produced to free the woman so that she would not have to live in adultery.

When a bill of divorcement was produced, the marriage was dissolved, severed, declared null and void. A copy of it would read:

On _____ day of the week _____ day of the month _____ in the year _____ I who am also called son of _____ of the city of _____ by the river of _____ do hereby consent with my own will, being under no restraint, and I do hereby release, send away, and put aside thee, my wife _____ who is also called daughter of _____ who is this day in the city of _____ by the river of _____ who has been my wife for some time past; and thus I do release thee, and send thee away and put thee aside that thou mayest have permission and control over thyself to go to be married to any man that thou mayest desire; and that no man shall hinder thee from this day forward, and thou are permitted to any man, and this shall be unto thee from me a bill of dismissal, a document of release, and a letter of freedom, according to the law of Moses and Israel.

_____ the son of _____ Witness

_____ the son of _____ Witness

Of course to be seen as an acceptable severance of marriage in God's eyes, it would have to be for 'indecency.' But this bill then freed a woman to marry again without committing adultery.

Deuteronomy 21:10-14 deals with the matter of an Israelite divorcing a non-believer. Divorce was permitted in that case.

> When you go out against your enemies and the Lord your God delivers them into your hands and you take captives, if you notice among the captives a beautiful woman and be attracted to her, you may take her as your wife. Bring her into your home and have her shave her head, trim her nails and put aside the clothes she was wearing when captured. After she has lived in your house and mourned her father and mother for a full month, then you may go to her and be her husband and she shall be your wife. If you are not pleased with her, let her go wherever she wishes. You must not sell her or treat her as a slave, since you have dishonored her.

One other Old Testament passage makes it clear when a person is absolutely forbidden to divorce. It was in the case when a man had raped a woman, then married her.

> If a man happens to meet a virgin who is not pledged to be married and rapes her and they are discovered, he shall pay the girl's father fifty shekels of silver. He must marry the girl, for he has violated her. He can never divorce her as long as he lives (Deuteronomy 22:28-29).

God's concession to man's sinfulness in no way altered His original intentions for marriage. He still detested divorce.

So guard yourself in your spirit, and do not break faith with the wife of your youth. "I hate divorce," says the Lord God of Israel, "and I hate a man's covering himself with violence as well as with his garment," says the Lord Almighty (Malachi 2:15b-16).

But His divorce laws did regulate divorce and protect women who otherwise were at the whim of their husbands.

New Testament

Jesus. By the time the New Testament era had been ushered in, the institution of marriage was at an all-time low, even among the Jews. Divorce was common. Seemingly nearly everybody had been divorced and remarried many times. Divorce and remarriage were far more common than in our day.

Palestine was no different than the rest of the Roman Empire. Adultery was common among the Greeks, although there was no legal process for divorce. Among the Romans, divorce was common. For example, Juvenal recorded one woman who had had eight husbands in five years. Seneca said, "People are getting married to get divorced, and they are getting divorced to get married again." It was in the midst of this kind of disregard for marriage that Jesus ministered.

Jesus' teaching on divorce is recorded in each of the Synoptic Gospels. The first entry is found in Matthew 5:31-33 in the Sermon on the Mount. Jesus' intent was to present the picture of kingdom folk whose righteousness is to be internal as well as external and will, therefore surpass the legalistic righteousness of the Pharisees. That righteousness would have profound effect on marriage.

It has been said, "Anyone who divorces his wife must give her a certificate of divorce." But I tell you that anyone who

149

divorces his wife, except for marital unfaithfulness, causes her to commit adultery, and anyone who marries a woman so divorced commits adultery.

Jesus spoke to the issue of divorce one again in a situation mentioned by all of the Synoptic writers.

Some Pharisees came to him to test him. They asked, "Is it lawful for a man to divorce his wife for any and every reason?"

"Haven't you read," he replied, "that at the beginning the Creator 'made them male and female,' and said, 'For this reason a man will leave his father and mother and be united to his wife, and the two will become one flesh'? So they are no longer two, but one. Therefore what God has joined together, let man not separate."

"Why then," they asked, "did Moses command that a man give his wife a certificate of divorce and send her away?"

Jesus replied, "Moses permitted you to divorce your wives because your hearts were hard. But it was not this way from the beginning. I tell you that anyone who divorces his wife, except for marital unfaithfulness, and marries another woman commits adultery" (Matthew 19:3-9).

Some Pharisees came and tested him by asking, "Is it lawful for a man to divorce his wife?"

"What did Moses command you?" he replied.

They said, "Moses permitted a man to write a certificate of divorce and send her away."

"It was because your hearts were hard that Moses wrote you this law," Jesus replied. "But at the beginning of creation God 'made them male and female. For this reason a man will leave his father and mother and be united to his wife, and the two will become one flesh.' So they are no longer two, but one. Therefore what God has joined together, let man not separate."

When they were in the house again, the disciples asked Jesus about this. He answered, "Anyone who divorces his wife and marries another woman commits adultery against her. And if she divorces her husband and marries another man, she commits adultery" (Mark 10:2-12).

Anyone who divorces his wife and marries another woman commits adultery, and the man who marries a divorced woman commits adultery (Luke 16:18).

The Pharisees had come to Jesus to inquire about divorce not because they had any real desire to know about the legality of it. But they were intent on ensnaring Jesus, and divorce was a sticky enough issue to do it. If He were to side with the Shammai interpreters, He would bring down the wrath of those who sided with Hillel. But if He were to side with the school of Hillel, the followers of Shammai would rise up in horror. It was a no-win situation.

Jesus refused to be trapped. Rather than dealing with any human interpretation of the practice of divorce, He took His interrogators back to the original intent of God for marriage. Divorce had never been God's plan, for marriage was to last a lifetime. The ideal never changes regardless of the circumstances.

The absolute ideal for marriage, then, was no divorce, no remarriage, no exceptions. However, the reality of a sinful world often falls far short of the ideal. It is because of this fallen condition that Jesus gave His teaching in Matthew 19:9. Because sin is real and sexual identity is sometimes misused, Jesus gave a practical application of the ideal: no divorce, no remarriage, one exception. That exception is *porneia*, translated as 'fornication' or 'adultery.'

Note what Jesus did. He refused to accommodate to the culture of the day and re-emphasized God's original

151

intention for marriage. He eased up the Old Testament requirement that a mate be executed for committing adultery. (He demonstrated that also in His attitude toward the woman of John 8:1-11 who was taken in adultery.) At the same time, He tightened the loose interpretation of Deuteronomy 24:1 by defining 'indecency' as *porneia* which could carry with it the idea not only of adultery, but also other sexual perversion.

Note, too, that Jesus did not command divorce for sexual aberration. But He did permit it. That should come as no real surprise, however, for if sexual union culminates a marriage, than adultery breaks it. Divorce would merely grant formal recognition of a marriage that was already severed. Given the meaning of *apoluo*, 'to release,' 'to set free,' 'to sever,' then the marriage is null and void, and remarriage is a possibility.

At the same time, divorce for any reason other than sexual perversion is outside of God's purposes for His people To remarry in such a circumstance is to commit adultery—and to cause the partner to commit adultery as well.

Does Jesus' teaching mean that a person who was divorced for something other than sexual unchastity and who then remarries lives in a continual state of adultery? The Bible does not deal with that issue. However, the New Testament seems to regard adultery as an *act*, not a *state*. That would seem to eliminate the idea of continual sin. It would seem that the initial sexual act would be an act of adultery in relationship to the first marriage. But it would also seem to cement a new relationship which God recognizes as marriage.

Jesus' teaching on divorce is demanding. The *only* acceptable grounds for divorce is sexual unchastity. To remarry when divorced on those grounds is permitted without adultery becoming an accompanying sin. But to divorce and remarry for any other reason involves the sin of adultery.

Paul. Paul, too, held forth the original intention of God for marriage.

> Do you not know, brothers—for I am speaking to men who know the law—that the law has authority over a man only as long as he lives? For example, by law a married woman is bound to her husband as long as he is alive, but if her husband dies, she is released from the law of marriage. So then, if she marries another man while her husband is still alive, she is called an adulteress. But if her husband dies, she is released from that law and is not an adulteress, even though she marries another man (Romans 7:1-2).

In I Corinthians 7, Paul replied to several questions about marriage. These were pressing practical problems confronting the infant Corinthian church. The Corinthians had come from a pagan background. In some homes, only one partner had come to Christ; the other still lived very much as a part of the pagan world. The questions were urgent then.

One of the questions must have been: is divorce among believers permissible? Paul's response was definite—he held forth the biblical ideal.

> To the married I give this command (not I, but the Lord): A wife must not separate from her husband. But if she does, she must remain unmarried or else be reconciled to her husband. And a husband must not divorce his wife (I Corinthians 7:10-11).

Note that should a Christian divorce without biblical reason, he is counseled to remain single.

Perhaps a second question was this: should a Christian divorce his pagan partner? Paul is once again very definite: the Christian is not to initiate divorce on that basis.

To the rest I say this (I, not the Lord), If any brother has a wife who is not a believer and she is willing to live with him, he must not divorce her. And if a woman has a husband who is not a believer and he is willing to live with her, she must not divorce him (I Corinthians 7:12-13).

However, Paul does offer an exception to the rule:

But if the unbeliever leaves, let him do so. A believing man or woman is not bound in such circumstances; God has called us to live in peace (I Corinthians 7:15).

Although Paul does not deal with the issue of remarriage in this case, the fact that he does not mention it would indicate that he understood divorce to permit remarriage. If a person is no longer bound by the law, it is as if the contract had never existed.

Paul, like Jesus, then, emphasized the original design of lifelong marriage. But he did hold out one additional allowable exception: when the unbelieving party initiates it.

Summary

The Bible firmly teaches God's intent for marriage: one man and one woman related to each other intellectually, emotionally, physically, and spiritually for a lifetime. Both the Old Testament and the New Testament affirm that design. However, the Bible realistically deals with sexual sin by permitting divorce and remarriage on that basis. Paul adds one other permissible exception for divorce and that is when an unbelieving partner initiates it.

The Church and the Divorced

It is one thing to hold out the God-given design for marriage, but quite another to minister to those people who experience marital difficulties and divorce. How can the church effectively minister in a sinful world?

Sometimes people are confronted with a scale of relative values. They know what the ideal is, yet they have to make tragic moral choices, any one of which falls far short of the ideal. It is possible that at times divorce may be the lesser of two evils.

But under any circumstances, divorce is a sin whenever it occurs. Usually both people participate in bringing about that failure, although one may have gone so far as to sever the relationship by sexual sin. It is probably not particularly helpful to try to determine the 'innocent party.' Rather, the church can minister best when it holds forth the ideal for marriage and calls for one who has failed to recognize his sin and confess it. Remarriage must always be accompanied by repentance.

Can one divorce and remarry and still be (or become) a Christian? Some would say absolutely not. But Jesus surely regarded divorce as a forgivable sin, for His first firm declaration of Messiahship was to a woman who had been married and divorced five times (John 4:1-42). She became a believer and brought others to Him. Divorce can be forgiven just as murder or lying or any other sin.

This is not to suggest an 'anything goes' mentality. The church is charged with the responsibility of maintaining a balance between *truth* and *grace*. Holding out for truth calls for repeated proclamation of the ideal for marriage, the responsibility of the Christian to seek the ideal, and the sin involved in divorce. But holding forth grace allows for redemptive care for the one who has failed. There is need for repentance when a divorce occurs, but there is also need for forgiveness and ministry.

Conclusion

The push for individual freedom, rights, and self fulfillment will continue to exert pressure on marriages. The easy divorce of this era will be tempting to Christians who can readily rationalize severance of marriage.

As the pressures mount, the church must remain faithful to God's word, declaring and supporting the Scriptural design for marriage. The church can prepare youth for marriage. The church can call for repentance when sin severs a marriage. The church can minister to folks who are experiencing failure. The church can assist people to put life back together again. The church can help people succeed in a subsequent marriage. The church can minister in grace and truth.

Summary Statements

1. God's design for marriage is a lifelong relationship.
2. The intrusion of sin marred God's original intent for marriage.
3. Divorce means to declare a marriage null and void.
4. In the Old Testament, adultery was to terminate a marriage, for the adulterer was to be stoned to death.
5. In the Old Testament, a marriage could also be severed because of 'indecency' which literally means naked-nakedness or exposure of oneself.
6. Jesus re-emphasized the original purpose of marriage.
7. Jesus did permit divorce and remarriage on the grounds of sexual unchastity.
8. Paul added an allowable grounds for divorce: when an unbeliever initiates it.
9. Divorce always involves sin and failure.
10. The church must minister to the divorced with grace and truth.

FOR DISCUSSION

1. What does the word 'divorce' mean?
2. On what basis does the Old Testament permit divorce?
3. Summarize Jesus' teaching about divorce.
4. What did Paul teach about divorce?
5. Suppose a Christian couple comes to you to talk about getting a divorce. They say that they are incompatible. What would you counsel?
6. Further assume that the couple gets a divorce. One begins to contemplate remarriage. He seeks your advice. What would it be?

REFERENCES

1. Boatman, Charles R. "Focus: Marital Crisis." *Journal of Christian Ministry.* n.d.
2. Bustanoby, Andre. "When Wedlock Becomes Deadlock." *Christianity Today.* June 20, 1975, p. 406, and July 18, 1975, pp. 11-14.
3. Cole, William Graham. *Sex and Love in the Bible.* New York: Association Press, 1959.
4. Duty, Guy. *Divorce and Remarriage.* Minneapolis: Bethany Fellowship, 1967.
5. Houlden, J. L. *Ethics and the New Testament.* New York: Oxford University Press, 1977.
6. Murray, John. *Divorce.* Philadelphia: Presbyterian and Reformed Publishing Company, 1961.
7. Olsen, V. Norskov. *The New Testament Logia on Divorce.* Tubingen, Germany. JCB Mohr, 1971.
8. "Saving the Family." *Newsweek.* May 15, 1978, pp. 63-90.
9. Small, Dwight Hervey. *The Right to Remarry.* Old Tappan, New Jersey: Fleming H. Revell, 1975.

10. Smoke, Jim. "Pastoring the Divorced: Caring Without Condoning." *Christianity Today.* June 6, 1980, pp. 36-37.
11. Staton, Knofel. *Divorce and Remarriage.* Lectures presented at the North American Christian Convention, St. Louis, Missouri, 1980.
12. Sutherland, Joseph. "Take Another Look at Marriage." *Lookout.* Reprint. 1980.

Chapter Thirteen

HOMOSEXUALITY: UNNATURAL FLESH

The sports world was stunned in May, 1981, when Billie Jean King, champion tennis pro, called a news conference to admit her lengthy homosexual affair with a woman who had also been her secretary. Although the affair had been over for some time, Miss King, who has been married to the same man since 1965, was being sued by her former female lover for lifetime support. The amazing thing is that Miss King would openly admit her homosexual activity. It is indicative of the era in which we live.

Less than a month later, Shelly Roberts, a free-lance columnist for *Newsweek,* wrote a response. It is even more of a reflection of the age, for she took King to task for saying that she had made a mistake. Roberts wrote:

> Billie Jean King, referring to her involvement with Marilyn Barnett, her former secretary, admitted on national television that she had made a "mistake" . . . Billie Jean was right. She did make a mistake. But I think it's important to see what that mistake really was. At first it seemed that Billie Jean was apologizing for the affront to conventional morality that a homosexual affair implies. Later she claimed that her mistake had been to break moral law by committing adultery— surely a transgression more forgivable and less offensive to many people than homosexuality. Her response to the "scandal" seemed to be designed to salvage whatever might be salvageable of a lucrative career. You can't fault Billie Jean for trying to survive, but I for one am disappointed that her statements did nothing to advance the feminist philosophy of tolerance which she has long and ardently supported.[1]

---

1. Shelly Roberts, "Bad Form, Billie Jean," *Newsweek*, May 25, 1981.

She proceeded to spell out what has been learned from the women's movement and concludes by saying:

> We learned to be more tolerant of differences among women. Some of us even learned that homosexuality just might not be an unspeakable abomination—not a lurid, pornographic subculture that never touched the lives of anybody we knew personally. We got to know women for whom homosexuality was a workable alternative to the traditional way of life. We came to believe that gay could be good for those who wished it, and it didn't have to be bad for those who would never make that choice themselves. It could simply be.[2]

Of course, homosexuality is not new. Nearly every culture in every age has dealt with it. The Greeks and Romans of New Testament times commonly practiced homosexuality.

The Christian lives in a world where sexual roles and values have been called into question. He hears about gays who 'come out,' 'gay power,' and 'gay bars.' He sees homosexuality propogated as a legitimate lifestyle, as Roberts did in her article. Such a lifestyle runs against the grain, but it seems impossible to argue against those who claim that they are constituted differently than heterosexuals.

But is homosexuality a viable alternative? How is a Christian to respond? What does the Bible teach?

Homosexuality Defined

Homosexuality refers to sexual activity with another of the same sex. Two specific words are used in the New Testament to denote homosexual behavior. The most commonly used word was *arsenokoites* which refers to all homosexual behavior. It is made up of two words, one meaning

---

2. *Ibid.*

'male,' and the other the word for 'sexual intercourse.' Literally, it could be translated as 'one who lies with a male as a female.' There is no distinction made between loving and casual sex. Paul could have used more specific terms such as *paiderastes* ('lover of boys') or *paidophthoros* ('corrupter of boys'), or *arrenomanes* ('mad after males'). But he selected the most general word available, presumably for specific purpose.

In I Corinthians 6, Paul also used the word *malakoi*. It literally means 'a male who submits his body to unnatural lewdness; a homosexual.'

Both words refer to male homosexuals. One could conclude, then, that the Bible does not speak about lesbianism. However, *arsenokoites* is a general word used for homosexuality. Paul dealt with lesbianism as well as male homosexuality in Romans 1:26-27, a passage that will be developed in greater detail later in this chapter.

At that, some distinctions must be made, for some people who engage in homosexual behavior are not homosexuals in preference nor in general practice. There are at least three categories of homosexuality:

1. Absolute invert. This person prefers and engages in only homosexual behavior. This may be the pattern for as many as four percent of all American males, probably a smaller percentage of women.
2. Bisexual. This person may be married and engage in heterosexual activity, but also seeks homosexual relations.
3. Contingent homosexuals. These are people who are basically heterosexual but who engage in homosexual behavior on some occasions. For example, some homosexual activity is experimental such as among teens.

It is generally a transitory stage. Others engage in homosexual activity to break boredom or when they are isolated from the opposite sex (such as in prison).

Origins of Homosexuality

How does a homosexual grow up to prefer sexual intimacy with a person of the same sex? Is it an accident of nature or something for which the person is responsible?

In Chapter 5, the development of sexual identity was examined in some detail. Factors that contribute to abnormal development were identified. A review of that chapter would be helpful to the reader at this point.

At least three theories about the origin of homosexuality have been proposed. One notion is that it is constitutionally inherited. The idea is that there is an organic factor, over which the individual has no control, that predisposes an individual to homosexual preference and behavior. Some have suggested that it is a hormonal imbalance; others believe it to be a genetic or chromosomal problem. Of course, if this is true, the weight of responsibility for his homosexual behavior is lifted from the person. Klaus Bockmuhl observed "The permissive attitude toward homosexuality came from the presupposition that it is constitutionally inherited . . . A further presupposition is that anyone with a 'constitutional' homosexuality cannot be considered morally responsible for his acts."[3]

However, no clearcut evidence has been found to support the idea that homosexuality is constitutionally inherited. Kinsey, whose sex research is classic, said:

---

3. Klaus Bockmuhl, "Homosexuality in Biblical Perspective," *Christianity Today*, February 16, 1973, pp. 12-18.

There is no need of hypothesizing peculiar hormonal factors that make certain individuals especially liable to engage in homosexual activity, and we know of no data which prove the existence of such hormonal factors. There are no sufficient data indicating that specific hereditary factors are involved.[4]

Nor has later research contradicted that conclusion. Clifford Allen observed: "I am reluctantly driven to the conclusion that there is, so far, no evidence upon which any reliance can be placed that is an endocrine difference between normal and homosexual."[5] Even more recently, Arno Karlen said, "The evidence is overwhelming that genes do not cause homosexuality."[6]

A second theory of the origin of homosexuality focuses on a person's relationship to his parents during his formative years. There is evidence to support this idea (see Chapter 5). Homosexuals report a higher than average incidence of one or more of the following factors:[7]

1. Rejection of the child by the parent of the opposite sex.
2. Seduction of the child by either parent.
3. Rejection of the parent of the opposite sex by the child.
4. Mistreatment of one parent by another.

It is rather clear that familial relationships do affect later sexual adjustment, either heterosexual or homosexual. But even so, that cannot totally explain what happens to produce a homosexual, for given the same family circumstances, one

---

4. Alfred C. Kinsey, *et al*, *Sexual Behavior in the Human Female* (Philadelphia: W. B. Saunders Co., 1953), p. 447.

5. Clifford Allen, *A Textbook of Psychosexual Disorders* (London: Oxford University Press, 1962), p. 169.

6. Arno Karlen, *Sexuality and Homosexuality* (New York: W. W. Norton and Company, 1971), p. 337.

child becomes a homosexual while another does not. It also focuses in a way that removes personal responsibility and permits blame to be extended to someone else.

A third theory insists that homosexuality, like heterosexuality, is learned behavior (see Chapter 5). This by no means discounts family influence, for it is a factor in learning, but it does put the responsibility where it belongs— with the individual.

Sexual behavior is learned behavior. Hormones may provide the initial drive, but from then on a person learns most of what he does to sexual acts. An indication of the truth of that is found in research done among boys who were sexually mature at ten or eleven. Even though they were sexually mature, they usually did not have sexual fantasies until about age fifteen. The hormones were fully operative, but the boys had yet to learn enough about sexual behavior to fantasize.[8]

The evidence is definite: a homosexual learns to be one. (What he has learned he can 'unlearn' if he wants to badly enough.) The position is stated very well in a letter to the editor in *Christianity Today,* June 6, 1980. Lorne Browne, a doctor at the University Health Center at the University of Nebraska, wrote:

> A homosexual becomes one by a series of choices. These choices may seem imperceptible to him because they are not at first conscious choices to overt homosexual activity. Most frequently they are those of social attraction, for reason other than sexual, to a person of the same sex. As the friendship becomes more intimate, some sexual stimulation occurs and

8. Frank B. McMahon, *Abnormal Behavior: Psychology's View* (Englewood Cliffs, New Jersey: Prentice-Hall, 1976), p. 323.

if there is not a prior commitment to the wrongness—or at least undesirability—of homosexual conduct, this develops into overt acts.

The pattern, if not abruptly broken off, develops more rapidly if the person or persons with whom the novice associates is already practicing homosexual activity. As the friendship deepens, the values and lifestyle of his friends are accepted. Then one day he 'discovers' that he really has a preference for homosexuality. This is entirely because of the conditioning that has taken place and has no basis whatever in his genetic, anatomic, or physiologic make-up.

What the Bible Teaches About Homosexuality

God made man and woman as sexual creatures. That statement, emphasized again and again during the development of this book, is descriptive of God's ideal and prescriptive for man's proper sexual behavior. The creation of sexual differentiation established heterosexuality as the normative direction for sexual activity. Homosexual behavior represents a choice to set one's desires in a way contrary to God's creation. The Bible implies that homosexuals are made, not born.

Old Testament

The first mention of homosexual behavior is in Genesis 19:1-11. The occasion was the destruction of Sodom and Gomorrah. God had become increasingly displeased with the terrible sin of the people of these two cities. He threatened to destroy them, but Abraham bargained for Him to save the cities if only ten righteous people were found to remain there. Two angels were sent to Sodom where they met Lot who hospitably greeted them and took them to his house.

165

Genesis 19:5 records one reason why the city had sunk to such a moral low:

> They called to Lot, "Where are the men who came to you tonight? Bring them out to us so that we can have sex with them."

The NIV translators have readily translated *yadha*, the Hebrew word 'to know,' as 'have sex.' The word was used in the Old Testament to denote sexual intercourse, although, of course, it had other uses as well.

Many today who would have Christians accept homosexuality as an alternative lifestyle argue that the word *yadha* should be translated as 'to know,' and then go on to explain that the request of the townsmen was not for homosexual intercourse at all, but to get acquainted with the heavenly visitors. Lot obviously understood it as a sexual advance, for he tried to appease them by offering his daughters for sexual activity. (It is interesting that Lot would be horrified at one sexual sin, yet suggest another.)

> "No, my friends. Don't do this wicked thing. Look, I have two daughters who have never slept with a man. Let me bring them out to you, and you can do what you like with them. But don't do anything to these men, for they have come under the protection of my roof" (Genesis 19:7-8).

Others say that Genesis 19:1-11 is a case of intended homosexual behavior. But, they insist, the sin was not homosexuality, but intended gang rape of the visitors, therefore a sin of inhospitality. But the context will not support that interpretation. The clear message of the passage is that at least part of the reason of God's judgment of Sodom and Gomorrah was their depraved sexual behavior. (To this day homosexuality is also called sodomy.) Jude 7 supports this idea:

> In a similar way, Sodom and Gomorrah and the surrounding towns gave themselves up to sexual immorality and perversion. They serve as an example of those who suffer the punishment of external fire.

One is not forced to learn God's mind about homosexual behavior by implication, however. His intolerance is stated explicitly in Leviticus:

> Do not lie with a man as one lies with a woman; that is destestable (Leviticus 18:22).
> If a man lies with a man as one lies with a woman, both of them have done what is detestable. They must be put to death; their blood will be on their own heads (Leviticus 20:13).

There is no question about it: covenant morality is not to be defined by the surrounding culture.

Another mention of homosexual behavior is made in Judges 19. A Levite from the hill country of Ephraim had taken a concubine from Bethlehem. She left him and returned home. After four months, the man went back to Bethlehem to reclaim her. On the return trip to the hill country, the man and his entourage decided to spend the night at Gibeah among fellow countrymen rather than in the alien city later known as Jerusalem. No one extended hospitality until a certain old man came in from work. He took the party into his home.

Then, in a Sodom-Gomorrah rerun, some citizens demanded homosexual relations with the guest:

> While they were enjoying themselves, some of the wicked men of the city surrounded the house. Pounding on the

door, they shouted to the old man who owned the house, "Bring out the man who came to your house so we can have sex with him: (Judges 19:22).

The host understood very well what they wanted and, like Lot, offered his daughter and the visitor's concubine instead:

> The owner of the house went outside and said to them, "No, my friends, don't be so vile. Since this man is my guest, don't do this disgraceful thing. Look, here is my virgin daughter, and his concubine. I will bring them out to you now, and you can use them and do to them whatever you wish. But to this man, don't do such a disgraceful thing" (Judges 19:23-24).

In this case, the townsmen did take the concubine and raped her, a sin in no uncertain terms. But the point for a study of homosexuality is that it was seen as a vile, disgraceful behavior—not just because it was a sin of inhospitality, as some would lead us to believe, but because it was a sin in and of itself.

Three references in I Kings refer to the idolatrous religions within the boundaries of Israel in which male prostitution was practiced:

> There were even male shrine prostitutes in the land; the people engaged in all the detestable practices of the nations the Lord had driven out before the Israelites (I Kings 14:24).
> He expelled the male shrine prostitutes from the land and got rid of all the idols his fathers had made (I Kings 15:12).
> He rid the land of the rest of the male shrine prostitutes who remained there even after the reign of his father Asa (I Kings 22:46).

Here, as in Leviticus, God regarded homosexuality as detestable.

New Testament

Jesus did not speak to the issue of homosexuality. All of the New Testament teaching comes from the pen of Paul. His first reference is found in Romans 1 where he expands upon the horrors of the human predicament. He clearly states that one consequence of continued disregard for God and seeking one's own pleasure was sexual impurity.

> Therefore, God gave them over in the sinful desires of their hearts to sexual impurity for the degrading of their bodies with one another. They exchanged the truth of God for a lie, and worshiped and served created things rather than the Creator —who is forever praised. Amen (Romans 1:24-25).

An evidence of the extreme of sexual impurity is homosexuality:

> Because of this, God gave them over to shameful lusts. Even their women exchanged natural relations for unnatural ones. In the same way the men also abandoned natural relations with women and were inflamed with lust for one another. Men committed indecent acts with other men, and received in themselves the due penalty for their perversion (Romans 1:26-27).

What does Paul mean by exchanging "natural relations for unnatural ones"? Many who argue that homosexuality is constitutionally inherited say that this passage applies only to those whose homosexual behavior is experimental and/or situational. It does not, they insist, apply to those who are true inverts.

But that is hardly Paul's argument. He is making a theological statement, one that refers back to God's original design for sexuality. The 'natural' refers to man and woman as God created them; 'unnatural' refers to what is unnatural

169

sexual behavior in relation to creation. Homosexuality is contrary to man's intrinsic nature and normal inclinations. Homosexuality is the cultural culmination of rebellion against God. It is described as perversion.

In I Corinthians 6:9-10, Paul includes both male prostitutes and homosexuals in general in the catalog of sinners who will not inherit the kingdom of God if they persist in their behavior:

> Do you not know that the wicked will not inherit the kingdom of God? Do not be deceived; Neither the sexually immoral nor idolaters nor adulterers nor male prostitutes nor homosexual offenders nor thieves nor the greedy nor drunkards nor slanderers nor swindlers will inherit the kingdom of God (I Corinthians 6:9-10).

Paul's teaching is the same in I Timothy 1:9-11:

> We also know that law is made not for good men but for law breakers and rebels, the ungoldy and sinful, the unholy and irreligious; for those who kill their fathers and mothers, for murderers, for adulterers and perverts (homosexuals), for slave traders and liars and perjurers—and for whatever else is contrary to the sound doctrine that conforms to the glorious gospel of the blessed God, which he entrusted to me (I Timothy 1:9-11).

Homosexual behavior infringes the demands of the Decalogue as certainly as heterosexual adultery.

One further observation does need to be made. The Biblical references are always to homosexual behavior, not homosexual inclinations. The intrusion of sin in the human arena makes the fact of improper sexual learning and development a reality. There are those people who have homosexual inclinations because of what they have learned in

170

the course of their growth. But a person need not accede to temptation, whether that is for homosexual behavior or for unacceptable heterosexual behavior. It is the act that is condemned.

Scriptures Used to Support Homosexuality

Those who would have us accept homosexuality as an alternative lifestyle have gone out of their way to draw out Scriptural examples which, they claim, support their position. Six are usually mentioned.

The first, in chronological order, is found in Genesis 4:7 in the case of Cain and Abel. It is built on tenuous evidence from the language of the King James Version:

> And unto thee shall be his desire, and thou shalt rule over him.

This is said to be homosexual desire. But the NIV uses a much clearer translation, making it clear that it was sin, not Abel, that desired Cain:

> But if you do not do what is right, sin is crouching at your door; it desires to have you, but you must master it.

Another incident used to support homosexuality is the relationship between Ruth and Naomi. Phrases like "she kissed them" (Ruth 1:9), "Ruth clung to her" (Ruth 1:14), and "where you go I will go, and where you stay I will stay" (Ruth 1:16) are said to be evidence of homosexual behavior. It is flimsy support, reading in something never explicitly stated in the passage. The best refutation of this argument is the pattern of behavior. If this were homosexual behavior, Ruth demonstrated an unusual pattern, for she would have been first heterosexual, then homosexual, and finally either heterosexual or bisexual. It is an highly unlikely pattern.

A third Old Testament incident used to support homosexuality is the friendship of David and Jonathan. The supporting evidence is found in the following verses:

> After David had finished talking with Saul, Jonathan became one in spirit with David, and he loved him as himself (I Samuel 18:1).
>
> And Jonathan made a covenant with David because he loved him as himself (I Samuel 18:3).
>
> Saul told his son Jonathan and all the attendants to kill David. But Jonathan was very fond of David (I Samuel 19:1).
>
> I grieve for you, Jonathan my brother; you were very dear to me. Your love for me was wonderful, more wonderful than that of women (II Samuel 1:26).

It is again as argument built on obscure references, none of which have the slightest support in any activity of Jonathan and David described in the Bible. Perhaps the best refutation is found in David's obviously heterosexual activity, some of it sinful, in other sections of I and II Samuel.

Advocates of homosexual activity cite Jesus' relationship with John as an example of homosexuality. It is again based on obscure evidence, this time in John 13:18-30 where a reference is made to John's leaning against Jesus' breast (13:23-25). Much is also made of the fact that John identified himself as the disciple whom Jesus loved. The context of 13:23-25 hardly suggests sexual activity, however. And the word used by John to describe Jesus' love for him was *agape*, love of the will, not *eros*, sensual love.

Another New Testament passage cited to provide a basis for homosexuality is Matthew 8:5-13. It is the occasion when the centurion asked Jesus to heal his servant boy, a request that Jesus fulfilled. The supposed evidence for homosexuality is the word Matthew used for servant. The word is *pais* which could be translated either as 'youth' or 'servant.' If, in fact, it were to be translated 'youth,' it would imply that the centurion was following a pagan practice of keeping a boy for sexual satisfaction. But when Luke reported the same incident, he used the word *doulos* which can be translated only as 'servant,' supporting the same translation in Matthew.

One last bit of Biblical material used to support homosexual activity is the relationship between Timothy and Paul. The alleged evidence is found in I Timothy 1:4:

> Recalling your tears, I long to see you, so that I may be filled with joy.

The joy is said to be sexual satisfaction. There is no explicit evidence to support such a theory. But if this were the case, it is alien to Paul's teaching in Romans 1:26-27, I Corinthians 6:9-10, and I Timothy 1:10.

Hope For Homosexuals

There is hope for homosexuals. The Bible condemns homosexual behavior, yet makes it clear that a person need not be hopelessly ensnared by it. The same passage that condemns it assumes that a person can be freed from it:

> Do you not know that the wicked will not inherit the kingdom of God? Do not be deceived: Neither the sexually immoral nor idolaters nor adulterers nor male prostitutes nor homosexual offenders nor thieves nor the greedy nor drunkards nor slanderers nor swindlers will inherit the kingdom of God. *And that is what some of you were. But you were*

173

washed, you were sanctified, you were justified in the name of the Lord Jesus Christ and by the Spirit of our God (I Corinthians 6:9-11).

The key to overcoming homosexuality is wanting to. Whatever has been learned can be unlearned or relearned. Jesus Christ can empower a person to be freed from homosexual behavior. It will not be easy, or course, for sexuality is such a deeply engrained part of personality. However, John Drakeford suggests a seven-step procedure that will permit the power of Christ to direct a person's life to new freedom:[9]

1. Admit awareness of the situation. "I am homosexual."
2. Accept personal responsibility for the situation. The person must quit blaming God for making him that way. "I am homosexual because I have chosen to be."
3. Genuinely desire to change. "I can change my sexual behavior if I want to."
4. Seek new company. A person attempting to build a new lifestyle needs association with those who encourage the new behavior.
5. Seek therapy. Because sexuality is so much a part of personality, Christian therapy will assist the relearning process.
6. Get involved in helping someone else. This puts the focus outside of self.
7. Realize that a complete 'cure' is unlikely. Temptation will probably always be present. But new responses to temptation are possible.

---

9. See John Drakeford, *A Christian View of Homosexuality* (Nashville: Broadman Press, 1977).

There is good news for those who are homosexuals. God will forgive the sin and redirect life into productive purposes designed to serve Him. It is a matter of choice.

Summary Statements

1. Homosexuality is sexual activity with a person of the same sex.
2. Although several theories for the origin of homosexuality have been proposed, the preponderance of evidence indicates that it is learned behavior.
3. The Old Testament unequivocally condemns homosexual behavior as detestable in God's sight.
4. The New Testament identifies homosexual behavior as unnatural, that is, alien to God's purposes for sexuality, and unacceptable for a kingdom person.
5. Although proponents of sexuality use Scripture to support their views, all arguments are based on obscure references.
6. Homosexual behavior can be forgiven and redirected by the power of God.

FOR DISCUSSION

1. How does a person become a homosexual?
2. Suppose a person confides in you that he is a practicing homosexual who also calls himself a Christian. He says that he will enjoy his homosexuality, using it responsibly, because God made him that way. How would you respond?
3. Summarize the Bible teaching about homosexual behavior.
4. Respond to the Scriptural evidence that homosexuals sometimes use to support their behavior.

5. Why is homosexuality so displeasing to God?
6. How would you respond to a person who tells you that he wants to be a Christian, but that he is a homosexual?

REFERENCES

1. Allen, Clifford. *A Textbook of Psychosexual Disorders.* London: Oxford University Press, 1962.
2. Bahnsen, Greg L. *Homosexuality: A Biblical View.* Grand Rapids: Baker Book House, 1978.
3. Bockmuhl, Klaus. "Homosexuality in Biblical Perspective," *Christianity Today.* February 16, 1973, pp. 12-18.
4. Cavanaugh, John R. *Counseling the Invert.* Milwaukee: Bruce Publishing Company, 1966.
5. Cole, William Graham. *Sex and Love in the Bible.* New York: Association Press, 1959.
6. Drakeford, John W. *A Christian View of Homosexuality.* Nashville: Broadman Press, 1959.
7. Field, David. *The Homosexual Way — A Christian Option?* Downers Grove, Illinois: InterVarsity Press, 1978.
8. Jones, H. Kimball. *Toward a Christian Understanding of the Homosexual.* New York: Association Press, 1966.
9. Karlen, Arno. *Sexuality and Homosexuality.* New York: W. W. Norton and Company, 1971.
10. Kinsey, Alfred C., *et al. Sexual Behavior in the Human Female.* Philadelphia: W. B. Saunders Co., 1953.
11. Lindsell, Harold. "Homosexuals and the Church." *Christianity Today.* September 28, 1973, pp. 8-12.

12. Lovelace, Richard. *Homosexuality and the Church.* Old Tappan, New Jersey: Fleming H. Revell Co., 1978.
13. McMahon, Frank B. *Abnormal Behavior: Psychology's View.* Englewood Cliffs, New Jersey: Prentice-Hall, 1976.
14. Scanzoni, Letha and Mollenkott, Virginia Ramey. *Is the Homosexual My Neighbor?* New York: Harper and Row Publishers, 1978.
15. Sims, Bennet J. "Sex and Homosexuality." *Christianity Today* February 24, 1978, pp. 23-30.
16. Smedes, Lewis B. *Sex for Christians.* Grand Rapids: William B. Eerdmans, 1976.
17. Twiss, Harold L. (ed.) *Homosexuality and Christian Faith: A Symposium.* Valley Forge, Pennsylvania: Judson Press, 1978.
18. White, John. *Eros Defiled.* Downers Grove, Illinois: InterVarsity Press. 1977.

Chapter Fourteen

LICENTIOUSNESS: MIND RULED
BY BIOLOGICAL SEX

Sex is everything—if you believe today's pleasure pitch. Sex is the ultimate experience, one to be sought at any price. A person exists to get pleasure, especially sensual titillation.

The appeal of advertising is to the gratification of every physical desire, and the vehicle used is sex. Razor blades, automobiles, shaving cream, you name it—all are sold with sex. It has become the epitome of the life of pleasure.

The movie and television industries picture promiscuity, homosexuality, and kinky sex as healthy and normal. People are seeking fun, vicarious thrills, a kick—and producers are more than happy to give it to them. Cable television now provides the most blatant of sexually-oriented movies that were once banned from the home screen.

Magazines, even the general newsstand variety, use sex to sell. Women's magazines nearly always include some kind of article on sex, and advertising uses sex appeal as well. But, of course, of far greater consequence is the multi-million dollar hard-core pornography business that poisons the minds of not only those who seriously seek such thrills, but also those who are tantalized into exploring simply because they are passing by. One need not go to a porn shop to be exposed to raw sex—the magazine stand in the corner grocery or drug store will do quite well.

Even the so-called family or general bookstores have enough sexually-oriented material to capture the mind of anyone who is susceptible. This author has made a point of spending an hour or so in reputable bookstores in major shopping malls in various places. In every case, there was a section on sex featuring such titles as *The Joy of Sex,*

The Joy of Gay Sex, and *The Joy of Lesbian Sex*—all complete with explicit diagrams, pictures, and instructions. Add to that all of the novels with detailed descriptions of sexual activity of all kinds—and one gets a picture of a society saturated, perhaps even ruled, by sex.

Edward Gibbon in his *Decline and Fall of the Roman Empire* observed that five characteristics marked Rome at her end, each contributing to her demise. They were:
1. Affluence;
2. Widening gap between the very rich and the very poor;
3. Obsession with sex;
4. Freakishness in the arts; and,
5. Increased desire to live off the state.
It could have been a commentary on our times, especially in obsession with sex.

It was into the midst of a decadent society, intent on sexual pleasure, that Christianity was born. The first century preachers and writers knew full well the depraved depths to which people could fall; they called it licentiousness. They pulled no punches about what happens when a person's mind is dominated by sexual activity. Their words are especially relevant to a later society in which the same kinds of obsession with sex are prevalent.

Licentiousness Defined

The word *licentious* is an interesting word, whether examined in the original language or in English. It comes from a Greek word *aselgeia* which literally means 'readiness,' or 'shamelessness.' The word describes a person's inner character: sex has become the ruling part of his personality.

Examination of a thesaurus reveals the same idea in English. A licentious person is one who is unrestrained, immoral,

179

unprincipled, unscrupulous, ungoverned, lewd, lustful, debauched, profligate, depraved, sleazy, dissolute.

It is not an appealing picture, for licentiousness describes a person whose every action and thought is motivated by sexual impulse. And the unfortunate fact is that it can and does happen—sometimes to Christians.

What the Bible Teaches About Licentiousness

Old Testament

The Old Testament does make reference to the depraved wickedness of men, even though the word licentiousness is not used. This implication is that men were so depraved that only evil rebellion against God motivated their actions. At least some of that evil motivation and activity was sexual in content.

The first reference to that kind of ungoverned self-seeking is found in Genesis 6:5:

> The Lord saw how great man's wickedness on the earth had become and that every inclination of the thoughts of his heart was only evil all the time.

The Bible says that God was so grieved that He had made man that He decided to obliterate mankind except for Noah, who was a righteous man, and his family.

Later in Genesis, in Chapter 18, God again grieved over His creation, this time because of the heinous sin of Sodom and Gomorrah:

> Then the Lord said, "The outcry against Sodom and Gomorrah is so great and their sin so grievous that I will go down and see if what they have done is as bad as the outcry that has reached me. If not, I will know" (Genesis 18:20-21).

180

It is obvious in the description of the events of Genesis 19 that at least a part of their depravity was a result of sexual desire and behavior (see Genesis 19:1-29).

New Testament

It is in the New Testament where the thrust of Biblical teaching examines a man's heart and motivation, even more than his outward behavior. The lewd, pleasure-seeking man whose every thought and action is immorally motivated is introduced.

Jesus spoke to the issue of licentiousness by identifying the source of immoral conduct:

> He went on: "What comes out of a man is what makes him 'unclean.' For from within, out of men's hearts, come evil thoughts, sexual immorality, theft, murder, adultery, arrogance, and folly. All these evils come from inside and make a man 'unclean'" (Mark 7:20-23).

A man's heart can become so ensnared in sexual thinking that he thinks of nothing else, resulting in behavior for which he no longer feels shame.

Paul wrote to the Romans pleading for Roman Christians to put off depraved sexual behavior in exchange for the clothing of Christ:

> And do this, understanding the present time. The hour has come for you to wake up from your slumber, because our salvation is nearer now than when we first believed. The night is nearly over; the day is almost here. So let us put aside the deeds of darkness and put on the armor of light. Let us behave decently, as in the daytime, not in orgies and drunkenness, not in sexual immorality and debauchery, not in dissension and jealousy. Rather, clothe yourselves with the Lord Jesus Christ, and do not think about how to gratify the desires of the sinful nature (Romans 13:11-14).

In this passage, Paul identifies six sins typical of a Christ-less life: revelry, drunkenness, sexual immoraltiy, shame-lessness, contention, and envy. Paul makes it clear that a person can think about sensual pleasures for so long and with such intensity that he finally becomes consumed by it. And when a person's every thought is consumed by sex, he no longer feels any shame for his conduct.

Paul again refers to the all-consuming passion of sex that results in lewd conduct for which no shame is felt in a passing reference in II Corinthians 12:21. It is in regard to his own grief over such conduct if it continues without repentance:

> I am afraid that when I come again my God will humble me before you, and I will be grieved over many who have sinned earlier and have not repented of the impurity, sexual sin and debauchery in which they have indulged.

The acts of the sinful nature are listed in Galatians 5:19-21. One is *aselgeia,* an inner character ruled by sex and resulting in conduct for which there is no sense of guilt and shame:

> The acts of the sinful nature are obvious: sexual immorality, impurity and debauchery; idolatry and witchcraft; hatred, discord, jealousy, fits of rage, selfish ambition, dissensions, factions and envy; drunkenness, orgies, and the like. I warn you, as I did before, that those who live like this will not inherit the kingdom of God.

Again, in Ephesians 4:17-19, Paul referred to unbridled lust and shamelessness:

> So I tell you this, and insist on it in the Lord, that you must no longer live as the Gentiles do, in the futility of their thinking. They are darkened in their understanding and separated from the life of God because of the ignorance that is in them

due to the hardening of their hearts. Having lost all sensitivity, they have given themselves over to sensuality so as to indulge in every kind of impurity, with a continual lust for more.

Note that Paul lists four characteristics of a depraved condition:

1. Darkened minds because of ignorance;
2. Petrified hearts—no longer aware of sinning;
3. Disregard for society so long as personal desires are gratified; and,
4. Insatiable lust.

It is a picture of a person so greedy for physical pleasure that he has given himself over entirely to the expression of physical appetites.

Peter refers to the same unbridled spirit as being unacceptable to God:

> But there were also false prophets among the people, just as there will be false teachers among you. They will secretly introduce destructive heresies, even denying the sovereign Lord who bought them—bringing swift destruction on themselves. Many will follow their shameful ways and will bring the way of truth into disrepute. In their greed these teachers will exploit you with stories they have made up. Their condemnation has long been hanging over them, and their destruction has not been sleeping.
>
> . . . .
>
> These men are springs without water and mists driven by a storm. Blackest darkness is reserved for them. For they mouth empty, boastful words and, by appealing to the lustful desires of sinful human nature, they entice people who are just escaping from those who live in error (II Peter 2:1-3, 17-18).

The cause of false teaching, in Peter's evaluation, was a desire to put self in place of Christ. The method was cunning, and the result was shamelessness that brings Christianity into disrepute. It is still true.

Finally, Jude also exposes the sin of pleasure domination:

> For certain men whose condemnation was written about long ago have secretly slipped in among you. They are godless men, who change the grace of our God into a license for immorality and deny Jesus Christ our only Sovereign and Lord (Jude 4).

He sees nothing but judgment reserved for those who have ceased to care for shame and decency and who have perverted the Word of God into an excuse for blatant immorality.

The Bible is explicit in its evaluation of those people who have become so dominated by sensual pleasure that they no longer feel any shame for sexual behavior that flaunts the teachings of God. To transgress moral values is one thing—serious enough, to be sure, but at least understandable when it occurs once in the midst of temptation—but to lose all sense of an objective moral order is quite another, according to Scripture.

Seneca once said, "To be enslaved to oneself is the heaviest of all servitudes." The licentious person, the one whose sensitivity is calloused, experiences that worst of slavery, for he is serving self and has lost his spiritual moorings.

Licentiousness Overcome

Can licentiousness be forgiven and overcome? Or has the person caught up in such base sexual sin and shamelessness reached such a depraved condition that he cannot be reclaimed?

The good news is that whatever the depths of sexual degradation to which a man can fall, he can be reclaimed. That was implied in II Corinthians 12:21 when Paul acknowledged the intensity of his grief if the people in Corinth failed to repent of their debauchery. It is obvious that he thought that they could be reclaimed. He states it again in Ephesians 4:17 when he urges the Ephesian Christians to no longer live as the Gentiles do (and one characteristic was licentiousness). Then he points out the possibility for new life in Christ:

> You, however, did not come to know Christ that way. Surely you heard of him and were taught in him in accordance with the truth that is in Jesus. You were taught, with regard to your former way of life, to put off your old self, which is being corrupted by its deceitful desires, to be made new in the attitude of your minds; and to put on the new self, created to be like God in true righteousness and holiness (Ephesians 4:20-24).

Emerson once said, "The key to every man is his thought." It is true. Deeds of shamelessness are preceded by deeds of shame. Deeds of shame are preceded by fantasies of shame. And fantasies of shame are preceded by thoughts that are retained in the mind, thought and spoken about, and finally acted upon.

The caution for Christians is that no man is immune. Tempting and lustful thoughts enter every mind. If they are permitted to remain undeterred by positive data that centers upon God, the thought process can be sabotaged. If immoral, ribald thoughts are planted in the mind by continued exposure to questionable books, television, movies, pornography, or whatever means, without equal or greater exposure to God's Word, thinking will be altered—and thoughts will then reappear to conduct and character.

185

The call for Christians is to observe the advice of the apostle Paul:

> Finally, brothers, whatever is true, whatever is noble, whatever is right, whatever is pure, whatever is lovely, whatever is admirable—if anything is excellent or praiseworthy—think about such things (Philippians 4:8).

Conclusion

Christians in a sexually stimulating society face particularly difficult temptations. One can become so enamored with sexual content, feelings, and thought that they begin to dominate the personality. A personality dominated by sexual impulse conducts itself in all kinds of behavior with no shame. The Bible clearly condemns licentiousness, ungoverned sexual passion. Yet it holds out the possibility of forgiveness and redirection for the genuinely repentant one who turns to Jesus Christ.

Summary Statements

1. Christians are bombarded with sex and sexual stimulation in American society that seems to be obsessed with sex.
2. Licentiousness refers to a personality so obsessed with sex that sexual misconduct no longer holds any shame.
3. The Bible explicitly condemns licentiousness.
4. Licentious conduct emanates from a person's heart.
5. Licentiousness can be forgiven.
6. A Christian must learn to fill his thoughts with God's thoughts in order to counteract the sexual stimulation that enters his mind.

FOR DISCUSSION

1. Cite examples from advertising, television, movies, and literature that fill the mind with sexual content and desires.
2. Why is licentiousness such a grave misuse of sexuality?
3. How can a Christian guard himself against the sin of licentiousness?

REFERENCES

1. Banowsky, William, *It's a Playboy World*. Old Tappan, New Jersey: Fleming Revell Co., 1969.
2. Piper, Otto A. *The Christian Interpretation of Sex*. London: Nisbet and Company, 1942.
3. Stott, John R. W. *Christian Counter-Culture*. Downers Grove, Illinois: InterVarsity Press, 1978.
4. White, John. *Eros Defiled*. Downers Grove, Illinois: InterVarsity Press, 1977.
5. Wright, H. Norman. *The Christian Use of Emotional Power*. Old Tappan, New Jersey: Fleming H. Revell, 1974.

Chapter Fifteen

OTHER DEVIANT SEXUAL BEHAVIOR

Sex is good, right, proper, and God-ordained. Sexuality, expressed as God has directed, is interwoven into personality to express what a person is and can be. But distortions of human sexuality make sexual contacts ugly and discordant and break up the splendor of human relationships.

William Banowsky, writing in *It's a Playboy World*, observed, and correctly so:

> Sex is not a biological appendage; it is an aspect of human existence by which every man, through his attitudes and actions, reveals something of his deepest convictions about life itself. . . . When we discover what men regard as right and wrong in sexual ethics, we learn what they believe about much else. Most important of all, it is in the relationships of sex that men mirror their basic beliefs concerning their own nature, their origin and dignity as man.[1]

If sex were nothing more than a physical act, it would make little difference how or when a person expressed his sexuality. In animals, the automation of the sexual approach cannot be interrupted by the animal itself. But man can. When the automatic sex process is interrupted in an animal, aggression increases, but man can translate interrupted or lack of overt sexual expression into creativity.

For man, sexuality and its expression are a matter of will and relationship. A great part of the joy of a sexual relationship is the presence of the other person, his physical caresses and verbal expressions of love and caring. (An all-too-common complaint of women is that their husbands

---

1. William Banowsky, *It's A Playboy World* (Old Tappan, New Jersey: Fleming Revell Co., 1969). p. 73.

take too little time to verbalize caring, to touch, to lovingly caress, before and after intercourse.) It is as Ruel Howe observed, "A holy sexual relationship is one in which the interrelatedness and wholeness of *function* and *being* are preserved and honored in thought and act."[2] It is as simple as this: genuine love forbids impersonal sexual behavior.

One unfortunate outcome of sin is the way in which sex becomes depersonalized and irresponsibly expressed. Those misuses of sexual identity already examined in the preceding chapters are perhaps the more common ones. But the Bible deals with several others less frequently expressed. It is those that are examined in the remainder of this chapter.

Immodesty

The Bible spells out that sexuality is good and its expression is right and proper in appropriate circumstances. Yet it also indicates that an individual's sexuality is intensely private, something to be discreetly revealed in all relationships outside of marriage. The sex organs were made by God and are an essential part of everything a person is, but they are to be reserved for the individual and his lifetime partner. Sexuality is not something to be flaunted in order to tempt, to manipulate, or to harm another. It is to be under the control of the will to be used as God has given sanction and direction.

The Bible spends little time expressly speaking of immodest behavior, but several references are made or narratives used to illustrate the point. The first is in Genesis 9:20-27.

---

2. Ruel L. Howe, "A Pastoral Theology of Sex and Marriage," *Sex and Religion Today,* ed. Simon Doniger (New York: Association Press, 1953), p. 99.

The setting was shortly after the flood. Noah and his family had abandoned the ark and had settled into a routine. Noah has planted a vineyard, then misused its produce by getting drunk. In his drunkenness he lost all sense of propriety (let sexuality slip from the domain of the will) and lay naked in his tent. The Bible narrates the account:

> Noah, a man of the soil, proceeded to plant a vineyard. When he drank some of its wine, he became drunk and lay uncovered inside his tent. Ham, the father of Canaan, saw his father's nakedness and told his two brothers outside. But Shem and Japheth took a garment and laid it across their shoulders; then they walked in backward and covered their father's nakedness. Their faces were turned the other way so that they would not see their father's nakedness. When Noah awoke from his wine and found out what his youngest son had done to him, he said, "Cursed be Canaan! The lowest of slaves will he be to his brothers." He also said, "Blessed be the Lord, the God of Shem! May Canaan be the slave of Shem. May God extend the territory of Japheth, may Japheth live in the tents of Shem, and may Canaan be his slave."

Noah's behavior was shameful because he failed to preserve his sexuality for no one other than himself and his wife.

An example of immodesty that tempted another is found in II Samuel 11:1-5 when Bathsheba bathed in plain sight of the palace of David.

> In the spring, at the time when kings go off to war, David sent Joab out with the king's men and the whole Israelite army. They destroyed the Ammonites and besieged Rabbah. But David remained in Jerusalem. One evening David got up from his bed and walked around on the roof of the palace. From the roof he saw a woman bathing. The woman was

190

very beautiful, and David sent someone to find out about her. The man said, "Isn't this Bathsheba, the daughter of Ellam and the wife of Uriah the Hittite?" Then David sent messengers to get her. She came to him, and he slept with her. (She had purified herself from her uncleanness.) Then she went back home. The woman conceived and sent word to David saying, "I am pregnant."

Whether her behavior was intended to tempt or not, the fact is that it did—and the result was adultery, murder, and an illegitimate pregnancy. None of the recorded events would likely have happened had Bathsheba been modest enough to bathe in private.

The law explicitly prohibited immodest behavior that was intended to harm another:

If two men are fighting and the wife of one of them comes to rescue her husband from his assailant, and she reaches out and seizes him by his private parts, you shall cut off her hand. Show her no pity (Deuteronomy 25:11-12).

A man's genitals are a private part of his person, and a violation without provocation is an intrusion on that privacy.

Paul expressed the same idea when he wrote to Timothy and expressed his desire for women:

I also want women to dress modestly, with decency and propriety, and with braided hair or gold or pearls or expensive clothes, but with good deeds, appropriate for women who profess to worship God (I Timothy 2:9-10).

A woman is not to flaunt her sexuality indiscriminately. It is beautiful and must be kept for one person—her lifetime partner.

With a little observation, the importance of this teaching for today becomes evident. The person of God is still to seek modesty. Some people, both men and women, leave little about their sexuality to imagination. All too often nearly everything that a person is sexually is open to public inspection. Unfortunately, sexuality is used to tempt, to manipulate, to inflict cruelty. But God wants a people who so respect their sexuality that they preserve it for revelation and expression in God-ordained circumstances.

Rape

Rape is a depraved, impersonal, cruel expression of sexuality. There is no love nor relationship involved in it. It is a horrible, selfish invasion of the privacy of another. The Bible minces no words about its regulation and condemnation.

A case of rape is recorded in Genesis 34:1-2:

> Now Dinah, the daughter Leah had borne to Jacob, went out to visit the women of the land. When Shechem son of Hamor the Hibite, the ruler of that area, saw her, he took her and violated her.

The result was that Shechem wanted to marry Dinah (an uncommon result in this day and age when rape is involved). He pleaded with Hamor to get her as his wife.

The sons of Jacob were rightfully indignant that their sister had been violated:

> Now Jacob's sons had come in from the fields as soon as they heard what had happened. They were filled with grief and fury, because Shechem had done a disgraceful thing in Israel by lying with Jacob's daughter—a thing that should not be done (Genesis 34:7).

Unfortunately, they returned evil for evil by deviously suggesting that Dinah could marry Shechem if the Hivites would be circumcised (making them participants in God's covenant). Hamor agreed, and every male in the city was circumcised. Then, on the third day after the circumcision rite, when they were in pain and unable to fight, the sons of Jacob plundered the city and killed every male. When Jacob rebuked them for such vicious behavior, they responded, "Should he have treated our sister like a prostitute?" (Genesis 34:31).

Another narrative that illustrates the tragedy of rape is found in II Samuel 13 when David's son, Amnon, raped his half-sister, Tamar. It is a tale of deception and plotting to invade the privacy of forbidden sexual territory:

> In the course of time, Amnon son of David fell in love with Tamar. The beautiful sister of Absalom son of David. Amnon became frustrated to the point of illness on account of his sister Tamar, for she was a virgin, and it seemed impossible for him to do anything to her. Now Amnon had a friend named Jonadab son of Shimeah, David's brother. Jonadab was a very shrewd man. He asked Amnon, "Why do you, the king's son, look so haggard morning after morning? Won't you tell me?"
>
> Amnon said, "I'm in love with Tamar, my brother Absalom's sister."
>
> "Go to bed and pretend to be ill," Jonadab said. "When your father comes to see you, say to him, 'I would like my sister Tamar to come and give me something to eat. Let her prepare the food in my sight so I may watch her and then eat it from her hand.'"
>
> So Amnon lay down and pretended to be ill. When the king came to see him, Amnon said to him, "I would like my sister Tamar to come and make some special bread in my sight, so I may eat from her hand."
>
> David sent word to Tamar at the palace: "Go to the house of your brother Amnon and prepare some food for him." So

Tamar went to the house of her brother Amnon, who was lying down. She took some dough, kneaded it, made the bread in his sight and baked it. Then she took the pan and served him the bread, but he refused to eat.

"Send everyone out of here," Amnon said, So everyone left him. Then Amnon said to Tamar, "Bring the food here into my bedroom so I may eat from your hand." And Tamar took the bread she had prepared and brought it to her brother Amnon in his bedroom. But when she took it to him to eat, he grabbed her and said, "Come to bed with me, my sister."

"Don't, my brother!" she said to him. "Don't force me. Such a thing should not be done in Israel! Don't do this wicked thing. What about me? Where could I get rid of my disgrace? And what about you? You would be like one of the wicked fools in Israel. Please speak to the king; he will not keep me from being married to you."

But he refused to listen to her, and since he was stronger than she, he raped her (II Samuel 13:1-14).

The immediate outcome of this case of rape was hatred and isolation.

Then Amnon hated her with intense hatred. In fact, he hated her more than he had loved her. Amnon said to her, "Get up and get out!"

"No!" she said to him. "Sending me away would be a greater wrong than what you have already done to me." But he refused to listen to her. He called his personal servant and said, "Get this woman out of here and bolt the door after her." So his servant put her out and bolted the door after her. She was wearing a richly ornamented robe, for this was the kind of garment the virgin daughters of the king wore. Tamar put ashes on her head and tore the ornamented robe she was wearing. she put her hand on her head and went away, weeping aloud as she went.

> Her brother Absalom said to her, "Has that Amnon, your brother been with you? Be quiet now, my sister; he is your brother. Don't take this thing to heart." And Tamar lived in her brother Absalom's house, a desolate woman (II Samuel 13:15-20).

The longer term outcome was a rift within the king's household, resulting in the murder of Amnon, the attempted of David by Absalom, and Absalom's violent death (see II Samuel 13:23—18:18).

The Old Testament law made it clear that rape was totally unacceptable to God and was to be dealt with severely.

> But if out in the country a man happens to meet a girl pledged to be married and rapes her, only the man who has done this shall die. Do nothing to the girl; she has committed no sin deserving death. This case is like that of someone who attacks and murders his neighbor, for the man found the girl out in the country, and though the betrothed girl screamed, there was no one to rescue her. If a man happens to meet a virgin who is not pledged to be married and rapes her and they are discovered, he shall pay the girl's father fifty shekels of silver. He must marry the girl, for he has violated her. He can never divorce her as long as he lives (Deuteronomy 22:25-29).

Invasion of personal sexual privacy called for immediate, definite action.

Rape is no less a distorted penetration of personality today. Its incidence is rising, and often it is linked with other physical violence as well. Although the New Testament does not mention rape specifically, every teaching about sexuality supports the Old Testament view that sexuality is personal and private and is to be expressed voluntarily in an act of love with a partner selected for a lifetime commitment. Rape is still unacceptable to God.

195

Incest

The basic law regarding sexual relations with relatives is stated in Leviticus 18:6, "No one is to approach any close relative to have sexual relations." Much of the rest of this chapter defines who is to be regarded as a close relative: parent, child, step-parent, sibling, stepsister or stepbrother, grandchild, half-sister or half-brother, aunt or uncle, daughter-in-law or son-in-law, mother-in-law or father-in-law. Leviticus 20:11-21 specifies the punishment for incest. It was death in the case of a step-parent, daughter-in-law, or son-in-law. In the case of a sister, brother, half-sister or half-brother, the violater is to be cut off from the people. If it was an aunt, sister-in-law, or brother-in-law, the result was dishonor and childlessness. Curses are pronounced for such behavior in Deuteronomy 27:20, 22, 23.

Genesis 19:30-38 records a violation of this law when Lot's daughters duped their father into having intercourse with each of them:

> Lot and his two daughters left Zoar and settled in the mountains, for he was afraid to stay in Zoar. He and his two daughters lived in a cave. One day the elder daughter said to the younger, "Our father is old, and there is no man around here to lie with us, as is the custom all over the earth. Let's get our father to drink wine and then lie with him and preserve our family line through our father."
>
> That night they got their father to drink wine, and the older daughter went in and lay with him. He was not aware of it when she lay down or when she got up.
>
> The next day the older daughter said to the younger, "Last night I lay with my father. Let's get him to drink wine again tonight, and you go in and lie with him so we can preserve our family line through our father." So they got their father

196

to drink wine that night also, and the younger daughter went and lay with him. Again he was not aware of it when she lay down or when she got up.

So both of Lot's daughters became pregnant by their father. The older daughter had a son, and she named him Moab; he is the father of the Moabites of today. The younger daughter also had a son, and she named him Ben-Ammi; he is the father of the Ammonites of today (Genesis 19:30-38).

Although an evaluation of the behavior is not given in the text, examination of the development of Biblical history reveals the enmity that existed between Moab and Ammon and Israel. Violation of God's regulations results in tangled relationships.

The principle forbidding incest must have been understood from the beginning. When Jacob lay dying, he called his sons to himself to foretell the coming days. To Reuben, he said:

"Reuben, you are my firstborn, my might, the first sign of my strength, excelling in honor, excelling in power. Turbulent as the waters, you will no longer excel, for you went up onto your father's bed, onto my couch and defiled it" (Genesis 49:3-4).

It was this principle that doubly condemned Amnon (II Samuel 13:1-22).

The New Testament does deal with incest—and in no uncertain terms. It was a blatant case of immorality in the church at Corinth:

It is actually reported that there is sexual immorality among you, and of a kind that does not occur even among pagans: A man has his father's wife. And you are proud! Shouldn't you rather have been filled with grief and have put out of your fellowship the man who did this? (I Corinthians 5:1-2).

197

Paul was appalled at their naive acceptance of such immoral conduct in the name of Christian liberty. He reasoned with them by saying that even heathen fail to condone incest. In the succeeding verses, they were instructed to purge the man from their assembly if he persisted in his sin and refused to repent.

The incidence of incest is increasing in American society, a sad commentary on our age, if, as Paul says, even pagans refuse to condone such behavior. This author heard one person recently state that her marriage was dissolved, at least in part, because of the sexual relationship between her former husband and his mother. Another case came to the author's attention through a student who was attempting to help a cousin who had been taken away from her parents by the court because of incest.

It is a direct violation of God's design for marriage and appropriate use of sexuality to assume that family relationships permit a person to use his sexual identity indiscriminately. A child need not be introduced to sexual techniques by a parent, step-parent, or sibling; he will learn how to express sexuality well enough by observing a positive, loving relationship between his parents. To deviate from that is to invite difficulty in sexual adjustment. God's person observes the principle of exclusiveness in his sexual relationships.

Bestiality

It is possible for a human to seek sexual relationships with an animal. It often happens in a pastoral society where sex among animals is open for all to see and where a person sometimes spends long periods of time isolated from other people. It was not merely a sin of Old Testament times, although the New Testament says nothing about it, for psychological literature has recorded such incidents in modern times.

The Bible is explicit in its condemnation of bestiality. It is in no way acceptable. The Old Testament punishment was death—just as it was for adultery, homosexuality, and some cases of incest.

> Anyone who has sexual relatons with an animal must be put to death (Exodus 22:19).
>
> Do not have sexual relations with an animal and defile yourself with it. A woman must not present herself to an animal to have sexual relations with it; that is a perversion (Leviticus 18:23).
>
> If a man has sexual relations with an animal, he must be put to death, and you must kill the animal. If a woman approaches an animal to have sexual relations with it, kill both the woman and the animal. They must be put to death; their blood will be on their own heads (Leviticus 20:15-16).
>
> Cursed is the man who has sexual relations with any animal (Deuteronomy 27:21).

Bestiality, then and now, is absolutely forbidden.

Conclusion

This chapter concludes where it began. Sex is good, proper and God-ordained. Expressed as God has directed, it is beautiful. But distorted by misdirected activity, it is ugly. As Banowsky said, how a person expresses his sexuality reveals his basic beliefs about himself.

Depersonalized, irresponsible sex is a violation of God's intentions for expression of sexuality. Fornication, adultery, homosexuality, licentiousness, immodesty, rape, incest, and bestiality—all are distortions of God's design. All are soundly condemned.

Yet God can deliver a person from sexual sin and distortion. No sin, however base, is unforgivable if a person seeks God in repentance. He can remake that one through Jesus Christ. That is why Paul recommended discipline for the incestuous man of I Corinthians 5:

> When you are assembled in the name of our Lord Jesus and I am with you in spirit, and the power of our Lord Jesus is present, hand this man over to Satan, so that the sinful nature may be destroyed and his spirit saved on the day of the Lord (I Corinthians 5:4-5).

It must have worked, too, for many scholars believe that II Corinthians 2:5-11 refers to the same man who by now had repented:

> If anyone has caused grief, he has not so much grieved me as he has grieved all of you, to some extent—not to put it too severely. The punishment inflicted on him by the majority is sufficient for him. Now instead, you ought to forgive and comfort him, so that he will not be overwhelmed by excessive sorrow. I urge you, therefore, to reaffirm your love for him. The reason I wrote you was not to see if you would stand the test and be obedient to everything. If you forgive anyone, I also forgive him. And what I have forgiven in the sight of Christ for your sake, in order that Satan might not outwit us. For we are not unaware of his schemes (II Corinthians 2:5-11).

If that speculation is true, then any kind of sexual sin can be forgiven.

Perhaps Paul thought of people with every kind of sexual sin when he wrote:

Do you not know that the wicked will not inherit the kingdom of God? Do not be deceived: Neither the sexually immoral nor idolators nor adulterers nor male prostitutes nor homosexual offenders nor thieves nor the greedy nor drunkards nor slanderers nor swindlers will inherit the kingdom of God. *And that is what some of you were. But you were washed, you were sanctified, you were justified in the name of the Lord Jesus Christ and by the Spirit of our God.* (I Corinthians 6:9-11).

The same offer extends to this day.

Summary Statements

1. Man reveals his basic personality in his sexual behavior.
2. Because sexuality is private, an essential part of a person's personality, immodest behavior is a violation of God's purpose for sexual behavior.
3. Rape is a violent invasion of another's sexual nature and is a violation of God's design for sexuality.
4. The Bible sets forth a principle banning sexual relationships with close relatives.
5. Sexual relations with animals are absolutely forbidden in the Bible.
6. Although sexual deviation is a violation of God's law, it can be forgiven when a person seeks God's forgiveness in genuine repentance.

FOR DISCUSSION

1. Do you agree or disagree with Banowsky's statement that "it is in the relationships of sex that men mirror their basic beliefs concerning their own nature, their origin and dignity as man"? Why?

2. Why would immodesty be a violation of God's design for sexuality?
3. Summarize the Biblical teaching about rape.
4. Why is incest a serious sin?
5. Why is bestiality a distortion of human sexual design?

REFERENCES

1. Banowsky, William. *It's a Playboy World*. Old Tappan, New Jersey: Fleming Revell Co., 1969.
2. Cole, William Graham. *Sex and Love in the Bible*. New York: Association Press, 1959.
3. Feucht, Oscar E.; Goines, Harry G.; von Rohr Sauer, Alfred; and Hanson, Paul G. (ed.). *Sex and the Church. St. Louis: Concordia, 1961.*
4. *Hollis, Harry, Jr. Thank God for Sex*. Nashville: Broadman Press, 1975.
5. Horner, Tom. *Sex in the Bible*. Rutland, Vermont: Charles E. Tuttle Co., 1974.
6. Howe, Ruel. "A Pastoral Theology of Sex and Marriage." *Sex and Religion Today*. Ed. Simon Doniger. New York Association Press, 1953.
7. Piper, Otto A. *The Christian Interpretation of Sex*. London: Nisbet and Co., 1942.
8. Pittenger, Norman. *Love and Control in Sexuality*. Philadelphia: Pilgrim Press, 1974.
9. Thielecke, Helmut. *The Ethics of Sex*. New York: Harper and Row, 1964.

Part III

A NEW TESTAMENT VIEW OF SEXUAL IDENTITY

The Bible is straightforward when it comes to sex. This book has examined that information in some detail. The Scriptures present a beautiful picture of the nature and purposes of sexuality as men and women were made sexual creatures with the divine intention for them to use every facet of their personalities to glorify God. But man sinned, and sexuality, as every other aspect of life, became distorted in its misuse.

A book on sexuality would hardly be complete without perusing the uniquely New Testament teachings. Previous chapters have looked at New Testament material, of course. But one cannot ignore Galatians 3:28, "There is neither Jew nor Greek, slave nor free, male nor female, for you are all one in Christ Jesus." It calls for a consideration of what that principle means to sexuality as it has already been defined.

The other uniquely New Testament idea must also be examined. It is Jesus' teaching about lust, for it is in that teaching that He recognizes that sexuality can be made subject to the will and, therefore, controlled in expression. It is to these two topics that the following section is addressed.

Part III — A New Testament View Of Sexual Identity

Chapter Sixteen

NEITHER MALE NOR FEMALE

Imagine a world in which there were no racial, economic, or sexual distinctions. It isn't easy, for we live in a world in which there are distinctions of all kinds. Black and white, Oriental and European, Jewish and Gentile, management and labor, rich and poor, men and women—all are designations that cause divisions in the world, even in the church at times. Angry, raucous voices demand their 'rights.' It sometimes seems almost hopeless to believe that divisive distinctions can be obliterated.

But the New Testament makes an unequivocal assertion: in Christ human distinctions, whatever their basis, are overcome. A distinctive newness is to be found in Christ, a newness so revolutionary that it erases racial, economic, and sexual distinctions. It is a teaching that requires examination in the midst of a study on sexual identity. What does the Bible mean when it says that there is 'neither male nor female' once a person puts on Jesus Christ?

The New Testament Principle

To discover what the New Testament says about sexual distinctions, one must consider as a unit three great theological themes. These are creation, the fall, and redemption. The first two have already been considered in some detail, but they will be briefly reviewed once again.

Creation

Two creation accounts are included in the Old Testament. The first, Genesis 1:26-28, focuses on the chronology of creation:

204

Then God said, "Let us make man in our image, in our likeness, and let them rule over the fish of the sea and the birds of the air, over the livestock, over all the earth, and over all the creatures that move along the ground." So God created man in his own image, in the image of God he created him; male and female he created them. God blessed them and said to them, "Be fruitful and increase in number; fill the earth and subdue it. Rule over the fish of the sea and the birds of the air and over every living creature that moves on the ground."

Man, male and female, were the supreme result of God's creative work.

Neither man nor woman is said to be superior to the other. There were no distinctions in role functions stated: both Adam and Eve were to care for the garden. The only distinction made in this text was biological.

A second creation account, found in Genesis 2:4-8, 18-24, focuses not on chronology, but on the unique relationship of man and woman:

This is the account of the heavens and the earth when they were created. When the Lord God made the earth and the heavens, no shrub of the field had yet appeared on the earth and no plant of the field has yet sprung up; the Lord God had not sent rain on the earth and there was no man to work the ground. And the Lord God formed man from the dust of the ground and breathed into his nostrils the breath of life, and man became a living being. Now the Lord God had planted a garden in the east, in Eden; and there he put the man he had formed.

. . . .

The Lord God said, "It is not good for the man to be alone. I will make a helper suitable for him." Now the Lord God had formed out of the ground all the beasts of the field and all the birds of the air. He brought them to the man to see what he would name them; and whatever the man called each living creature, that was his name. So the man gave names to all of the livestock, the birds of the air, and all the beasts of the field. But for Adam no suitable helper was found. So the Lord God caused the man to fall into a deep sleep; and while he was sleeping, he took one of the man's ribs and closed up the place with flesh. Then the Lord God made a woman from the rib he had taken out of the man, and he brought her to the man. The man said, "This is now bone of my bones and flesh of my flesh; she shall be called 'woman,' for she was taken out of man." For this reason a man will leave his father and mother and be united to his wife, and they will become one flesh.

The core of the whole matter is found in verse 18 when God said, "It is not good for man to be alone." (That is the only negative commentary on creation.) In this account, to emphasize the uniqueness of the male/female relationship, the animals are said to be created one by one in an effort to find a helper for Adam. None would do—not until God made Eve from Adam's own flesh.

It is important to notice that woman was not an inferior creature. Compare Genesis 1:28, when God mandated both man and woman to manage the earth, and Genesis 2:23, when man exclaimed, in effect, "Now I have an adequate helper!"

Fall

The second theological theme is the fall of man into sin when chaos was introduced in the order of creation. Both Adam and Eve sinned, and both fell under God's judgment.

206

The pronouncement of punishment is recorded in Genesis 3:16-19:

> To the woman he said, "I will greatly increase your pains in childbearing; with pain you will give birth to your children. Your desire will be for your husband, and he will rule over you." To Adam he said, "Because you listened to your wife and ate from the tree about which I commanded you 'You must not eat of it,' cursed is the ground because of you; through painful toil you will eat of it all the days of your life. It will produce thorns and thistles for you, and you will eat the plants of the field. By the sweat of your brow you will eat your food until you return to the ground, since from it you were taken; for dust you are and to dust you will return."

Redemption

A third theological theme found in the Bible is redemption. This redemptive work was intended to be so revolutionary that a person who had been reconciled to God was described as a 'new creature:' "Therefore, if anyone is in Christ, he is a new creation: the old has gone, the new has come!" (II Corinthians 5:17). The word translated 'new,' here as in other Pauline writings, indicates a newness of kind.

Paul applied this principle of newness to several social distinctions common in the first century world.

1. He insisted that the Gentile is not a second-class kingdom citizen. When he became a Christian, he ceased being primarily a Gentile to become a kingdom man:

> For he himself is our peace, who has made the two one and has destroyed the barrier, the dividing wall of hostility, by abolishing in his flesh the law with its commandments and regulations. His purpose was to create in

207

himself one new man out of the two, thus making peace, and in this one body to reconcile both of them to God through the cross, by which he put to death their hostility (Ephesians 2:14-16).

2. Furthermore, distinctions of the flesh were no longer to be observed:

So from now on we regard no one from a worldly point of view. Though we once regarded Christ in this way, we do so no longer (II Corinthians 5:16).

Neither circumcision nor uncircumcision means anything; what counts is a new creation (Galatians 6:15).

3. Economic distinctions were transcended:

Perhaps the reason he was separated from you for a little while was that you might have him back for good —no longer as a slave, but better than a slave, as a dear brother. He is very dear to me but even dearer to you, both as a man and as a brother in the Lord (Philemon 15-16).

My brothers, as believers in our glorious Lord Jesus Christ, don't show favoritism. Suppose a man comes into your meeting wearing a gold ring and fine clothes, and a poor man in shabby clothes also comes in. If you show special attention to the man wearing fine clothes and say, "Here's a good seat for you," but say to the poor man, "You stand there," or, "Sit on the floor by my feet," have you not discriminated among yourselves and become judges with evil thoughts (James 2:1-4).

4. Sexual distinctions were also transcended:

You are all sons of God through faith in Christ Jesus, for all of you who were baptized into Christ have been clothed with Christ. There is neither Jew nor Greek, slave nor free, male nor female, for you are all one in Christ Jesus (Galatians 3:26-28).

Does Paul's teaching about newness totally obliterate all differences? The answer is an obvious no. Becoming a new creature does not erase the biological distinctions of ethnicity. A black man does not change colors when he becomes a Christian. Nor does a European begin to look and act Oriental. Created distinctions remain, but Paul insists that they are no longer the basis upon which a person is evaluated or allowed to participate in the church once he has been united with Christ in Christian baptism.

Neither does newness require that the church practice a kind of welfare state, taking from the rich to give to the poor. Never was wealth—or lack of it—commended or disparaged on its own merits. Actual differences in economic status exist—and will no doubt continue to do so. But brotherhood in Christ is to transcend the differences and revolutionize the relationships.

Slaves, obey your earthly masters with respect and fear, and with sincerity of heart, just as you would obey Christ. Obey them not only to win their favor when their eye is on you, but like slaves of Christ, doing the will of God from your heart. Serve wholeheartedly, as if you were serving the Lord, not men because you know the Lord will reward everyone for whatever good he does, whether he is slave or free. And masters, treat your slaves in the same way. Do not threaten them, since you know that he who is both their master and yours is in heaven, and there is no favoritism with him (Ephesians 6:5-9).

If you really keep the royal law found in Scripture, "Love your neighbor as yourself," you are doing right. But if you

209

show favoritism, you sin and are convicted by the law as lawbreakers (James 2:8-9).

Once a person is united with Christ in Christian baptism, the master and the slave, the rich man and the poor man stand on equal footing before God.

Nor does newness call for a unisex society. Created sexual differences are not to be obliterated. Women are still women; men are still men. Both act as men and women according to the definition of a given culture, which is not wrong at all as long as it does not violate any Biblical principle. But quite in contrast to rabbinic opinion that regarded women as inferior, unworthy to be taught the Torah, and totally unable to confront God directly, the New Testament does teach that woman and man stand before God and each other equal in regard to sin and salvation.

A first century Jewish man was likely to be heard praying and thanking God that "Thou has not made me a Gentile, a slave, or a woman." Paul's revolutionary principle in Galatians 3:25-28 nullified every part of that prayer.

Galatians 3:26-28 indicates that redemption through Jesus Christ is intended to restore the relationships that existed before sin created chaos. That is the intention—and should be our goal. Yet, in spite of that, there always exists a tension between the 'already' and the 'not yet.' The church lives in a fallen world. Try as the redeemed will to transcend social distinctions, the presence of sin makes the progress uneven at best. What is 'already' and what is 'not yet' have to be worked out in the sinful world in which the church lives.

New Testament Practice

Jesus

Women in the first century were not treated as women are today. Rather, some rabbis regarded women as inferior, unworthy of receiving an education, incapable of challenging thought, and the property of their husbands—all in distinct contrast to the creation intentions. These rabbis would forbid women to listen to teaching, be seen talking to a man in public, or be considered one of those counted as adults in order to have a synagogue. Many first century women were downtrodden, persons with little worth beyond satisfying a man's sexual appetites and bearing his children.

Jesus' treatment of women was radically different than the way the others in His culture treated them. An examination of His ministry grants insight into what it means for men and women to stand equally before God:

1. He taught both men and women in the same audience, Matthew 14:13-21, 15:29; Mark 6:30-44; Luke 9:10-17; John 6:1-15.
2. He claimed sisters and brothers in the kingdom, Matthew 12:46-50; Mark 3:31-35; Luke 8:19-21.
3. He healed both men and women, Matthew 8:5-15, 9:1-8, 18:26; Luke 7:1-17.
4. He regarded women as capable of thinking, Matthew 15:31-38; John 4:1-42, 11:1-44.
5. He forgave women as well as men, John 8:1-11.
6. He had men and women friends, Luke 10:38-42.
7. He commended the faith of women, Mark 14:1-11; Luke 7:36-50; John 12:1-11.
8. He appeared first to a woman after His resurrection and made her a spokesman to tell about the resurrection, John 20:10-18.

Jesus understood what it meant for there to be 'neither male nor female' before God.

Early Church

A look at the early church also provides helpful insight to determine how to apply 'neither male nor female.' The

211

practice of the early church stood in direct contrast to the custom of others who still saw women as inferior.

1. Women and men were fully members of the church, Acts 5:14; 6:12; 9:36; 16:1, 13-15; 17:4, 12, 34. In the Old Testament order only men could partake of the initiatory rite of circumcision, the outward sign that they were God's people. But now, in the church, *every* believer, man or woman, was baptized into Christ.

2. Both men and women joined in prayer meetings. Acts 1:14, 12:1-19. There seemed to be no distinctions between men and women in regard to praying.

3. Women as well as men helped establish and support local churches, Acts 16:40.

4. Both men and women were persecuted for their faith, Acts 8:3, 9:2, 22:4.

5. Women as well as men were held accountable for their sins, Acts 5:1-11.

6. Women as well as men could pray in public, I Corinthians 11:5.

7. Women could instruct, Acts 18:26; Titus 2:4-5.

8. Paul regarded both men and women as fellow workers in the gospel, Romans 16:1-15; Philippians 4:2-3.

Tertullian wrote, "Together they pray, together they prostrate themselves, together they perform their fasts, mutually teaching, mutually exhorting, mutually sustaining. Equally they are found in the church of God."[1] The early church apparently knew what it meant for sexual distinctions to be erased.

---

1. Tertullian, *Ante-Nicene Fathers* (New York: Charles Scribners Sons, 1885) 4:48.

On the other hand, the New Testament in no way suggests a unisex society that overthrows every male/female distinction. Men and women were equal before God. Both had ministries to perform. But they were still distinguishable as men and women as suggested in Chapters 6 and 7 in this book.

On two occasions Paul did tell women to be silent. In at least one of those cases it was to deal with a specific congregational problem. The church at Corinth was beset with problems of all kinds, not the least of which was disorderly worship (I Corinthians 12-14). Paul appealed to propriety (one mark of a Christian woman), not so much because women should never speak in worship (that right had already been recognized in 11:5), but because misuse of that possibility was creating havoc within the church.

Again, in I Timothy 2:12, Paul prohibited a woman to "teach or have authority over a man." The wording in the original language prohibits a spirit of arrogance and wresting authority from its rightful owner. Such a spirit is in direct contradiction to the standards set for God's ideal woman. Presumably, men, too, are disqualified from teaching should they demonstrate the same spirit.

At the same time, one cannot escape the fact that the major positions of leadership in the early church were filled by men. No women were apostles. The eldership was male, probably to picture the relationship of Christ and the church in much the same way that a husband's leadership in the home presents the same symbolism. Evangelists were men.

The Biblical teaching was radical for the first century world. "Neither male nor female" was revolutionary. Both men and women stood equally before God without regard to sex. Within the bounds set for God's ideal man and woman,

213

both participated fully in the church, quite in contrast to its forerunner, the synagogue.

Conclusion

How is Paul's statement, "There is neither male nor female," to be applied in this age? Are all sexual distinctions to be obliterated?

Women are still to be women, and men are to be men. Paul's assertion is no call for men and women to look alike, think alike, and/or act alike. Biological distinctions remain as do many of the cultural expectations taught from birth. These need not be indiscriminately discarded.

But women and men stand before God equal, absolutely no different in His eyes in regard to sin and salvation. Both have equal worth. Both are thinking, reasoning people with specific talents and abilities to be developed for His service. Both are free to make choices as to marriage, vocation, and avocation on the basis of their needs and abilities. The choice determines, in part, the proper 'feminine' and 'masculine' responsibilities and behaviors.

Both men and women operate within a given cultural milieu. The principle of "neither male nor female" never varies. But its actualization will vary according to the locale and the cultural dictates of the age. Freedom may have to be restricted so that the church can successfully penetrate the world.

Women and men must work out their choices and ministries within the Biblically-established standards for femininity (few, but definite) and masculinity (also few, but certain). Neither should despise his sexuality, but accept it as an integral part of his personality to carry out his particular ministry and use it to bring glory to God who made him a

NEITHER MALE NOR FEMALE

man or a woman, yet treats him equally with every other believer.

Summary Statements

1. In Christ, all human distinctions are erased.
2. When human distinctions are erased, created differences (color and sex, for example) remain.
3. "Neither male nor female" means that both men and women stand equally before God in regard to sin and salvation.
4. Jesus demonstrated the principle of "neither male nor female" when He treated women as He did men.
5. Men and women were both fully members of the church in the New Testament.
6. Men and women are to involve themselves in the church within the boundaries established by God for the ideal man and woman.

FOR DISCUSSION

1. What does it mean for there to be "neither male nor female" in Christ?
2. Cite New Testament evidence to show that there is "neither male nor female" in Christ?
3. What boundaries must be considered in actualizing the idea that there is "neither male nor female" in Christ?
4. How does "neither male nor female" affect sex roles?

REFERENCES

1. Cole, William Graham. *Sex in Christianity and Psychoanalysis.* New York: Oxford University Press, 1966.

215

2. Foster, Lewis A. "Marks of the Christian Woman." *Christian Standard.* August 2, 9, 16, 23, 30, 1981.

3. Heine, Ronald. "The Biblical Teaching about the Role of Women in the Church." Chapel Address, Lincoln (Illinois) Christian College, February 11, 1975.

4. Keister, Dorothy. "Jesus and Women." Ladies' Day Address, Midwest Christian College, Oklahoma City, Oklahoma, April 9, 1981.

5. Pape, Dorothy R. *In Search of God's Ideal Woman.* Downers Grove, Illinois: InterVarsity Press, 1976.

6. Scanzoni, Letha, and Hardesty, Nancy. *All We're Meant To Be.* Waco, Texas: Word Books, 1974.

7. Stouffer, Austin H. "The Ordination of Women: Yes." *Christianity Today.* February 20, 1981.

8. Williams, Don. *The Apostle Paul and Women in the Church.* Glendale, California: Regal, 1977.

Chapter Seventeen

THE WILL: CONTROLLING SEXUAL BEHAVIOR

It is quite possible to misuse sexuality without commiting an overt sexual act. It is not only possible; it happens often. It is possible to let òne's thoughts dwell on sexual activity with another person to the point where he is as guilty of sexual misconduct as one who actually engages in sexual intercourse with someone with whom he has no legal or moral right.

Jesus pointedly presented a hard teaching when He said in the Sermon on the Mount, "You have heard that it was said, 'Do not commit adultery.' But I tell you that anyone who looks at a woman lustfully has already committed adultery with her in his heart" (Matthew 5:27-28). Re-emphasizing the Old Testament law, He proceeded beyond observable behavior to penetrate the heart. He made it clear that proper use of sexuality is more than merely keeping a law: it is a matter of using the will to control sexual thought and behavior.

It has been said before in this book, but it bears repetition: ours is a society that sees no need for restraint in any area of life, certainly not in sexual expression. A secular society has demoted man to the status of an animal, no different than other animals, which then permits him to express his sexual instincts as he wills. But the Biblical view of man is far loftier than that of contemporary society. The Bible pictures man as a thinking, reasoning individual, capable of choosing to do good or evil, as he wills. Man is more than a mass of instincts to be acted out as he is motivated by physical needs. He can control his behavior by controlling his thinking. Jesus' teaching about lust is important, then, for it reminds us of man's potential to will his conduct.

217

Lust Defined

The word translated as 'lust' in the New Testament is the Greek word *epithumeo*. It indicates a direct impulse toward food, sexual satisfacton, and desire in general. It is a motion of the will that is self-seeking for immediate gratification of its desire. It is a life dominated by the senses: food, luxury, sex, possessions. It is never to be confused with the work of God, as John made clear:

> Do not love the world or anything in the world. If anyone loves the world, the love of the Father is not in him. For everything in the world—the cravings of sinful man, the lust of his eyes and the boasting of what he has and does—comes not from the Father but from the world. The world and the desires pass away, but the man who does the will of God lives forever (I John 2:15-17).

It is obvious from John's statement that *epithumeo* is an act of the will. Contrary to a will that seeks immediate gratification, John calls for a person to love God, another act of the will, for the word he used was *agape*.

Neither Jesus nor John are to be understood as condemning thoughts that sometimes clamor for satisfaction. The word *epithumeo* does *not* refer to fleeting thoughts. Nearly everyone can bear witness to having tempting thoughts, some related to food, sex, luxury, or possessions. But the condemnation is for nurturing those thoughts, deliberately stimulating them, intentionally looking, dwelling upon satisfaction of them.

Man has two distinct sides. He is a person with instinctual motivations, but he is at the same time a spiritual being made to serve God. Nowhere are physical needs condemned in the Bible. Quite by contrast, they are good when they are

218

controlled by the will to be used in a way that is pleasing to God.

What The Bible Says About Lust

Jesus introduced the topic of lust in the Sermon on the Mount. He stated:

> You have heard that it was said, "Do not commit adultery." But I tell you that anyone who looks at a woman lustfully has already committed adultery with her in his heart (Matthew 5:27-28).

Jesus is certainly not speaking of normal desires. But He is referring to deliberate stimulation of the mind to imagine or desire sexual intercourse with a specific person to whom he is not entitled. He simply called for control of the body through discipline of the mind.

The writers of the epistles also dealt with a man's control of the will. For example, Paul minced no words when he wrote to the church at Thessalonica:

> Finally, brothers, we instructed you how to live in order to please God, as in fact you are living. Now we ask you and urge you in the Lord Jesus to do this more and more. You know what instructions we gave you by the authority of the Lord Jesus. It is God's will that you should be holy; that you should avoid sexual immorality; that each of you should learn to control his own body in a way that is holy and honorable, not in passionate lust like the heathen, who do not know God; and that in this matter no one should wrong his brother or take advantage of him. The Lord will punish men for all such sins, as we have already told you and warned you. For God did not call us to be impure, but to live a holy life (I Thessalonians 4:1-7).

James clarifies why it is so essential for a man to control his thoughts:

> When tempted, no one should say, "God is tempting me." For God cannot be tempted by evil, nor does he tempt anyone; but each one is tempted when, by his own evil desire, he is dragged away and enticed. Then, after desire has conceived, it gives birth to sin; and sin, when it is full-grown, gives birth to death (James 1:13-15).

It is more than a matter of eliminating desire merely to exercise the will. Desire is something that can be nourished or stifled by an act of the will. If desire is nourished long enough, it is translated into *action*. Lucian once said, "All the evils which come upon man—revolutions and wars, stratagems and slaughter—spring from desire. All these things have as their fountainhead the desire for more."

No person can prevent a tempting thought from entering his mind. But he can decide whether to entertain that thought or not. Should he choose to nurture the thought, he will not forever be content to merely contemplate the sexual behavior. Sooner or later, that contemplation will become reality. That is why Jesus instructed a person to eliminate such thinking at first sight.

Peter carefully delineated the results of a life dominated by lust:

> For if God did not spare angels when they sinned, but sent them to hell, putting them into gloomy dungeons to be held for judgment; if he did not spare the ancient world when he brought the flood on its ungodly people, but protected Noah, a preacher of righteousness, and seven others; if he condemned the cities of Sodom and Gomorrah by burning them to ashes, and made them an example of what is going to happen to the ungodly; and if he rescued Lot, a righteous man,

who was distressed by the filthy lives of lawless men (for that righteous man, living among them day after day, was tormented in his righteous soul by the lawless deeds he saw and heard;—if this is so, then the Lord knows how to rescue godly men from trials and to hold the unrighteous for the day of judgment, while continuing their punishment. This is especially true of those who follow the corrupt desire of the sinful nature and despise authority. Bold and arrogant, these men are not afraid to slander celestial beings; yet even angels, although they are stronger and more powerful, do not bring slanderous accusations against such beings in the presence of the Lord. But these men blaspheme in matters they do not understand. They are like brute beasts, creatures of instinct, born only to be caught and destroyed, and like beasts they too will perish (II Peter 2:4-12).

How to Stifle Lust

How can a Christian who is intent on using his sexuality to glorify God wage a battle to counteract any tendency toward lust? How can he master his instinctual needs?

Every era has had its thinkers who sought to describe how to achieve the self-controlled life. Most have relied on reason, intelligence, even good sense, for the mind to move the will, only to find that personal effort alone fails.

However, the Bible makes it clear that the will can direct sexual thinking and behavior (as well as other physical needs). The beginning point is to see sexuality as a God-given facet of personality, a necessary and good part, yet an aspect that need not be expressed in intercourse indiscriminately, or even at all, for a full human life. That frame of reference frees a person to do what God desires.

Then a man must recognize that God is willing to provide whatever a person needs to overcome any tendency toward lust.

221

His divine power has given us everything we need for life and godliness through our knowledge of him who called us by his own glory and goodness. Through these he has given us his very great and precious promises, so that through them you may participate in the divine nature and escape the corruption in the world caused by evil desires (II Peter 1:3-4).

He has given us what is needed—but we must use it.

Paul gave yet another hint in Galatians 5:16: "So I say, live by the Spirit, and you will not gratify the desires of the sinful nature." One secret to control of the will is to fill the mind and heart with the things of God, to keep close to God and His people, to become saturated with God's ways. When that happens, one has resources at his command— and in his mind—to counteract illicit desires.

Paul provides further guidance in I Corinthians 10:1-13:

For I do not want you to be ignorant of the fact, brothers, that our forefathers were all under the cloud and that they all passed through the sea. They were all baptized into Moses in the cloud and in the sea. They all ate the same spiritual food and drank the same spiritual drink; for they drank from the spiritual rock that accompanied them, and that rock was Christ. Nevertheless, God was not pleased with most of them; their bodies were scattered over the desert.

Now these things occurred as examples, to keep us from setting our hearts on evil things as they did. Do not be idolaters, as some of them were; as it is written: "The people sat down to eat and drink and got up to indulge in pagan revelry." We should not commit sexual immorality, as some of them did—and in one day twenty-three thousand of them died. We should not test the Lord, as some of them did—and were killed by snakes. And do not grumble, as son of them did—and were killed by the destroying angel.

These things happened to them as examples and were written down as warnings for us, on whom the fulfillment of the ages has come. So, if you think you are standing firm, be careful that you don't fall! No temptation has seized you except what is common to man. And God is faithful; he will not let you be tempted beyond what you can bear. But when you are tempted, he will also provide a way out so that you can stand up under it.

Using examples from Israel's history to illustrate negative outcomes when evil desires are allowed to ferment and finally find expression, he concludes with three guidelines for victory (verses 12-13):

1. Recognize that temptation is inevitable. One cannot eliminate temptations that come to satisfy physical needs. One will never rise above the fleeting thoughts that appeal to physical desires. Some will experience greater sexual temptation than others. As long as a person lives in the world, he will be tempted.

2. Be assured that no temptation is unique. As much as a person may try to convince himself that his situation is different, that he cannot overcome, that he is entitled to special consideration for nururturing his tempting thoughts, he cannot take that leisure. At the same time, it is a source of strength to realize that every person experiences temptation at one time or another.

3. Claim the promise that with temptation there is always a route of escape provided by God. But a person must actively seek that way out. God will never force him to take it. There is a point when one can overcome— if he exercises his will and casts out the thoughts that would take up permanent residence in his mind.

223

God does expect a kingdom man to discipline himself to use his body, mind, his emotions, his talents to glorify his Creator. He wants transformed men who use the resources of God to control sexuality so it can be used to glorify Him.

Lust Overcome

The Bible makes it clear that a person can be transformed in his mind to control his sexual thoughts and behavior.

At one point we too were foolish, disobedient, deceived and enslaved by all kinds of passions and pleasures. We lived in malice and envy, being hated and hating one another. But when the kindness and love of God our Savior appeared, he saved us, not because of righteous things we had done, but because of his mercy. He saved us through the washing of rebirth and renewal by the Holy Spirit, whom he poured out on us generously through Jesus Christ our Savior, so that, having been justified by his grace, we might become heirs having the hope of eternal life. This is a trustworthy saying. And I want you to stress these things, so that those who have trusted in God may be careful to devote themselves to doing what is good. These things are excellent and profitable for everyone (Titus 3:3-8).

It is extremely good news to those who struggle to overcome temptations.

Conclusion

It is possible to commit adultery in one's mind if he harbors and nurtures physical desires that enter the mind. Jesus knew very well that to continue to nurture a forbidden physical response was to finally seek overt expression of it. He called for responsible exercise of the will, empowered by His guidance, to quickly erase lustful thoughts before they find physical completion.

Summary Statements

1. Lust is a motion of the will to satisfy physical impulses, one of which is sex. It is deliberately stimulating and nurturing thoughts of illegal or immoral satisfaction.
2. The Bible calls for a Christian to control his thoughts, not to permit his thoughts to control him.
3. It is important to combat lust, for illicit thoughts savored and nurtured eventually find overt expression.
4. God provides what is necessary to overcome temptation.
5. Lust can be overcome and left behind as a person is transformed in Jesus Christ.

FOR DISCUSSION

1. What is the difference between a tempting thought and lust?
2. Summarize the Biblical teaching about lust. Is lust strictly sexual in nature?
3. How can a person overcome lustful desires?

REFERENCES

1. McCracken, Robert J. *What Is Sin? What Is Virtue?* New York: Harper and Row, 1966.
2. Piper, Otto J. *The Christian Interpretation of Sex.* London: Nisbet and Company, 1942.
3. Stott, John R. W. *Christian Counter-Culture.* Downers Grove, Illinois: InterVarsity Press, 1974.
4. Thielecke, Helmut. *The Ethics of Sex.* New York: Harper and Row, 1964.

Part IV

HANDLING SEXUAL IDENTITY
IN AN AMORAL WORLD

The Christian lives in an amoral world. It is a world with no fixed values, no absolutes, no standard by which to evaluate life or behavior. It is, as one author calls it, a "culture of narcissism" in which the prevailing passion is to live for oneself.[1]

Sex in American society is valued for its own sake. It has lost all reference to the future, all hope of cementing permanent relationships. Sexual liaisons can be terminated at a whim. Sexual excitement is expected to satisfy every emotional need.

But the Christian is moral; his point of reference is the Bible. His behavior is to be evaluated by the norm of God's Word. He is to live for God, not self. He is to care for the needs of others. Commitment is valued. Sexual chastity is to be guarded.

Therein lies the conflict for a Christian. How can he live as a Christian in a world gone awry? How can he value sexuality and properly express it within the context of a society that seeks to erode his Biblical foundations? The following three chapters examine the dilemma and suggest how a Christian, single or married, can handle sexuality in an amoral world.

---

1. See Christopher Lasch, *The Culture of Narcissism* (New York: W. W. Norton and Company, 1978).

Part IV — Handling Sexual Identity In An Amoral World

Chapter Eighteen

SEXUAL IDENTITY FOR THE SEXUAL CELIBATE

Single people create discomfort in a world made for pairs. And a world made for pairs elicits equal discomfort among singles.

It is a world made up of families. At the grocery, try buying meat or frozen vegetables for one—everything comes in 'family size.' At church, classes are for young marrieds, older marrieds, or pairs and spares. At work, invitations to company affairs are issued with a call to respond, "Yes, my spouse and I will attend"; "I can attend, but my spouse cannot;" or "Sorry, neither my spouse nor I can attend." Old maid jokes abound, even today. And some insist that a single person is an anomaly. One person said, "Every game has its losers. Every game has those who refuse to play. In short, some females never marry."[1]

The English language has no polite word to describe an unmarried person past thirty. 'Old maid,' 'bachelor girl,' 'spinster'—all have negative connotations. 'Bachelor' used to be an acceptable term, but even it conjures up some negative images in this day. In the case of either the never-married man or the single woman, there is at least a hint that his/her sexuality is out of kilter, else he/she would no longer be single.

---

1. Evelyn Goldfield, Sue Munsher, and Naomi Weistein, "A Woman is a Sometime Thing," *The New Left,* ed. Priscilla Long (Boston: Porter Sargent Publisher, 1969), p. 255.

To live as a single in a sex-saturated society is not easy. The never-married person is led to believe that he is somehow inferior or missing out on something profound if he maintains his celibacy. Those who were once married and have become single again because of divorce or death are confronted with powerful temptations to actively express the sexual nature that once was expressed in marriage.

The Bible does make a strong case for marriage, of course. Man and woman were created to complement each other, to minister to each other, to satisfy each other sexually. Man and woman were designed with a sexual nature, a powerful permeating facet of their personalities. God did sanctify marriage, and He said that the partners should become one flesh, a unity that is expressed in sexual intercourse, although that oneness extends beyond the physical to include unity of purpose, emotional harmony, and social complementarity.

Even if everyone wanted to marry, they could not, for women outnumber men in American society. The laws of mathematics simply eliminate the possibility of marriage for some. But not everyone does seek to marry, and according to the Bible, those people are very much within God's design.

What The Bible Says About Celibacy

The Bible speaks very little regarding the sexual celibate, probably because the societal norm is marriage. But when the Bible does speak, it clearly states that a singleness is not a pitiful, abnormal state for inferior folk who have a serious personality flaw that precludes marriage. It does not identify these folk as losers. Singleness can be honorable.

229

Jesus spoke about celibacy in Matthew 19:10-12:

> The disciples said to him, "If this is the situation between a husband and wife, it is better not to marry." Jesus replied, "Not everyone can accept this teaching, but only those to whom it has been given. For some are eunuchs because they were born that way; others were made that way by men; and others have renounced marriage because of the kingdom of heaven. The one who can accept this should accept it."

The occasion was Jesus' teaching on divorce in Matthew 19:8-9 in which He had said that divorce was permitted only for unfaithfulness. It sounded like a hard teaching in view of the marital laxity of the day, so much so that the disciples concluded that if marriage was so binding, it would would be preferable not to marry at all. Jesus' response was that only kingdom men could live by a kingdom ethic.

Then Jesus listed three reasons why a person might choose not to marry, to live as a single:

1. Some people are born with a physical deformity that makes it impossible to have sexual intercourse.
2. Some have been castrated by another. This practice was especially common in ancient Oriental societies where a man would be put in charge of the king's harem. The king often had the attendant castrated so that he could not approach any of his wives sexually.
3. Others choose not to marry for the sake of the kingdom. They opt to sublimate sexual needs in order to give themselves for service in the kingdom. Clement of Alexandria expressed it this way, "The true eunuch is not he who cannot, but he who will not indulge in fleshly pleasures." There are those places and kinds of services that can be done most effectively without the encumbrances of a spouse and children. Every reader can name someone whose kingdom service

has been deterred not because of his own lack of devotion and talent, but because of a spouse whose devotion failed to match his or whose needs siphoned off his energy for service.

Jesus demonstrated in His own life that singleness is an acceptable option. Quite obviously, marriage is not an essential state for a person to be fully human or to be considered normal. If it were, Jesus could hardly be considered a complete person. But Jesus was perfect and complete; He demonstrated that it is possible to live successfully as a celibate. He sublimated physical needs to the greater need to do His Father's will. He demonstrated the idea of being a eunuch for the sake of the kingdom.

Paul also dealt with the issue of singleness in his letter to the church at Corinth. He, too, considered singleness a viable option:

> I wish that all men were as I am. But each man has his own gift from God; one has this gift, another has that. Now to the unmarried and the widows I say: It is good for them to stay unmarried, as I am. But if they cannot control themselves, they should marry, for it is better to marry than to burn with passion.
>
> . . . .
>
> Now about virgins: I have no command from the Lord, but I give a judgment as one who by the Lord's mercy is trustworthy. Because of the present crisis, I think that it is good for you to remain as you are. Are you married? Do not seek a divorce. Are you unmarried? Do not look for a wife. But if you do marry, you have not sinned. But those who marry will face many trials in life, and I want to spare you this.
>
> . . . .
>
> I would like you to be free from concern. An unmarried man is concerned about the Lord's affairs—how he can please the

231

Lord. But a married man is concerned about the affairs of the world—how he can please his wife—and his interests are divided. An unmarried woman or virgin is concerned about the Lord's affairs: Her aim is to be devoted to the Lord in both body and spirit. But a married woman is concerned about the affairs of this world—how she can please her husband. I am saying this for your own good, not to restrict you, but that you may live in a right way in undivided devotion to the Lord (I Corinthians 7:7-9, 25-28, 32-35).

Paul's teaching is simply this: singleness may be better than marriage in a time of crisis. He wrote urging Christians always to be ready for the second coming. But he understood very well that for some not to marry would be to court temptation perhaps too heavy to bear. He suggests, then, that the ability to live as a celibate is a gift not enjoyed by everyone. Celibacy is no real virtue if a person cannot harness his sexual passions. He will be forever susceptible to sexual temptation.

Paul understood both marriage and singleness as honorable estates. He was wise enough to know that the married person has many decisions to make, many distractions, many troubles, all of which in crisis times may divert his attention from essential kingdom matters. A married person is bound by oath to God to concern himself with the needs of his partner; in one sense, then, devotion to the Lord can never be totally undivided for him.

The teaching of I Corinthians 7:7-9, 25-28, 32-35 can be summarized with the following statements:

1. Both marriage and singleness are acceptable to the Lord.
2. Self-discipline and continence are good.
3. A person is not to make an unnatural thing of his religion. Christianity was meant to glorify the normal life.

232

For most people marriage is the best way to express
their sexuality.

4. A person is never to make an agony of his religion.
Celibacy is not for everyone. Just as marriage is not
to be a Christian's goal, neither is celibacy. The Bible
destroys two equally erroneous myths. One is that
marriage is essential for a person to be fully human.
The other myth is that celibacy is holier than marriage.
Neither is true. Holiness is demonstrated by being devoted to glorifying God whether single or married.

Living Successfully as a Single

The Bible does hold our singleness as an option, especially in crisis times and to devote oneself to kingdom service.
But not everyone is single because he originally chose to be
Those singles must learn to accept their singleness and trans-
slate it into effective living. How, then, can a single person
live as a celibate in a sex-saturated society? Paul Tournier
defines the problem, "The real problem is to make a success
of one's marriage if one does marry, and to make a success
of the celibate life if he does not.[2]

Accept Sexuality

The celibate must come to grips with himself as a sexual being. He must realize that sexuality is a powerful, demanding,
but controllable element that does not have to be expressed
in intercourse. That sexual force is more powerful for some
than it is for others. But every person must acknowledge
his sexual needs, then plan ways to sublimate those needs

2. Paul Tournier, *The Adventure of Living* (New York: Harper and Row,
1965), p. 135.

into creative living, a process that is possible when the will controls physical activities.

Too many singles make the mistake of trying to deny sexuality, to act as if it did not exist, to insist that they have no sexual inclinations. The result of that behavior pressed to the extreme is a man or a woman who thwarts meaningful facets of their personalities. Women often lose their vibrancy, their gentleness, their femininity. Men frequently become calloused, even subhuman in their treatment of and concern for others.

Other singles appear to be constantly on the search for a potential partner, to the point where they cannot relate naturally to the opposite sex. They evaluate every member of the opposite sex as a potential partner. Some fantasize about sexual activity.

A part of a person's acceptance of sexuality is to see his virginity as a way to imitate Christ and to follow the dictates of the Spirit without any encumbrance. He must take responsibility for his own attitudes toward life, sexuality, and singleness. To do so is to put oneself at God's disposal to make life what He wants. Paul Tournier said, "The biggest difference [between marrieds and singles] is not between those who are married and those who are not, but between those who live their real lives with conviction and those who live them unwillingly."[3]

When a person comes to grips with his sexuality, he is no longer dependent upon his marital status, or lack of it, to give him feelings of worth. He can go right on living with purpose and excitement, regardless of the stereotypes others may hold. He is well aware that he is neither biologically

---

3. *Ibid*, p. 137.

abnormal nor totally unattractive if he isn't married. He need not be frustrated sexually—he simply finds creative, moral channels by which to express his sexuality. Self-acceptance is the key.

Develop Relationships

What a single person perceives as sexual needs may, in fact, be desires for companionship, emotional security, closeness, affirmation, love. Very often, a person's specific physical needs are significantly reduced when the other needs are met.

Every person has touch needs. This is difficult in a society that permits touch only through ritualized conditions. Husband and wife usually meet those needs with a quick hug, a supportive arm around the waist, holding hands. Psychologists call it "skin hunger." Singles have to be very discreet in handling this need, but it can be done.

Single folks also have affirmation needs. Every person needs to feel worthwhile and valued as a person. It is at this point that the single person's home and job are so important. A comfortable, well-kept home raises self-esteem. A satisfying job gives a sense of worth. It is also helpful to develop relationships with children, for they are loving and affirming.

Single people have a battle with loneliness because man was made for community. Yet loneliness is by no means unique to singles, for not all marriages can be held up as epitomes of intimate sharing. Celibates do have to seek ways to build relationships to meet the need for sharing.

Friendship is a special gift of God to celibates to provide for the need for affirmation and sharing. God's love and life's joys become all the more real when a person shares in a significant relationship with at least one other person. Close friends who love us as we are ease loneliness, give us a pat on the back when we need it, affirm us as a person. C. S. Lewis said:

> Friendship arises out of mere companionships when two or more companions discover that they have in common some insight or interest or even taste which others do not share and which, till the moment, each believe to be his own unique treasure (or burden). The typical expression of opening friendship would be something like, "What? You too? I thought I was the only one . . ."[4]

This author can testify to the power of friendships in enabling one to live a successful single life. Good friends of all ages, some married, others single, have met the needs of affirmation and sharing. There was Pat, a supervisor of teaching assistant work in graduate school, who built self-confidence. There is Dorothy who has taught the meaning of purposeful living. There is Ellen who listens. There is Altice who encourages. There is another Dorothy who listens, gently affirming and/or correcting. There is Bonnie who always believes in and affirms the best motives even when behavior is sometimes discordant. There was Marie who showed how to be a lovely, gracious, purposeful single lady. These friends have been a representation of God, so different than others who are friends, yet cannot accept inadequacies and weaknesses. Indeed, they are gifts of God to help another be able to use singleness to His glory.

Yet, a word of caution must be sounded, for only in marriage is there the right to a unique relationship of sharing. Friends sometimes disappoint; they sometimes misunderstand

---

4. C. S. Lewis, *Four Loves* (Glasgow, Scotland: Fontana Books, 1960), p. 61.

Friendships, as important as they are, can never substitute for a relationship with God.

Find a Place of Service

A single person must discover his place of service to God, his way to glorify and praise God. God wants the single to use his capabilities for Him

The single may well find a place of service where it would be extremely difficult for a couple to serve. Leah Moshier and Dolly Chitwood have served for over thirty years at Kulpahar Kids Home, a children's work in a remote village of India. Couples have gone there to serve, but only Leah and Dolly have remained over the years. One reason is because of the difficulty a couple finds in educating their children who have to be sent away to school. The celibate has the option of finding a place of service anywhere God leads him. The single who prepares to serve God and seeks to find a place to serve has a distinct asset: he has the freedom to do what he feels to be God's will for him.

Live Victoriously

The celibate life is not devoid of problems. There will always be cruel jokes, and they sometimes hurt. There are times of loneliness. There is sometimes rejection because people do not know how to relate to a single. There are physical needs. None of these problems are ever settled once and for all. But they can be met and overcome.

Ada Lum suggests eight practical guidelines for meeting the problems of celibacy:[5]

---

5. Ada Lum, *Single and Human* (Downers Grove, Illinois: InterVarsity Press, 1976), pp. 34-61.

1. Give self completely to Christ. He will help to transform sexual energy into creative expressions.
2. Extend self to others. Become involved in their lives. When that is done, attention is diverted from self and selfish needs.
3. Enjoy children. They have an amazing capacity to entertain, to give love, to affirm.
4. Seek new experiences. Avoid falling into a secure rut.
5. Plan for recreation, especially somewhat strenuous play.
6. Have friends of the opposite sex to whom you relate genuinely, yet discreetly.
7. Make good friends.
8. Grow old gracefully.

In short, develop life to its fullest. That reduces self-pity and helps one to live positively in the midst of temptations.

Conclusion

Celibacy is not an impossible task for those who seek to use their singleness to glorify God. It does not deny nor suppress one's sexuality. A single man still should be a godly man; a single woman should be a godly woman. It is simply a matter of controlling sexual expression for a greater purpose—to advance the kingdom. It is directing sexual energy into other channels and using those channels to bring glory to God.

Summary Statements

1. Singleness is an acceptable lifestyle.
2. Jesus said that celibacy is a gift that is to be used to bring glory to God.

3. Paul advised celibacy in crisis times.
4. A celibate must accept his sexuality and direct it into proper channels.
5. A celibate will meet most of his personal needs by developing friendships.
6. The single is freer to do God's work than is his married brother.
7. The single is called to glorify God.

FOR DISCUSSION

1. How is it possible for a person to live as a celibate?
2. What reasons for singleness are listed in the Bible?
3. How would you adivse a celibate to live victoriously?

REFERENCES

1. Anders, Sarah Frances. *Woman Alone: Confident and Creative.* Nashville: Broadman Press, 1976.
2. Evening, Margaret. *Who Walk Alone.* Downers Grove, Illinois: InterVarsity Press, 1974.
3. Goergan, Donald. *The Sexual Celibate.* New York: Seabury Press, 1974.
4. Grimm, Robert. *Love and Sexuality.* New York: Association Press, 1964.
5. Lewis, C. S. *Four Loves.* Glasgow, Scotland: Fontana Books, 1960.
6. Lum, Ada. *Single and Human.* Downers Grove, Illinois: InterVarsity Press, 1976.
7. Pape, Dorothy. *In Search of God's Ideal Woman.* Downers Grove, Illinois: InterVarsity Press, 1976.
8. Peter, George W. "Jesus, Paul, and the Divorce Court." *Whatever Happened to Marriage?* Ed. Marshall Shelley. Elgin, Illinois: David C. Cook, 1976.

9. Piper, Otto. *The Christian Interpretation of Sex*. London: Nisbet and Company, 1942.
10. Scanzoni, Letha, and Hardesty, Nancy. *All We're Meant To Be*. Waco, Texas: Word Books, 1974.
11. Tournier, Paul. *The Adventure of Living*. New York: Harper and Row, 1965.
12. Trevett, R. F. *The Church and Sex*. New York: Hawthorn Books, 1960.
13. White, John. *Eros Defiled*. Downers Grove, Illinois: InterVarsity Press, 1977.
14. Williams, Terri. "The Forgotten Alternative in First Corinthians 7." *Christianity Today*. May 25, 1973.

Chapter Nineteen

CHASTITY: PRIDE IN SEXUAL IDENTITY

Chastity and purity seem to be words from a bygone era. In an age in which people feel compelled to openly parade knowledge and experience in sexual matters, one wonders if there is any such thing as sexual purity today.

Americans act as if sexual knowledge and behavior were the ultimate goal of life. They worship sex, display sex, talk sex, think sex, all to prove that they understand sexuality and have their identity squared away.

The gurus of this age are the sex-knowledge dispensers who tell us what we should feel and do if we are to glory in our sexual identity. David Reuben, writing in *Everything You Always Wanted To Know About Sex**, defined his purpose in writing:

> One problem among others is to make an individual aware of the capabilities and potential of his sexual organs so he can utilize them to their fullest capactiy. The average person has not even begun to experience the range of sexual gratification of which he is capable. . . . The purpose of this book is to tell the reader what he wants to know and what he *needs* to know to achieve the greatest possible degree of sexual satisfaction.[1]

Then he proceeded to answer nearly every conceivable question about the sexual act itself, never once referring to the significance of sexuality beyond the pleasurable implications. Of course, he sold thousands of copies.

The central theme of this book has been that sexuality is a gift of God and that its expression is beautiful and sacred

---

1. David Reuben, *Everything You Always Wanted to Know About Sex** (New York: David McKay Co., 1971), p. 3.

—and pleasurable—when it fits within the parameters established by God. But beautiful, sacred things, as important as they are, are not intended to be flaunted, displayed indiscriminately, nor cheapened. That is especially true of human sexuality.

This era demands a call for chastity, not just in where and when one has sexual intercourse, but also in other overt expressions, thought, and speech. This chapter is an examination of the idea of chastity in an amoral world.

Chastity Defined

The word translated as "chaste," or sometimes "pure," in the New Testament is *hagneia* or *hagnos*. The word originally meant "that which awakens religious awe." Later it came to denote things connected with deity. Still later the meaning came to be used to denote "ritually clean." Finally, it came to be used to denote "morally blameless."

Three shades of meaning are used in the New Testament:

1. Moral purity and sincerity: "Keep yourself pure," I Timothy 5:22b, or, "But the wisdom that comes from heaven is first of all pure," James 5:17a, or "Set an example for the believer in speech, in life, in love, in faith and in purity," I Timothy 4:12.

2. Innocence:

> See what this godly sorrow has produced in you:what earnestness, what eagerness to clear yourselves, what indignation, what alarm, what longing, what concern, what readiness to see justice done. At every point you have proved yourselves to be innocent in this matter (II Corinthians 7:11).

3. Wholehearted inward dedication to Christ:

> I am jealous for you with a godly jealousy. I promised

242

you to one husband, to Christ, so that I might present
you a pure virgin to him. But I am afraid that just as Eve
was deceived by the serpent's cunning, your minds may
somehow be led astray from your sincere and pure devotion to Christ (II Corinthians 11:2-3).

The word chastity or purity is commonly used to denote
one who has not had sexual intercourse. But the original
language does not demand that condition. Chastity is a
matter of attitude. One could very well technically be a virgin, yet be impure because of his attitudes toward sex, his
thoughts about sex, his speech that debases and cheapens
sex, his other behavior that ignores divine purpose for sex,
especially in petting and necking. And one could have had
sexual intercourse innumerable times, yet be chaste because
his attitudes, thought, speech, and behavior demonstrate
that he takes pride in his sexual identity, expressing it in the
way God has defined. Chastity is not a puritanical attitude
that denies sexuality. It is recognition that the most beautiful
and sacred things are not open to public scrutiny.

Chastity, then, is an attitude toward one's sexual identity.
It is acceptance of the sexual nature as a gift of God. It is
recognition of God's design for sexuality. It is observance of
God's guidelines for sexual expression. It is pride in being
a man or a woman made by God. It is unmixed, unadulterated thoughts and behavior. It is proudly accepting a
standard of self-control.

Gladys Hunt observed in her book *MS Means Myself* that
". . . a person's attitude toward his sexuality manifests itself in all his behavior,"[2] not just in sexual intercourse or
lack of it. She pointed out that chastity is demonstrated in
at least four areas of behavior.

---

2. Gladys Hunt, *MS Means Myself* (Grand Rapids: Zondervan, 1972), p. 33.

The first is the way the person finds fulfillment. Some people find fulfillment in titillating their sensual nature. Many women, and some men, are hooked on television 'soaps' where sexuality is debased. Many men, and some women, fill their time with suggestive literature, erotic movies, crude talk, and cheap behavior. That person is far from chaste, for he takes no pride in his sexuality.

A second area is the ability to give oneself in relationships. Some men and women are unable to relate comfortably to others. They are 'takers,' seldom, if ever, 'givers,' especially in relationships with the opposite sex. Such egocentric behavior is an indication that they have yet to feel at ease with their sexual identity.

A third area is attitude toward those of the opposite sex. Some people cannot endure healthy friendships with the opposite sex; every contact is interpreted sexually. Some withdraw from contacts with the opposite sex and become prudish, but others see their sexuality as a seductive instrument to accumulate sexual conquests. The uncomfortably harsh attitudes of militant feminists are an indication of a lack of adequate sexual identity. But so are male chauvinistic attitudes that see women as little more than sex objects.

A fourth area is treatment of those of the same sex. Women who have failed to make a successful sexual identity do not relate to other women very well, especially in work relationships when a woman is in a position of authority. Men sometimes do the same.

Indeed, a person's pride in his sexual identity—or lack of it—colors the remainder of life.

What the Bible Says About Chastity

The Bible is clear that chastity is a desirable goal for a Christian. Not always is the word *hagneia* used; sometimes

244

it is *hagios* (holiness) which carries the idea of devotion to God. God wants His people to be people who remember who they are, men or women, sexual creatures, made by Him to use every facet of personality, sex included, to show His praise and power and goodness.

> Do you not know that your body is a temple of the Holy Spirit, who is in you, whom you have received from God? You are not your own; you were bought at a price. Therefore honor God with your body (I Corinthians 6:19-20).

God calls His people to a different way of life, to a lifestyle that is in tune with His purposes, even in sexual pride and expression.

> It is God's will that you should be holy; that you should avoid sexual immorality; that each of you should learn to control his own body in a way that is holy and honorable, not in passionate lust like the heathen, who do not know God; and that in this matter no one should wrong his brother or take advantage of him. The Lord will punish men for all such sins, as we have already told you and warned you. For God did not call us to be impure, but to live a holy life. Therefore, he who rejects this instruction does not reject man but God, who gives you his Holy Spirit (I Thessalonians 4:3-8).
>
> Therefore, prepare your minds for action; be self-controlled; set your hope fully on the grace to be given to you when Jesus Christ is revealed. As obedient children, do not conform to the evil desires you had when you lived in ignorance. But just as he who called you is holy, so be holy in all you do; for it is written: "Be holy, because I am holy" (I Peter 1:13-16).

God called for transformed minds that do not deny sexuality, but control its expression as God designed.

You, however, did not come to know Christ that way. Surely you heard of him and were taught in him in accordance with the truth that is in Jesus. You were taught, with regard to your former way of life, to put off your old self, which is being corrupted by its deceitful desires; to be made new in the attitude of your minds; and to put on the new self, created to be like God in true righteousness and holiness (Colossians 4:8-10).

Unadulterated devotion, undivided allegiance, is the key to achieving and keeping a chaste spirit.

Submit yourselves, then, to God. Resist the devil, and he will flee from you. Come near to God and he will come near to you. Wash, your hands, you sinners, and purify your hearts, you double-minded (James 4:7-8).

How Chastity Affects Sexuality

The chaste person knows—and remembers—who he is. His basis for pride is not in himself, but in the fact that he was made by God. He is not merely matter, nor is his sexuality a matter of chance. He is a man or a woman because God made him that way.

Many psychologists are convinced that it is the person most lacking in self-esteem who can most easily be drawn into a promiscuous sexual liaison. The individual who sees himself as God-designed has no hostility toward the body and can live in harmony with his sexual impulses and needs.

The chaste person will also discard non-Biblical attitudes toward sex. Some see it as a necessary evil, but not the person who is proudly a man or a woman. Sex is not evil; it is a profound giving and expression of self. Others see sex as a simple biological function meant to be enjoyed wherever and whenever one wants. But the Christian rejects that as a cheap expression of a beautiful gift. Rather, he sees his sexual identity as good, its expression to be enjoyed within the context of marriage and responsibility.

The person who sees sexuality as good, but set apart with the rest of his life to glorify God, understands that his behavior, his attitudes, his thought, his speech reveal his fundamental attitude toward sexuality. His every behavior reflects a sense of comfort with his sexual nature. He will be concerned with more than mere technical virginity.

Indeed, the chaste Christian, the one who understands and accepts sexual identity as God intended, brings his thoughts, behaviors, attitudes, and speech under control to bring glory to God.

> Do not be yoked together with unbelievers. For what do righteousness and wickedness have in common? Or what fellowship can light have with darkness? What harmony is there between Christ and Belial? What does a believer have in common with an unbeliever? What agreement is there between the temple of God and idols? For we are the temple of the living God. As God has said: "I will live with them and walk among them, and I will be their God, and they will be my people." "Therefore, come out from them and be separate," says the Lord. "Touch no unclean thing, and I will receive you. I will be a Father to you, and you will be my sons and daughters," says the Lord Almighty (II Corinthians 6:14-18).

The greatest gift that anyone can give to God is to be as wholeheartedly devoted to Him in accepting and expressing sexuality as he is in his formal worship, prayer, or giving.

Conclusion

Although chastity is sometimes defined as lack of sexual activity, the Biblical idea is that of a person who proudly accepts sexual identity, expressing it within God-defined boundaries. The Biblical call is for a life of holiness, a life in which sexuality, as every other aspect of life, is devoted to God. Sexual identity is a matter of gender; it results from learning. But it is something of which to be proud because God made people this way.

Summary Statements

1. Chastity as it refers to sexuality means a state of moral purity and sincerity, a state of innocence, a wholehearted dedication of his sexual identity to God.
2. Chastity is an attitude toward sexuality, an acceptance of sexual identity as a gift from God.
3. Chastity, pride in sexual identity, is expressed in the way a person finds fulfillment, his ability to give self in relationships, his attitude toward those of the opposite sex, and his treatment of those of the same sex.
4. God calls men and women to a sense of pride in sexual identity and control of sexual expression.

FOR DISCUSSION

1. How does a person's self-concept affect his chaste behavior—or lack of it?
2. What is chastity?
3. Draft a definitive paragraph about sexual identity and its expression by the Christian.
4. Cite examples of how sexual identity is expressed in:
   a. the way a person finds fulfillment;
   b. the ability to give self to relationships;
   c. the attitudes toward those of the opposite sex; and,
   d. the treatment of those of the same sex.
5. How does chastity affect behavior? Speech? Thought? Attitudes?

REFERENCES

1. Banowsky, William. *It's A Playboy World.* Old Tappan, New Jersey: Fleming H. Revell Co., 1969.
2. Goergan, Donald. *The Sexual Celibate.* New York: Seabury, 1974.
3. Hunt, Gladys. *MS Means Myself.* Grand Rapids: Zondervan, 1972.
4. Larson, Bruce *Ask Me To Dance.* Waco, Texas: Word, 1972.
5. Trobisch, Walter. *Love Yourself.* Downers Grove, Illinois: InterVarsity Press, 1976.
6. Wood, Frederic C., Jr., *Sex and the New Morality.* New York: Association Press, 1968.

Chapter Twenty

"WHATSOEVER IS PURE: THINK ON THESE THINGS"

The real secret of handling sexual identity in an amoral world is to learn to manage the mind. When we know what a person thinks, we can ascertain his commitments and self-identity and predict his behavior. When we know what a person thinks, we can determine how well he has achieved mind management.

Indeed, the Christian must learn to manage his mind. Otherwise, his mind will manage him. The mind is like a computer, collecting data from every direction, some of it positive and good, but other of it negative, suggestive, and immoral. Although a person has some control over the data to which he is exposed, he cannot eliminate all negative input. But he can determine what thoughts are retained to later order his conduct.

The mind is a fascinating creation, for it absorbs everything a person sees and hears. And whatever goes into the mind has the potential of reappearing in conduct and character. Yet the mind does classify all information that enters, sorting it out for active use, assigning it to ready recall, or pushing it into cold storage, not to be recalled under normal circumstances.

Each person decides where the data that enters his mind goes. If he chooses, he can send unwelcome messages into cold storage, assuming that his mind is not satiated with negative material. But that material that he retains to think about, speak about, and act upon is in his active mind to stay. Even if such material is not constantly on active duty, it is poised for ready recall.

James describes the subtle way in which thoughts permeate a person's consciousness, then drag him away into sin when he lets those thoughts stay on active or reserve duty in his mind:

> When tempted, no one should say, "God is tempting me." For God cannot be tempted by evil, nor does he tempt anyone; but each one is tempted when, by his own evil desire, he is dragged away and enticed. Then, after desire has conceived, it gives birth to sin; and sin, when it is full-grown, gives birth to death (James 1:13-15).

Deeds of shame are preceded by fantasies of shame.

What The Bible Teaches About Mind Management

The Biblical writers knew full well the powerful influence of the mind. Two words are used interchangeably in the Bible: heart and mind. They are synonomous terms. So the writer of Proverbs could say:

> As water reflects a face, so man's heart reflects the man (Proverbs 27:19).

A person's thoughts reveal what he really is.

Jesus insisted that it is a person's mind that directs his conduct:

> But the things that come out of the mouth come from the heart, and these make a man "unclean." For out of the heart come evil thoughts, murder, adultery, sexual immorality, theft, false testimony, slander. These are what make a man "unclean"; but eating with unwashed hands does not make him "unclean" (Matthew 15:18-20).

His response was directed to Pharisees who meticulously observed the law and foolishly ignored their own thought processes.

James suggested also that a man's mind directs his conduct:

> Who is wise and understanding among you? Let him show it by his good life, by deeds done in the humility that comes from wisdom. But if you harbor bitter envy and selfish ambition in your hearts, do not boast about it or deny the truth. Such "wisdom" does not come from heaven but is earthly, unspiritual, of the devil. For where you have envy and selfish ambition, there you find disorder and every evil practice. But the wisdom that comes from heaven is first of all pure; then peace loving, considerate, submissive, full of mercy and good fruit, impartial and sincere. Peacemakers who sow in peace raise a harvest of righteousness (James 3:13-18).

Jesus called for a kingdom man to manage his mind:

> Blessed are the pure in heart, for they will see God (Matthew 5:8).

His call is evidence that an unadulterated thought life is possible, though it will mean that a person must apply a full measure of self-discipline to achieve it.

Paul made the same plea in his letter to the Colossian Christians:

> Since, then, you have been raised with Christ, set your hearts on things above, where Christ is seated at the right hand of God. Set your minds on things above, not on earthly things (Colossians 3:1-2).

A Christian must put undersirable thoughts in cold storage in his mind. Otherwise, they will reappear to direct his conduct.

> Put to death, therefore, whatever belongs to your earthly nature: sexual immorality, impurity, lust, evil desires and greed, which is idolatry (Colossians 3:5).

Practicing Mind Management

Paul set the pattern for mind management when he instructed the Philippians:

> Finally, brothers, whatever is true, whatever is noble, whatever is right, whatever is pure, whatever is lovely, whatever is admirable—if anything is excellent or praiseworthy—think about such things. Whatever you have learned or received or heard from me, or seen in me—put it into practice. And the God of peace will be with you (Philippians 4:8-9).

The human mind sets itself on something. Paul urged every Christian to make it the right things, for he knew that if a person thinks of something often enough and long enough, he finally cannot keep from thinking of it. His mind is no longer his to control.

So upon what is the Christian to focus his mind?

The mind must be centered on true thoughts, the things upon which a person can rely. One way to do that is to fill the mind with God's teaching. The sage of Proverbs wrote:

> My son, if you accept my words and store up my comments within you, turning your ear to wisdom and applying your heart to understanding, and if you call out for insight and cry aloud for understanding, and if you look for it as for silver and search for it as for hidden treasure, then you will understand the fear of the Lord and find the knowledge of God (Proverbs 2:1-5).

> My son, do not forget my teaching, but keep my commands in your heart, for they will prolong your life many years and bring you prosperity (Proverbs 3:1-2).

Furthermore, the mind must retain noble, honest thoughts, those things which have the dignity of holiness about them. Peter must have had that idea in mind when he wrote:

Therefore, prepare your minds for action; be self-controlled; set your hope fully on the grace to be given to you when Jesus Christ is revealed (I Peter 1:13).

Right, just thoughts are fit for God. They give to God His due. Other thoughts need to be sent to the permanent inactive file. Good thoughts are also said in this passage to be admirable—fit for God to hear.

The Christian is to strive to retain only pure thoughts, only those thoughts that are fit for the presence of God. Not all thoughts need be 'religious' in nature, but all should be in keeping with the expression of one's personality to praise God in every facet of life.

Attractive, winsome thoughts should permeate the mind of the follower of Jesus. Those are the thoughts that call forth love and respect. They are in contrast to the negative, deprecating thoughts and remarks some feel compelled to make about others. Recently I mentioned some new-found acquaintances, outstanding, respected leaders in a congregation where I had visited, to a woman whose husband was once their preacher, only to be informed of their faults in the previous congregation. My joy in their friendship momentarily evaporated—until I began to control my thoughts. But isn't it interesting that a person would remember only the negative, never once mentioning the positive leadership qualities so clearly evidenced when I met the couple?

Paul summed up his teaching by insisting that negative, impure immoral thoughts be recognized for what they are, then removed from active or reserve duty in the mind. Rather, he said, fill the mind with excellent data that God would entertain.

But how can a person exercise the discipline of himself in such a way that he actually manages his mind? What helpful tips would assist him to change his current policy of mind management?

The Christian must first feed his mind on godly teaching.

Apply your heart to instruction and your ears to words of knowledge (Proverbs 23:12).

Careful study of God's Word brings joy as well as purity.

Your statutes are my heritage forever; they are the joy of my heart (Psalm 119:111).

One can live sexually pure in an amoral world if he will stick relentlessly to his Bible reading schedule, really *listen* to sermons and lessons, and take advantage of every opportunity to worship and pray.

But the one who would manage his mind must also manage his television set. No one need fill his mind with violence, lewd talk, or sexual innuendoes. He must learn to be selective with the channel selector button!

A Christian must then control what he reads. It is really very simple to buy titillating or pornographic literature in nearly any community. 'Girlie' magazines, gossipy news sheets, and off-color books lodge undesirable material in the mind, requiring that the reader dispense with it in some way. It is far wiser to save the mind the strain of having to classify information. If the information is never there, it cannot ever come back to direct conduct.

One must also control what he hears both in words and with music. Many of the popular songs of the day cheapen sex and love. Much rock music appeals to and arouses the sensual nature. How much better it is to avoid that kind of arousal rather than to be forced to banish it to permanent inactivity in the mind.

Finally, the believer must surround himself with Christian friends.

> As iron sharpens iron, so one man sharpens another (Proverbs 27:17).

Friends profoundly influence a person, for good or for evil. A person must carefully select those people with whom he spends much time, for his friends also provide data for the mind and a model for behavior. Good friends reinforce the good while bad friends undermine Christian thoughts and lifestyle.

This is not to insist that it is necessary to isolate oneself from all non-Christian acquaintances. But it is to recognize the influence of peers on what one thinks and finally does.

Conclusion

It is possible—even desirable—for a Christian to learn to manage his mind. No one can eliminate contact with all ugly, immoral data. But he can turn his thought life to the Lord who will renew his mind.

> Therefore, I urge you, brothers, in view of God's mercy, to offer your bodies as living sacrifices, holy and pleasing to God—which is your spiritual worship. Do not conform any longer to the pattern of this world, but be transformed by the renewing of your mind. Then you will be able to test and approve what God's will is—his good, pleasing and perfect will (Romans 12:1-2).

Summary Statements

1. The Christian must manage his mind or his mind will manage him.

2. A person's thoughts are controllable—and affect his behavior.
3. The mind absorbs everything it sees or hears. But a person can assign thoughts to active use, inactive use, or permanent inactivity.
4. The Christian can control his thought life by dwelling upon God's Word, then controlling what he reads, hears, and watches, and also by carefully selecting his friends.

FOR DISCUSSION

1. Explain how a person's mind operates when data enters it.
2. Summarize the Bible teaching about mind management.
3. Give examples of how television, books, music, and friends can affect a person's thoughts and behavior. Be specific.
4. How can filling the mind with God's Word help a person to control his mind?

REFERENCES

1. Banowsky, William. *It's A Playboy World*. Old Tappan, New Jersey: Fleming Revell, 1969.
2. Goergan, Donald. *The Sexual Celibate*. New York: Seabury Press, 1974.
3. Pittenger, Norman. *Love and Control in Sexuality*. Philadelphia: Pilgrim Press, 1974.
4. Staton, Knofel. *Check Your Lifestyle*. Cincinnati: Standard Publishing Company, 1979.
5. Stott, John R. W. *Christian Counter-Culture*. Downers Grove, Illinois: InterVarsity Press, 1978.
6. Wright, H. Norman. *The Christian Use of Emotional Power*. Old Tappan, New Jersey: Fleming Revell, 1974.

Epilogue

MAN'S PURPOSE — TO GLORIFY GOD

Man is unique. Nothing else in creation is like him. God made him for specific purpose. He was to provide companionship for God Himself. It is a noble picture of man given by the Bible.

The thesis of this entire book has been man's uniqueness, his design to bring glory to his Maker, his sharing the very image of God in rationality, emotionality, decision-making, morality, and immorality of spirit. Because man was made like God and bears the mark of quality workmanship, his most intense desire must be to please the One who made him.

Although man's biological nature, his flesh and blood, show him to be the created, not the Creator, still his body is his vehicle for pouring forth a life of praise to God. Because his sexual identity is very much a part of him, he must take control of his sexual nature, his thought life, his desires to direct his body to live within God's design.

But man lives in a world tainted by sin, so deadly that it distorts every aspect of life. A prime target for sin is man's sexuality. If a person can be convinced that the essence of life lies in bodily functons, he is doomed because he will see no reason to deny bodily impulses whenever they appear. The very heart of temptation is for Satan to get man to believe that his body is somehow apart from the remainder of personality.

God was unwilling that man be consigned to an eternal destiny with sin. He sent Christ to free him to use his body, mind, and spirit to once again glorify Him. There is a way back to the tree of life.

What a person does with his body is important. He need not deny normal biological functioning, normal sexual desires.

Sexual identity is no cause for shame. But it is cause for a person to bring his mind *and* body into subjection to God's design for him. Sexual behavior is to be accompanied by sexual control in thinking, both used as God intended.

> For you were once darkness, but now you are light in the Lord. Live as children of light (for the fruit of the light consists in all goodness, righteousness and truth) and find out what pleases the Lord (Ephesians 5:8-10).

Man's purpose has yet to change. God still desires his praise and honor. He still seeks man to use every facet of personality to live for Him. He still promises judgment for those intent on seeking their own ends.

> Blessed are those who wash their robes, that they may have the right to the tree of life and may go through the gates into the city. Outside are the dogs, those who practice magical arts, the sexually immoral, the murderers, the idolaters and everyone who loves and practices falsehood (Revelation 22:14-15).

Sexual identity is a precious gift of God. How He longs for His followers to value it, take pride in it, and use it as He intended, as a vehicle of praise to Him.

Appendix I

CHRIST AND WOMEN

By Seth Wilson[1]

This outline is prepared to assist you in reading what Christ in the Gospels and through the apostles says about the place of women in salvation, in Christ's ministry, in the church, and in service for Christ.

I. JESUS FREELY ASSOCIATED WITH WOMEN, MINISTERED TO THEM AND WAS HELPED BY THEM.

John 4:7-9	Jesus talked to the woman at the well. In 4:27, the disciples marvelled that he was speaking with a woman.
John 4:28-30, 41, 42	This woman had success in interesting the people of her village in Jesus.
Luke 7:37-50	A notorious sinner washed and kissed His feet. He said that she was forgiven and she loved much.
Matt. 15:21-28	In a foreign land, He granted a request for a Gentile woman and praised her faith. (Mark 7:25-30).
Matt. 19:13-15	He received little children when they were brought to Him, probably by their mothers, and taught, "See that ye despise not one of these little ones" (18:3-14).
Matt. 20:20-28	The mother of James and John dared to come to Him and ask for her sons to sit in the chief seats in His kingdom.
Luke 10:38-42	He upheld Mary for sitting to hear His teaching when Martha wanted her to help with serving.

---

1. Seth Wilson is Dean Emeritus of Ozark Bible College, Joplin, Mo., where he has served for forty years.

Luke 8:1-3   Some women traveled about with Him and provided for His entourage out of their own means.

Matt. 21:31   Jesus said the harlots would go into the kingdom ahead of the Pharisees, because they were willing to repent.

Matt. 14:21;   There were women and children in
15:38   the crowds (5,000 and 4,000 men) which He fed miraculously.

Luke 11:27, 28   A woman dared to speak up in public to praise the blessedness of His mother. Jesus answered her, offering the same blessedness to anyone who would hear the word of God and keep it.

Mark 12:41-44   He pointed out the humble woman who had only two mites to give, and said she had given more than the rich men, for it was all she had. (Luke 21:1-4).

Matt. 26:6-13   He let Mary of Bethany anoint Him with precious ointment at a public feast and upheld her as doing a good deed which would always be remembered to her credit. (John 12:1-8; Mark 14:3-9).

Matt. 27:55, 56   There were women at the cross who had followed Him from Galilee and ministered to Him. (Mark 15:40, 41; Luke 23:49; John 19:25).

John 19:26, 27   From the cross He assigned to John the care of His mother.

Luke 23:27-29   On the way to the cross He tried to comfort and warn the women who wept and mourned for Him in His sufferings.

II. JESUS ACCEPTED WOMEN INTO THE FAVOR OF GOD AND THE FELLOWSHIP OF THE FAITHFUL.

   A. In His teaching, he showed sympathy and kindness for them. Sometimes He made them examples in His teaching.

Matt. 12:42	"The queen of the South will rise up in judgment with this generation and condemn it." (Luke 11:31).
Matt. 12:46-50	He offered to all women the privilege of being as important in His sight as His mother or sisters, if only they would do the will of His Father in heaven. (Mark 3:32-45; Luke 8:20, 21).
Matt. 24:16-21	In predicting the extreme hardships of the days of the destruction of Jerusalem, Jesus told the Christians to flee from the city; at the same time He expressed deep sorrow for the mothers with young babies and those about to be delivered. (Mark 13:14-17; Luke 21:20-23).
Matt. 24:40, 41	He speaks of women being chosen for rescue before the world's destruction in the same manner as men. (Luke 17:34, 35).
Matt. 19:4-6	Jesus emphasized the unity of man and wife, and the obligation of a husband to his wife as above that to his father. (Mark 10:6-9).

262

B. Later women received salvation in the same manner as men.

Gal. 3:25-28	All become children of God by faith and baptism into Christ, regardless of race, slavery, or sex.
Rom. 3:23-26	There is no distinction. All have sinned and are saved through the death of Christ and faith in the gospel.
Acts 5:14	Crowds of both men and women believed the gospel and were added to the Lord.
Acts 6:1-6	Foreign-born widows were numerous in the church very early.
Acts 8:12	Both men and women at Samaria believed and were baptized.
Acts 8:3; 9:2	Both men and women were persecuted and imprisoned for their faith.
Acts 16:14, 15	Lydia, a businesswoman, obeyed the gospel and furnished lodging to the preachers.
Acts 17:4, 12	At Thessalonica, many chief women believed and joined with the Christians.
Acts 17:34	At Athens, a woman was among the first few converts.

III. AFTER JESUS' DEATH AND IN HIS RESURRECTION APPEARANCES, WOMEN WERE MOST FAITHFUL AND HIGHLY FAVORED.

Matt. 27:61	Although two men who were prominent rulers of the Jews took charge of the body of Jesus and

263

buried it, women disciples of His watched how it was done and determined to add their contribution toward completing the care of it. (Mark 15:47; Luke 23:55, 56).

Matt. 28:1, 5-8   Women came early on the first day of the week to the tomb, received from angels the first report of the resurrection, and were told to tell the apostles. (Mark 16:1-8; Luke 24:1-9; John 20:1, 2).

John 20:11-18   Jesus appeared first to Mary Magdalene. (Mark 16:9).

Matt. 28:9   His second appearance was to the other women as they were obeying the angel's instructions to tell the apostles of His rising.

Mark 16:10, 11   These women did deliver the message faithfully, although they were disbelieved. (Luke 24:10, 11, 22-25; John 20:18).

Acts 1:14   The women continued in prayer and expectation with the apostles after Jesus had ascended, before the day of Pentecost.

IV. JESUS CHOSE MEN, NOT WOMEN, TO BE SPIRITUAL LEADERS.

Jesus did not appoint any woman to be an apostle, or to be one of the seventy other miracle-working witnesses whom He sent out in Judea before His death (Luke 10: 1-20). There is no indication that women received directly the great commission, on any of the several occasions when He gave it, or when He promised the divine powers and authority by which they would be empowered to carry it out. (Read John 20:21-23; 21: 15-23; Matt. 28:18-20; Mark 16:15, 16; Luke 24:45-49; Acts 1:2-11.) There is no indication that any women received the outpouring of the Holy Spirit on the day of Pentecost, by which the apostles' message was attested. Of course, those who obeyed that day in repenting and being baptized in water, did receive the gift of the Holy Spirit which is part of the new birth of every Christian. But all of the following verses indicate that those who were baptized in the Holy Spirit and spoke in tongues on that occasion were apostles: Acts 1:26; 2:1; 2:7, 14, 37, 42. On Pentecost and following it, it was the apostles who bore the witness, worked the miracles, taught the people, bore the persecution, etc. Acts 3:6; 4:3, 33, 35; 5:12, 13, 18, 29, 40-42; 6:2, 6.

V. THE PLACE OF WOMEN IN THE EARLY CHURCH

   A. New Testament passages which show service by women in the church:

      1. Women workers:

         Rom. 16:1, 2 Phoebe was a *deaconess or minister.*

         Rom. 16:3-5 Prisca (Priscilla) and Aquila, Paul's *fellow workers* deserve gratitude of many, and have a church in their home in Rome.

         Acts 18:18, 19 Priscilla and Aquila had worked with Paul at Corinth and at Ephesus (I Cor. 16:19), and had a church in their house.

         Rom. 16:6 "Mary worked hard among you." (R.S.V.)

I Cor. 11:5-16   Women were expected to pray or prophesy under the right conditions (but not in the main assembly; read I Cor. 14:26, 33;35).

Phil. 4:2, 3   Euodia and Syntyche "labored side by side with me." (R.S.V.)

Col. 4:15   Nympha had a church in her home.

Acts 21:8-10   Philip had four daughters who prophesied, but the message was given to Paul by Agabus.

Acts 5:1, 7:10   Sapphira shared with her husband in giving property to the church, and shared in the penalty for misrepresenting it.

Acts 12:12-16   Mary held a prayer meeting in her house, and Rhoda, a maid, kept the door and informed the Christians of Peter's arrival.

Acts 9:36-41   Dorcas served in good works and *almsdeeds* and was loved for it.

2. Instructions concerning women:

I Tim. 5:4-10   Dedicated women were supported by the churches if they had no family to support them and they had served well at home, in hospitality, benevolence, and every good work and continued in prayers day and night (and were at least 60 years old).

I Tim. 5:11-15   Younger widows are not likely to

266

serve as well, but should marry, bear children, rule their household.

Note: Women are to "rule their household" (I Tim. 5:14) in submission to their husbands (Eph. 5:21-33). God commands their husbands to love and honor them (I Pet. 3:7); and their children to respect and obey them (Eph. 6:1; Col. 3:18-20).

I. Tim. 3:11   Qualifications for women (either wives of elders, or women who serve somewhat as deacons serve).

Titus 2:3-5   The preacher is to instruct older women to train younger women in godliness and in exemplary family life, so that the word of God will not be spoken against.

Acts 2:17, 18   The powers of the Spirit, especially prophecy, are promised to daughters and handmaidens (not necessarily in the same degree or for all the same functions).

I Cor. 7:34, 35   An unmarried woman may be more careful for the things of the Lord than one who is concerned to please her husband.

I Cor. 7:39, 40   If a husband dies, the widow is free to marry another in the Lord but may be happier to remain unmarried, under the circumstances of that time.

In general a Christian woman serves her Lord in serving her husband and children, but in many situations the demands made by her family may conflict with her highest ideals or desire for single-minded devotion to Christ. She can be holy, even with an un-Christian husband, but she could have less conflicts and distress in being holy without him. Yet, if she is married, she must live out her faith in that condition and not desert her family responsibility. (I Cor. 7:10-17).

B. Passages of the New Testament which direct and limit the area of service by women.

    1. I Cor. 14:33b-37   Women are not to speak among the prophets in the public gathering of the whole church (see 14:26-33).

    a. I Cor. 11:5-10   In the same book, conditions are stated under which they may pray or prophesy, evidently in some kind of private or semi-private situations.

    b. I Cor. 11:3-12   The explanation for excluding women from speaking revelations for the church is found in divine order of headship by which God's authority is graciously administered to us.

    (1) Eph. 5:21-33   As verse 21 says, all of us are to be subject to one another out of

reverence for Christ. Wives are to be subject to the husbands because Christ has so designed for them to live in good order and to help their husbands practice the responsibility which is assigned to them by God and which is good for all the family. This works well when husbands love their wives "as Christ loved the church and gave Himself up for her." To acknowledge and follow God's wisdom in this divine order (of submission and responsible oversight) brings a blessing to the whole human family.

(2) Col. 3: 18, 19   "Wives, be subject to your husbands, as is fitting in the Lord. Husbands, love your wives, and do not be harsh with them." (R.S.V.)

(3) Gen. 3: 16   "He shall rule over thee." This was probably what Paul referred to in "as also saith the law" (I Cor. 14:34).

(4) I Pet. 3: 1-6   Women are to be in subjection to their husbands, live chastely, adorning themselves with a meek and quiet spirit.

Note on I Pet. 3:1-6 and Eph. 5:21-33:

When people are doubtful about the rightness of Christian wives being in subjection to ungodly husbands who expect them to participate in sinful deeds,

269

they may be helped by reading Acts 4:19, 20 and 5:29. Notice that Peter taught Christians to be subject to every human institution as a general rule (I Pet. 2:13-17). But Peter himself set a good example of obeying God rather than men, when his rulers commanded him to disobey Christ (Acts 4:18-20; 5:29 -32). And God upheld him and the other apostles in this resistance to authority (Acts 4:23-33; 5:17-25). Yet the apostles were submissive to the rulers in taking the punishment which their resistance brought on them. They bore the penalty patiently and without railing or retaliation.

2. I Tim. 2:8-15. Women are not to teach or exercise authority over a man.

   a. Extent of teaching or leadership done by women.

(1) Acts 18: 26	Priscilla apparently aided Aquila in "expounding the word of the Lord more perfectly" to Apollos, whether she took part in the discussion or just opened her home to him. Either way, it was done privately with no thought of domination over him.
(2) II Tim. 1:5, 3: 14, 15	Timothy's grandmother Lois and mother Eunice were quite probably responsible for teaching him the "sacred writings."

Women certainly have the responsibility to teach and guide their own children, and that does not entirely cease at a certain birthday; yet the propriety and effectiveness of her teaching diminishes as the young man takes on the independence and

270

responsibilities of a man. She should then rely upon her teachings of earlier years (and perhaps indirect or gentle reminders of them) and do her best to respect and use and build up the manhood of young men.

(3) Titus 2: "To train younger women to love
3-5 their husbands and children, to be sensible, chaste, domestic, kind, and submissive to their husbands." (R.S.V.)

(4) I Tim. 2: It is not wrong for a woman to
12-14 have information and to give it, but it is not well for her to assume the position of boss or director over men. This is a valid distinction, although either could be called teaching. There is a real difference between sharing knowledge modestly, and assuming authority in leadership, although the word "teaching" might be applied to either one. The women to whom Jesus appeared after His resurrection were told to tell the apostles that good news. But they were not given the position of apostles or leadership in the church. On the whole it seems that the Lord is not trying so much to limit the rights of anyone as He is trying to teach a better order and to make known the relative duties He wants men and women

271

to perform. It seems that I Tim. 2:12-14 connects the teaching a woman is not to do with serving in authority over a man, and with being a guide who may not always be reliable in times of moral crisis. ("The woman being beguiled hath fallen into transgression.")

(5) I Tim. 2: 12   The meaning of "teach" is more than merely to give information; perhaps it means something more like setting standards for the church, or as in Titus 2:15: These things speak and exhort and reprove with all authority. Let no one despise you."

The kind of situation which we have in a Sunday School class (or a home Bible study) is not described in the New Testament at all. It is hard to be sure whether or not it should be regarded as the assembly of the church in which a woman is not to speak, even to ask a question. (I Cor. 14:34; 35). Probably it is more like the situations in which Paul expected women to pray or prophesy (I Cor. 11:5), or to be active in training younger women and children. (Titus 2:3-5).

It is not fitting for us to make exact rules about what is permitted and what is not, where the Lord has not made it plain for us. But the principles of modesty, submission, and helpfulness must be put into practice.

In New Testament churches women ministered of their time, substance, hospitality, and labors in a variety of ways. Their part in the service of the church was appreciated and important, but it was not a leading part, not directive or managerial.

Although there is no distinction between Jew or Gentile, slave or slaveowner, woman or man in the matter of being welcomed into the family of God (Gal. 3:22-29), there is in God's sight a difference in the lines of service for which men and women are fitted and in which they make their best contribution to the whole family of God.

The most important thing to understand is this. The teachings of the Scriptures are not to be made a strict set of rules to set exact limits on a woman's activities, but to give the principles by which each Christian is to be guided in contributing the most to others in any situation.

The Christian woman must accept the fact that God has made her "for the man" (I Cor. 11:9). She was not created to be just like a man, but to be a helper and fill a need (Gen. 2:18-24).

She will be just as important and just as great in God's sight, without being as dominant or as much a public leader as the man. Jesus taught that the one who is servant of all is the greatest of all (Matt. 20: 26-28; 23:11, 12; Mark 10:43-45). *Submission does not mean inferiortiy.* Jesus submitted to God and became a servant to all of us and God exalted Him for it (Phil. 2:5-11). Jesus would not consider a woman inferior because she is subject to her husband and is servant to her family. According to Jesus'

273

teaching and example she will be exalted for it.

She must recognize man's God-given responsibility to lead in the family, in the church, and in society; and she should do her best to help him fulfill that responsibility.

Yet God, who established this order in the family of man and gave to women their greatness in a subordinate position, has shown in His word that women can sometimes serve outside their usual area of subordination. Consider the examples of Miriam (Exodus 15:20 , 21); Deborah (Judges 4:4-10); Huldah (II Kings 22:14-20; II Chron. 34:22).

Is there really any need for a struggle between men and women to prove their importance, rights, or superiority? Should the man try to suppress the woman, or the woman resist her special calling and try to prove that she has unlimited rights and powers? Both must submit to the Lord Jesus.

Let both value each other, as God has valued every human being, and serve each other as it is His will for us to do: "in honor preferring one another" (Rom. 12:10). "For ye, brethren, were called for freedom; only use not your freedom for an occasion to the flesh, but through love be servants (slaves) one to another. For the whole law is fulfilled in one word, even in this: Thou shalt love thy neighbor as thyself. But if ye bite and devour one another, take heed that ye be not consumed one of another" (Gal. 5: 13-15).

Let us accept the teachings and the challenges in the word of our loving Father that guide and stimulate each of us to fill a place that will richly bless us with the highest fulfillment of our God-given natures.

For Further Study:

Elliott, Elizabeth. *Let Me Be A Woman.* Wheaton: Tyndale Press, 1976. Response to those advocating a Christian feminism.

Hurley, James B. *Man and Woman in Biblical Perspective.* Grand Rapids: Zondervan Publishing House, 1981. Competent, scriptural study.

Knight, George W., III. *The New Testament Teaching on the Role Relationship of Men and Women.* Grand Rapids: Baker Book House, 1977. A careful exegetical study.

Ryrie, C. C. *The Role of Women in the Church.* Chicago: Moody Press, 1958. Basic study on the New Testament teaching concerning women.

Appendix II

MARRIAGE, DIVORCE, AND REMARRIAGE
By Seth Wilson

INTRODUCTION: This is intended to be a brief summary of what is revealed of God's will on this much disputed subject. An effort is made to present every pertinent passage of scripture and to bring to consideration every permissible interpretation. But space is not given to refute or to support every interpretation.

I. Marriage
   A. Marriage Was Instituted and Blessed by God.
      It was a part of God's design in the creation of man, and is central or basic in His will for human society (Gen. 1:27, 28; 2:18-25). Marriage is honorable for all, or is to be kept honorable by all (Heb. 13:4). To forbid marriage is a doctrine of demons or conscienceless men (I Tim. 4:1-3).
   B. The Positive Rule of Marriage for Life.
      "Leave father and mother and cleave unto his wife" (Gen. 2:24). Jesus quoted Genesis 2:24 and added, "What God hath joined together, let no man put asunder" (Matt. 19:5, 6; Mark 10:6-9). A wife is bound by law to her husband while he lives (Rom. 7:1-3). A wife is bound for so long time as her husband lives (I Cor. 7:39).
   C. Remarriage Permitted After Death of a Spouse.
      "If the husband be dead, she is free to be married to whom she will; only in the Lord" (I Cor. 7:39, cp. Rom. 7:3). Paul recommends marriage for younger widows (I Tim. 5:14).

II. Adultery
   A. Prohibition of Adultery.
      "Thou shalt not commit adultery" (Exod. 20:14).

276

Adultery comes from the heart and defiles the man (Mark 7:21). An adulterer cannot enter the kingdom, but can be justified (I Cor. 6:9-11). "Fornicators and adulterers God will judge" (Heb. 13:4). No fornicator . . . hath any inheritance in the kingdom of Christ" (Eph. 5:3-5). Adultery is frequently included in lists of sins in the New Testament (Gal. 5:19-21; I Thess. 4:3-8). The word translated "fornication" includes adultery and is not distinct from it. It is used in I Thessalonians 4:3-8 apparently of married persons, and seems to include adultery in I Corinthians 6:18; Colossians 3:5; Ephesians 5: 3-5; Galatians 5:19; and Revelation 21:8.

B. In the Old Testament Adulterers Were to be Put to Death. "And the man that committeth adultery with another man's wife, even he that committeth adultery with his neighbor's wife, the adulterer and the adulteress shall surely be put to death" (Lev. 20:10; cp. 11:21; Deut. 22:21-24). Adultery is a very serious matter. How can one who believes God's word take it lightly? It nullifies God's plan for the very important relations and responsibilities of the family unit. It defies His will and disrupts lives. It takes what God made holy and makes it common and profane. It degrades the soul of a being made in the image of God. What was made to be enobling and a means of spiritual strength is diverted to the practice of self-gratification. It is a crime against individual persons, against society, and against the wise will of God.

277

III. Divorce

    A. Teaching Against Divorce.

        While divorce was permitted in Mosaic law, Jesus said that it was only because of the hardness of men's hearts and was not God's will even in the Old Testament society (Matt. 19:8). Deuteronomy 24: 1-4 was given for the protection of the woman who was cast out, and to prohibit wife-swapping back and forth. In this text the first three verses furnish a protasis (condition) for the fourth verse, which is the law under these conditions. (This is evident in these translations: Revised Standard Version; New American Standard Bible; New English Bible; Modern Language Bible; An American Translation; New American Bible; and Jerusalem Bible.) The passage implies that men will put away their wives, but it does not so much give permission to put one away as it prohibits taking one back who has been married to anyone else. God says, "I hate divorce" (Mal. 2:16). Some would point out that the context emphasizes the treachery of Israelites putting away their wives.

    B. Dealing with the Divorced.

        1. Avoid disputes about words to no profit, questionings and strife (II Tim. 2:14-26; I Tim. 1:5-11; 6:3-5; Titus 3:9, 10).

        2. Avoid being unnecessarily judgmental (Matt. 7:1-5; Luke 6:37-42; Rom. 12:16-21; 14:10-13; James 2:1-13; I Cor. 5:7-13), for we are sent to serve people more than we are to sort them for the Lord.

        3. Continue studying God's word to apply it with

278

true spiritual understanding, and accepting a dogmatic and legalistic church position or traditional view without discerning God's will. Try not to "go beyond what is written" (I Cor. 4:6).

a. Always realize and teach that:

(1) God does not want divorce.

(2) That every divorce represents some spiritual failure.

(3) That divorce and remarriage is not unforgivable.

(4) That these as well as other evils can be overcome, even prevented if we give God's word its place in our hearts.

b. Too often church people are studying only superficially, if at all, or trying to apply old opinions or unscriptural phrases, to determine how to judge divorced people, rather than how to save them and serve them.

4. We must be more concerned to succeed in helping them than we are to find excuses for our failure or for finding someone to blame for it (cp. Matt. 17:14-20; Mark 9:24-29). It should not be our aim to defend ourselves or make a name for ourselves in the minds of the unbelievers and the leaders of our society.

5. We must *communicate* to all God's grace and love. His truth, authority and righteousness, His reality and trustworthiness.

a. Not merely discourage,but encourage them.

b. Not only with words, but with what we are and do. Let Christ live in us and work through us.

c. Not to shirk, but to fulfill our responsibility to Christ.

    d. Not to excuse the sin, but to cure and heal the sinners.

    e. The cross shows that sinners are not worthless (Rom. 5:8); the cross of Christ draws men to Him (John 12:32); if we bear the cross we will draw more people, too.

  6. We must fulfill our calling as God's new creatures and ministers of reconciliation, knowing no one from a merely human point of view (II Cor. 5:11 —6:1). Try our best to represent Christ and all the transforming power of His love and truth.

IV. Adultery and Divorce

  A. Scriptural Statements.

    1. General — "And he said unto them, Whosoever shall put away his wife, and marry another, committeth adultery against her: and if she herself shall put away her husband, and marry another, she committeth adultery" (Mark 10:11, 12). "Every one that putteth away his wife, and marrieth another, committeth adultery: and he that marrieth one that is put away from a husband committeth adultery" (Luke 16:18).

    2. Exception — "but I say unto you, that every one that putteth away his wife, saving for the cause of fornication, maketh her an adulteress: and whosoever shall marry her when she is put away committeth adultery" (Matt. 5:32). "And I say unto you, Whosoever shall put away his wife, except for fornication, and shall marry another, committeth adultery: and he that marrieth her when she is put away committeth adultery" (Matt. 19:9).

B. Exception Interpreted. Various views of this exception and of conclusions drawn from it.

1. Some think this applied only to Jews under the law, and it is not to be considered for Christians at all. The law decreed death for adultery, so of course a man could put away an adulterous wife and remarry because she would be executed. If he put away any other (an innocent wife) he would be guilty of adultery and cause anyone who married her to commit adultery.

2. Some think this term fornication applied only to sex before marriage, and she could be put away because the marriage was not a genuine one. Commentaries and lexicons generally agree that fornication in these passages includes and probably specifies the sin of adultery.

3. Does the fornication refer to any illicit sex, homosexuality, etc.?

4. Does the sexual unchastity of a mate make the other obligated to divorce, or is it better to forgive and to restore the sinful mate?

   a. Some think that an adulterer becomes one flesh with even a harlot, so that the original wife must divorce him or she will be living in a "polygamous union" (I Cor. 6:16).

   b. Some think that since the law decreed death for adulterers that they are unforgivable. But didn't Jesus know that the Samaritan woman at the well was unforgivable (if that be so)? See John 4:10—what would Jesus give her, if she knew who He was? Does John 6:37 really mean to leave out as exceptions at least 1/10th of the people because of divorce or adultery, when Jesus said, "Him that cometh

281

unto me I will in no wise cast out"? Why did
Jesus say, "harlots go into the kingdom" (Matt.
21:31)? Why did Paul write (I Cor. 6:9-11)
that adulterers were washed and justified and
sanctified? Compare Ephesians 2:1-9 and
4:17-19.

c. Divorce on the ground of fornication may be
permitted, but it is nowhere commanded or
even recommended.

5. Does this exception contradict Paul's statement
"a wife is bound to her husband as long as she
lives" (Rom. 7:2; I Cor. 7:2; I Cor. 7:39)? Does
it contradict Mark 10:6-12?

a. Jesus' statements in both Matthew 5:32 and
19:9 are complete, clear and specific. There
is no manuscript evidence to support any
doubt about their being an original part of the
book of Matthew.

b. A simple statement of a general truth cannot
contradict limitations on or exceptions to that
truth when they are given on equal authority
elsewhere.

c. Paul's purpose in Romans was not to teach all
about divorce and remarriage, but to illustrate
the fact that Christians have been discharged
from the law to be joined to Christ. In Corinthians also he states the general rule without
having any reason to deal with a possible
exception under bad or abnormal conditions.

6. How does one who divorces a wife, not for the
cause of adultery, make her an adulteress (Matt.
5:32)?

    a. He gives her his permission to be joined to
       another, and it will seem to the woman that
       she has a legal right to marry; also it may be-
       come a necessity to find a way of living.

    b. Some think this only means that she will be
       made to bear the stigma of an adulteress, or
       appear to be an adulteress.

V. Is Remarriage Adultery?

  A. Divorce under the law explicitly gave permission to
     marry someone else (Deut. 24:1-3). If no one has a
     right to remarry, why did Jesus state an exception to
     the rule that one who puts away a wife and marries
     another commits adultery? If divorce and remarriage,
     except for the cause of fornication, constitutes adul-
     tery, then divorce and remarriage for that cause
     does not amount to adultery.

  B. Then why does Jesus say that anyone marrying her
     that is put away commits adultery? Is there an ex-
     ception *implied* in this statement to conform to the
     exception *stated* in the preceding statement? Does
     this mean that only the sexually faithful spouse who
     puts away an unfaithful one may marry another?
     Some think that if the marriage bond is really broken
     for one of the pair it can no longer be binding upon
     the other, but of course the guilty one has already
     committed adultery to be forgiven or punished.
     Since the Jews in Jesus' day did not have the power
     under Roman rule to execute the death penalty
     upon adulterers, divorce was the only way of escape
     for innocent parties to intolerable marriages to im-
     moral mates. Did Jesus give His consent to this kind

of statement? If the person who puts away a faithful spouse remarries, then the innocent partner has no chance of reconstructing that marriage and can consider the divorce valid in God's sight, and hence can remarry. One whose companion has given himself (or herself) over to sexual immorality can divorce that person and marry another without being guilty of adultery. If this is not true, then the only exception to remarriage being adultery is when the unfaithful mate is executed for adultery.

C. Summary of Possible Conclusions:

1. All marriages of divorced persons are adulterous.

2. All marriages after a divorce where fornication was not the cause of the divorce are adulterous.

3. An innocent spouse who has been put away not for fornication may not marry just because he or she is put away; but if the mate who got the divorce marries, then the divorce may be considered valid in God's sight because there is no chance of that marriage being reconstructed.

4. If a marriage has been dissolved, even the one who committed adultery may repent and be forgiven, and later marry again. (If this be so, how then does anyone who marries a divorced person commit adultery?) It may be granted that neither party is married any longer after a divorce for fornication has been secured; but it is not necessarily true that any unmarried person has an automatic right to marry.

D. Is divorce merely a legal separation under human law for protection of property and personal freedom or preservation of peace?

1. The Old Testament spoke of divorce as permitting remarriage. The Jews seem to have always had that concept, and asked Jesus with that in mind. There is no evidence that any ancient society had a practice of legal separation from bed and board without the right of remarriage.
2. If that is all Jesus intended divorce to mean, it would be unlikely that He would state only one cause for which it would be permitted. I Corinthians 7:11 seems to allow a Christian wife to depart from her husband but to remain unmarried or else be reconciled to her husband.

E. Does I Corinthians 7:27 say that a divorced person may marry without sinning? The person who was "loosed from a wife" might have been loosed by the death of the wife? It seems possible that Paul may have used the perfect passive of the verb to refer to a state of singleness without referring to any past action by which they became loosed. Therefore, it is a doubtful text to prove that one divorced may marry innocently.

F. Does I Corinthians 7:15 say that a marriage is dissolved if a non-Christian (unbelieving) husband is not willing to live with his Christian wife? If the nonbeliever departs, how is the Christian brother or sister "not in bondage in such cases"? Does the bondage here refer to the marriage contract? Or does it refer to a bondage in which a Christian would have to yield to any demands by the pagan mate in order to get him or her to live with the Christian and not depart?

1. Some say that Paul uses the same word "bound"

in reference to the marriage contract and its responsibility in Romans 7:2 and I Corinthians 7:39. But there is some difference between being "bound" as by a contract and being in bondage of slavery to a manner of life? Paul does not use the same word in Greek in both of these expressions. The fact is that in I Corinthians 7:15 he used a verb which means to be enslaved. It could refer to the total bondage of a life that could not separate from the unbeliever. If does mean at least that much. It is doubtful whether it was intended to mean that the Christian is set free to be remarried to anyone else.

2. Many believe that "not in bondage" was intended to include dissolution of the marriage obligation in every sense. If the unbeliever who departs subsequently commits adultery or marries someone else, many would conclude that the believer's obligation to the marriage was certainly broken.

G. Did the apostles ever teach anything about divorce and remarriage? What did they do about people who wanted to become Christians after they had divorced and remarried not according to God's law? If the apostles required everyone who was not still married to their first spouse to break up the marriage they had and live without marriage, does it seem reasonable that no mention is ever made of such drastic teaching?

1. Some think that non-Christians were not subject to any of Christ's teaching for they could not be responsible to any law they had not been taught. Then it is inferred that at baptism their old sins

and marriage bonds are blotted out; they are simply to live faithfully in the marriage in which they are involved when they become Christians. Others are afraid that this means that the non-Christians had no sin in any of his actions that were against Christ's teaching, which He did not know.

3. When a pagan accepts Christ as Lord, does he not accept Christ's standards in judgment over his past life as well as for direction of his present actions? Thus he repents and is forgiven, and serves under the rule of Christ as well as he can in the state in which he was called. He does not try to escape the responsibility for his former sins; neither can he change them. Our problem arises from the assumption that God could not forgive him and let him live with a second wife.

4. Is it God's purpose to punish all who married contrary to His law by making them remain unmarried all their lives? Or is it His purpose to make new creatures who will live according to His will in family relationships?

5. It is true that one should not plan to profit by sin. A Christian should not lust after a different woman and plan to commit adultery by divorce and remarriage then expect to repent and be forgiven and be able to keep the second for which he lusted. But how do we know that no one can repent of a wrong marriage without breaking it up? The Bible does not use the phrase "living in adultery." Neither does it say that a man who has divorced and remarried "has two living wives."

Do we distort our thinking by using expressions that beg the question? In I Corinthians 6:9-11 Paul mentions adultery along with other sins which were forgiven. In Corinth there were probably many who had been involved in divorces and remarriages. Paul can see them as former adulterers, but ones who are now cleansed and forgiven. There is no indication that they had separated from all illegal partners. For a Christian to marry an unbeliever is a sin by New Testament standards; yet those who are married to unbelievers are taught to continue faithful to their marriages where the unbeliever is willing. One who tries to apply an Old Testament example (see Ezra 10:3) might conclude that a Christian must put away the unbelieving spouse. But Paul says not to (I Cor. 7:12, 13). John the Baptist did tell Herod that it was not lawful for him to have his brother's wife. This close relationship was expressly forbidden in Leviticus 20:21.

6. Does the rule of I Corinthians 7:24 state a principle broad enough to apply to a second marriage?

7. Do the instructions of I Corinthians 7:26 not apply at all to persons who have been divorced?

8. If the first marriage cannot be restored (see Deut. 24:4) what command of God is served by sinning against the second wife or husband? The remarried husband is not bound to his first wife, if adultery is just cause for breaking up the marriage (Matt. 19:9). If the first marriage was not broken up by fornication before, then it was after the second marriage. And God forbids it to be

reformed after a second marriage (Deut. 24:4).

9. Was the sin of adultery in breaking the vows and the union of the first marriage, or is it adultery to live faithfully with a second partner after one has a real change of heart? Must the sinful attitudes and actions that destroyed the marriage be continued? Or if their damage cannot be fully repaired, can they be repented of and forsaken in the context of a marriage of forgiven sinners?

10. Does forgiveness of the sin of divorce and remarriage become the same thing as approval of adultery, as if it were no sin at all? Does the church which welcomes repentant thieves to forgiveness admit that thieves did no wrong? Does a man who forms a legal, business partnership for bad motives have to break his contract, or can he change his sinful purposes and live up to his contract in a righteous way?

H. What shall we do in actual practice of marrying people?

1. Shall we act as an agent of state law without reference to morality of the marriages performed?

2. Shall we refuse to marry any divorced persons?

3. Shall we marry only the "innocent party" of a broken marriage?

4. Shall we teach the words of the Lord to each couple and lay upon them the responsibility to decide whether their marriage is in obedience to God?

VI. Concluding Observations

1. Let us beware of striving to be strict in interpreting and applying the words of scripture in order that we may feel merit in holding a more perfect legal standard. God may want to teach a kind of character in men more than a strict set of limitations on the legal status of a marriage.

2. Let us beware also of looking for loopholes to allow a lenient application of God's statements. Our leniency may be used to help men feel relieved of obligations to do what God wants.

3. Let us leave judging to God, as far as possible. When we try to decide exactly how men should be judged, we need to ask questions why we want to settle the matter. Did God intentionally leave His word so that it was not easily settled and so that we hesitate to judge others? Teach God's will against divorce; but we may not be sure how God will judge those who have been guilty.

4. Preach God's mercy, repentance as needed, and forgiveness as available.

5. Expect the fruit of repentance in the continued seeking of God's will and in obedience to it as we can determine it. But beware of going beyond what is written in decreeing harsh terms as necessary fruit of repentance when God has not given a hint of such application in the word.

6. If divorced and remarried persons can become accepted and active members of the church, does that make the church teach that there is nothing really bad about divorce and remarriage? Does

290

it need to? Let's not let it.

7. Let us make far greater efforts to teach so that Christians will avoid divorce.

For Further Study:

Duty, Guy. *Divorce and Remarriage*. Minneapolis: Bethany Fellowship, Inc., 1967. Balanced study on the interpretation and application of the relevant Biblical texts.

Meredith, Maurice. *The Divorce Question*. Bound together with Alva Hovey's *The Scriptural Law of Divorce*. Rosemead, Cal.: Old Paths Book Club, n.d. Both very fine words but are now out of print.

Schubert, Joe D. *Marriage, Divorce and Purity*. Abilene: Biblical Reserach Press, 1966. A study guide on the Bible's teaching in regard to the whole area of marriage, divorce and sexual purity.

Stott, J. R. W. *Divorce*. Downers Grove: InterVarsity Press, 1971. Brief booklet which carefully deals with the problems in interpreting the texts on divorce.

Annotated Bibliography

Achtemeier, Elizabeth. *The Committed Marriage.* Philadelphia: Westminster Press, 1976.

Achtemeier presents marriage as a commitment to be made and lived out.

Anders, Sarah Frances. *Woman Alone: Creative and Confident.* Nashville: Broadman Press, 1976.

A valuable feature of this book is the author's statement of and refutation to common biological, psychological, and social myths that surround singles in general and single women in particular.

Bahnsen, Greg L. *Homosexuality: A Biblical View.* Grand Rapids: Baker Book House, 1978.

The foundational principle for this book is that the creation of sexual differentiation established heterosexuality as the normative direction for sexual behavior. Homosexuality, then, is a choice. The author then examines Biblical passages dealing with homosexuality.

Bailey, Derrick Sherwin. *The Mystery of Love and Marriage.* Westport, Connecticut: Greenwood Press, 1952.

This work examines the foundations for sexuality and marriage.

Banowsky, William. *It's A Playboy World.* Old Tappan, New Jersey: Fleming H. Revell Company, 1969.

Banowsky penetratingly analyzes the hedonistic sexual climate that permeates every facet of life and then calls for responsible Christian sexual behavior in its midst.

Barnhouse, Ruth Tiffany and Holmes, Urban T., III (ed.). *Male and Female.* New York: Seabury Press, 1976.

This compilation of articles looks at Biblical and sociological data about male and female roles.

Brown, Stanley C. *God's Plan for Marriage.* Philadelphia: Westminster, 1977.

Brown reviews the Biblical foundations for marriage.

Christenson, Larry. *The Christian Family.* Minneapolis: Bethany Fellowship, 1970.

The author's thesis is that marriage belongs to God. He asserts that a wife has the same relationship to her husband that Christ has with God. In his view, the headship of the husband and the submission of the wife are an order of creation rather than a result of sin as Thielicke and others assume.

Cole, William Graham. *Sex and Love in the Bible.* New York: Association Press, 1959.

Cole presents an overview of sexual practices and mispractices as presented in the Bible. The most valuable part of the work is the inclusion of a description of the sexual mores of the cultures surrounding the Israelites, and later the church.

DeJong, Peter and Wilson, Donald R. *Husband and Wife.* Grand Rapids: Zondervan, 1979.

This book is an effort to assist Christians in their response to the current social upheaval in sex roles. It presents three kinds of evidence: biological, social-scientific, and Biblical. By integrating the three types of evidence, the authors attempt to construct a Christian perspective on the changing roles of men and women.

Drakeford, John W. *A Christian View of Homosexuality.* Nashville: Broadman Press, 1959.

Drakeford surveys the Biblical teaching about homosexuality, using Genesis 19, Leviticus 18:22 and 20:13, Romans 1:26-27, I Timothy 1:10, and I Corinthians 6:9-10 to establish the principles. A section is also devoted to an examination of the Biblical material often used to support homosexual behavior as acceptable.

294

Duty, Guy. *Divorce and Remarriage*. Minneapolis: Bethany Fellowship, 1967.

Duty deals with this question: does divorce dissolve a marriage? His assumption is that if it does in fact dissolve the marriage, then there is no question about the right to remarry. He concludes that divorce for adultery as granted by Jesus absolutely severs the marriage bond and declares the former marriage null, void, and dead.

Engelsma, David. *Marriage: The Mystery of Christ and the Church*. Grand Rapids: Reformed Free Publishing Association, 1975.

This book examines marriage in its function as a microcosm of the church.

Field, David. *The Homosexual Way—A Christian Option?* Downers Grove, Illinois: InterVarsity Press, 1979.

Field's treatment of homosexuality begins with an examination of social attitudes toward it and then proceeds to the Biblical teaching and theological foundations. The author accepts that some will have homosexual orientation, yet calls for responsible, Biblical sexual behavior by them.

Getz, Gene A. *The Measure of a Man*. Glendale, California: Regal Books, 1974.

In his first "measure," Getz examines Titus 1:6-8 and I Timothy 3:1-12 to determine the qualities of a real man in God's sight.

Getz, Gene A. *The Measure of a Marriage*. Glendale, California: Regal Books, 1980.

The author provides exercises by which couples may analyze their marriages and seek to explore together to make them what Christ would have a marriage to be.

Getz, Gene A. *The Measure of a Woman*. Glendale, California: Regal Books, 1977.

Getz examines three New Testament passages—I Timothy 3:11, Titus 2:3-5, and I Peter 3:1-4—to determine those characteristics that the Bible assigns to Christian women.

Goergen, Donald. *The Sexual Celibate*. New York: Seabury Press, 1953.

The author presents celibacy as a viable Christian alternative to marriage. He examines theological and psychological foundations of sexuality, then determining how celibacy fits into those guidelines.

Howell, John. *Equality and Submission in Marriage*. Nashville: Broadman Press, 1979.

This book begins by examining Biblical material relating to the nature and importance of Christian marriage. With that theological perspective in view, he then examines the persons in marriage. He asserts that family relationships must be based upon a theology of voluntary mutual submission after which both husband and wife will readily find proper expression of their respective roles as defined in the Bible. He concludes by encouraging couples to develop their own marriage style within the parameters established by the Biblical text.

Hunt, Gladys. *Ms. Means Myself*. Grand Rapids: Zondervan, 1972.

Based upon acceptance of Biblical revelation as normative, this book provides guidelines for Christian women to find meaning in life, to maximize potential, and to achieve godliness. The Christian woman is truly free when she is related to God.

Lloyd-Jones, D. M. *Life in the Spirit.* Grand Rapids: Baker Book House, 1973.

This exegesis of Ephesians provides sound Biblical guidelines to structure modern marriage as God intended. The scope of the book is wider than merely the Ephesian passage on marriage.

Lovelace, Richard. *Homosexuality and the Church.* Old Tappan, New Jersey: Fleming H. Revell Company, 1978.

Another survey of the Bible teaching about homosexuality, this book asserts that homosexuality destroys God's purposes for sexuality.

Pape, Dorothy R. *In Search of God's Ideal Woman.* Downers Grove, Illinois: InterVarsity Press, 1976.

This book surveys women's roles and functions in the New Testament and the early church. The author then examines the ministries of contemporary women with final conclusions about the single woman, the married woman, and the mother. She concludes that godly women have no set roles or duties, but do possess the traits of meekness and a gentle spirit.

Piper, Otto. *The Christian Interpretation of Sex.* London: Nisbet and Company, 1942.

The author's foundations for a Biblical understanding of sex plus his fundamental ideas for a Biblical interpretation of sex make this treatment a classic work. He clearly outlines the purposes of sexuality and its profound permeation of every aspect of human personality whether expressed in intercourse or not.

Scanzoni, Letha and Hardesty, Nancy. *All We're Meant To Be.* Waco, Texas: Word, 1974.

This book carries a subtitle "A Christian Approach to Women's Liberation." The authors define their idea of liberation for the Christian woman, calling it a *state of mind* in which a woman comes to view herself as Jesus Christ sees her—a person created in God's image. Somewhat controversial in places, the book, nonetheless, deals very well with Genesis 1-3, then critically examines women's roles through the ages. The chapter entitled "The Single Woman" is the best treatment on the subject to be found anywhere.

Small, Dwight Hervey. *Christian, Celebrate Your Sexuality.* Old Tappan, New Jersey: Fleming H. Revell Company, 1974.

The thesis of this work is that the meaning of sexuality is the meaning of man himself, making him "infinitely larger than the current theories of sexuality take him to be." The author insists that human sexuality is a gift of God to be celebrated as part of man's worshipful response to Him in an act of responsible choice. A stated purpose of the book is to get behind sexual behavior to sexual being, to build Christian sexual ethics upon theology. *Only the informed and committed Christian can truly celebrate his sexuality,* according to Small. The task is accomplished by providing a history of Christian thought on sexuality, an outline of today's sexual milieu, and an examination of Biblical material dealing with sexuality.

Small, Dwight Hervey. *The Right to Remarry.* Old Tappan, New Jersey: Fleming H. Revell Company, 1975.

The author's position in this book may be summarized in this way: a) God's original intent envisions marriage as indissoluble, b) divorce and remarriage is neither a personal nor an absolute right, c) divorce and remarriage, although *never* God's intention, are nonetheless within

God's conditional will, and d) the church should seek a redemptive role among the divorced and remarried.

Smedes, Lewis B. *Sex for Christians*. Grand Rapids: William Eerdmans, 1976.

The author examines the normative statements for sexual conduct for Christians.

Thielicke, Helmut. *The Ethics of Sex*. New York: Harper and Row, 1964.

The author examines the theological foundations for sexuality, especially in Genesis 1-3, and provides an ethical guideline for viewing sexuality and sexual behavior.

Trobisch, Walter. *Love Yourself*. Downers Grove, Illinois: InterVarsity Press, 1976.

Although the author's stated purpose is to teach self-acceptance as a cure for depression, his chapter entitled "The Consequences of the Lack of Self-Love" points out the basic way self love affects sexual behavior.

White, John. *Eros Defiled*. Downers Grove, Illinois: Inter-Varsity Press, 1977.

White's stated purpose is to help sexual sinners. He accepts the reality of sexual standards for life, hence the reality of sexual sin. Sexual sin, being sin, calls for the sinner to repent in order to receive forgiveness from God. Yet he maintains a redemptive attitude to help those who have misused sex to help them to find forgiveness and new life in Christ.

Williams, Don. *The Apostle Paul and Women in the Church*. Glendale, California: Regal Books, 1977.

This book examines every Pauline reference to women —the occasion for the writing, what was said, and implications for contemporary application. The guidelines for women's roles are beneficial to women and to the church today.

Wright, H. Norman. *The Pillars of a Marriage.* Glendale, California: Regal Books, 1979.

This book deals with the realities of marriage: goals, fulfilling needs, stress, crises, decision-making, conflict, and forgiveness. It is a book intended for couples to read, discuss, evaluate, and apply together to bring their unions into harmony with God's purpose for marriage.

TOPICAL INDEX FOR *WHAT THE BIBLE SAYS ABOUT SEXUAL IDENTITY*

As arranged in *Monser's Topical Index and Digest of the Bible* edited by Harold E. Monser with A. T. Robertson, D. R. Dungan and Others.

ADULTERY. Commandments concerning.—Ex. 20:14; Lev. 18:20; Num. 5:12-31; Deut. 5:18; 22:22-27; 24:1-4; Jer. 3:1; 5:7-9; 29:21-23; Mt. 5:27-32; 19:3-9, 18; Mk. 10:19; Lu. 18:20; Jas. 2:11. Law of—Rom. 7:3.

Teaching of Jesus concerning.—Mt. 5:27-32; 15:19; 19:9, 18; Mk. 7:21; 10:11, 12, 19; Lu. 16:18; 18:20.

Punished with death.—Lev. 18:20, 20:10-12; Deut. 22:22-27; Pr. 9:18; Mt. 5:27-32; John 8:5; Gal. 5:19-21; Eph. 5:3-5; I Thes. 4:4-7; Heb. 13:4; Rev. 21:8; 22:15. By Jehovah—Jer. 7:9; Mal. 3:5.

Despoils life.—Deceives—Job 24:15; Ps. 50:18. Children of transgression—Pr. 6:26; 31:3; Is. 57:3.

Disgraces individual.—Path towards death—Pr. 2:18, 19. Woman deceives—Pr. 5:3, 4; 6:27-33; 22:14; 23:27, 28: 30:20; Eccl. 7:26.

Degrades a nation.—Lev. 19:29; Deut. 23:17; Job 31:9-12; Jer. 3:1; 7:9; Hos. 4:1-2, 11; Mt. 12:39; 16:4; Mk. 8:38; I Cor. 10:8; Jude 7; I Pet. 4:3; Rev. 2:14.

Debars fellowship.—Eph. 5:11, 12. With God—Jas. 4:4.

Dwarfs a soul.—Mk. 15:19; I Cor. 3:17; II Pet. 2:10, 14; Eph. 4:17, 19, 20; 5:3, 4.

Adulterers shall not inherit the kingdom of God.—I Cor. 6:9; Gal. 5:19, 21; Eph. 5:5; Rev. 21:8; 22:5. God will judge—Jer. 7:9; 29:23; Ez. 22:9-11; Eph. 5:6; Col. 3:6; I Thess. 4:3-5; Heb. 13:4; Jude 7; Rev. 2:20, 22.

Judged by righteous men.—Ez. 23:45; Job 31:11.

Examples of.—Shechem—Gen. 34:2. Reuben—Gen. 35:22. Judah—Gen. 38:1-24. Potiphar's wife—Gen. 39:7-12. Eli's sons—I Sam. 2:22. David—II Sam. 11:1-5. Absalom—II Sam. 16:22. Israelites—Jer. 5:7-9; 29:23; Ez. 22:9-11; 33:26. Herod—Mk. 6:17, 18. Samaritan woman John 4:18. A woman—John 8:3-11. Corinthians I Cor. 5:1. Gentiles—I Pet. 4:3.

Figurative.—Adulterous state of Zion—Jer. 9:2; 23:10; Hos. 2:2; 3:1; 7:4; Rom. 7:1-6.

SPIRITUAL ADULTERY—*i.e.*, **IDOLATRY. Fascinating.**—Parable—Num. 25:1-3; Ez. 16:30-34; Ch. 23; Hos. 4:18; 11:2.

Predicted.—Lev. 20:1-5; Deut. 31:16-18, 20, 29.

Prohibited.—Ex. 34:12-16.

Introduced by foreign wives.—I Ki. 11:1-8; II Ki. 9:22.

Practiced by Israel and Judah.—Ju. 8:27, 33; I Chr. 5:25; Ps. 106:38, 39; Jer. 3:1, 2; Ez. 16:16, 17, 20-29; Hos. 1:2; 2:2-5; 4:12, 13; 5:3, 4, 6, 10; Mal. 2:11. Nineveh—Nah. 3:4. Babylon—Rev. 17:1, 2.

Reproved.—Ju. 3:8-10; Gen. 13:27; Ez. 20:30-32, 39; Hos. 2:6-9; 4:14, 15.

Entreaty to return.—Jer. 3:14, 16; Ez. 43:7, 9.

Punished.—II Ki. 9:22; Ps. 73:27; Ez. 6:9; 16:35-43; Hos. 2:9-13; Rev. 17:16, 17; 18:2, 3, 5; 19:2.

BETROTHAL. Espousal among the Hebrews was something more than a marriage engagement is with us. It was the beginning of marriage, was as legally binding as marriage itself, and could be broken off only by a bill of divorce. Hence we find that Joseph is called the husband of Mary —Mt. 1:18, 19. Parents chose the companion—Gen. 21:21; 34:4-6; 38:6; Deut. 22:16.

The marriage was not consummated for some time after the betrothal. —Ju. 14:7-8. Brothers were consulted—Gen. 24:58.

The betrothal was accompanied with gifts.—Gen. 24:53; 34:12. A dowry was given—I Sam. 18:25.

The bride remained at her home till taken by the bridegroom.—Deut. 20:7.

The friend of the bridegroom kept up communication between the two.—John 3:29. Compulsory betrothal—Ex. 22:16; Deut. 22:28-29. Violated betrothal—Lev. 19:20; Deut. 22:23. A blameless woman—Deut. 22:25.

CHASTE, CHASTITY. Tit. 2:5; I Pet. 2:3; Eccl. 7:26. Enjoined—Pr. 21:3; Acts 15:20; Rom. 13:13; I Cor. 6:13-18; Col. 3:5; I Thess. 4:3; Tit. 2:5; Heb. 13:4; I Pet. 4:1-3. Heart, In—Pr. 6:24, 25. Look, In —Job 31:1; Mt. 5:28. Speech, In —Eph. 5:3. Unchaste shall not enter heaven—Eph. 5:5, 6; Heb. 13:4; Rev. 22:14. Unchaste, Shun company of—Pr. 5:3-11; 7:10-27; 22:14; Eccl. 7:26; I Cor. 5:11; I Pet. 3:1, 2. Wicked are not—Eph. 4:19; II Pet. 2:14; Jude 8.

CHILDREN: The chosen type of the kingdom.—Mt. 18:2-5; 19:14; Mk.

10:14, 15; Lu. 18:17; I Cor. 14:20; I Pet. 2:2.

Promised as an inducement to righteousness.—Gen. 15:5; 22:17; Ex. 32:13; Lev. 26:9; Deut. 7:12-14; 13:17; 30:5; Job 5:24, 25; Ps. 45:16, 17; 128:1-6; Is. 44:3, 4; 48:18, 19; Jer. 33:22; Rom. 4:18.

Come from God.—Gen. 4:1, 25; 17:20; 29:31-35; 30:2, 6, 17-20; 33:5; 48:9; Deut. 7:13; Ruth 4:13; I Sam. 1:19, 20; Ps. 107:41; 113:9; 127:3-5; 128:1-6.

Children a blessing.—Gen. 5:29; Ps. 113:9; 127:3-5; Pr. 10:1; 15:20; 17:6; 23:24; 27:11; 29:3.

Childlessness an affliction.—Gen. 15:2, 3; 30:1; I Sam. 1:6, 7; Jer. 20:30; 22:30; Lu. 1:25.

Given in answer to prayer.—Gen. 15:2-5; 25:21; I Sam. 1:10-20, 27; Lu. 1:13.

By special appointment.—Isaac— Gen. 15:2-6; 17:16; 21:1-3. Jacob and Esau—Gen. 15:21-26. Samuel —I Sam. 1:11, 19, 20. John the Baptist—Lu. 1:13-25, 57-80; Lu. 1:26-42. Jesus—Mt. 1:18-23; Lu. 1:26-38.

Children taken away in punishment. —Ex. 12:29, 30; Deut. 28:32, 41; II Sam. 12:14, 15; Job 27:14, 15; Ps. 21:10, 11; Hos. 9:12.

Covenant of circumcision.—Gen. 17:10-14; Lev. 12:3; Phil. 3:5.

Named.—Gen. 21:3; 30:6, 8, 10, 13, 18, 20, 21, 24; 41:51, 52; Ex. 2:22. Ruth 4:17; I Sam. 4:21. At circumcision—Lu. 1:59; 2:21. After relatives—Lu. 1:59, 61. From remarkable events—Gen. 21:3, 6; 18:13; Ex. 2:10; 18:3, 4. From circumstances connected with their birth —Gen. 25:25, 26; 35:18; I Chr. 4:9. Named by God—Is. 8:3; Hos. 1:4, 6, 9; Lu. 1:31.

302

Treatment at birth.—Ez. 16:4-6; Lu. 2:7, 12.

Brought early to the house of the Lord.—I Sam. 1:24.

Weaning of.—Gen. 21:8; I Sam. 1: 22-24; I Ki. 11:20; Ps. 131:2; Is. 11:8; 28:9.

Nurses of.—Gen. 24:59; Ex. 2:7, 9; Ruth 4:16; II Sam. 4:4; II Ki. 11:2.

Adopted.—Gen. 48:5, 6; Ex. 2:10.

Education of.—Gen. 18:19; Ex. 10: 2; 13:8-10; Deut. 4:9; 11:19; 31: 12, 13; Ps. 78:3-8; Pr. 4:1-22; 13: 1, 24; 22:6, 15; Is. 28:9, 10; Lu. 2:46; II Tim. 3:14, 15.

Training of.—Pr. 22:6, 15; 29:17; Eph. 6:4.

Parental authority.—Gen. 9:24, 25; 18:19; 21:14; 38:24; Pr. 13:1, 24.

Parental indulgence.—Gen. 27:6-17, 42-45; 37:3, 4. Indulgence forbidden—Deut. 21:15-17.

Parental example.—Gen. 18:19; II Tim. 1:5.

Duties of children to parents.—Ex. 20:12; 21:15, 17; Lev. 19:3; 20:9; Deut. 5:16; 27:16; Pr. 1:8; 6:20; 15:5; 23:22; 24:21; Is. 45:10; Eph. 6:2, 3; Col. 3:20; I Tim. 5:4; I Pet. 5:5.

Penalty for disobedience.—Deut. 21: 18-21; Pr. 30:17.

Prosperity of, greatly depended on obedience of parents.—Deut. 4:40; 12:25, 28; Ps. 128:1-3.

Amusements.—Job 21:11; Zech. 8: 5; Mt. 11:16, 17; Lu. 7:31, 32.

Fellowship with parents.—Gen. 6: 18; 13:15-16; Lev. 26:45.

Children sacrificed to idols.—Lev. 18:21; 20:2-5; Deut. 12:29-31; 18:10; II Ki. 17:31; II Chr. 28:3; 33:6; Ez. 16:20, 21.

Prayers for.—Gen. 17:18; I Chr. 29: 19.

Discriminations: Male.—Redeemed as belonging to God—Ex. 13:13-15. Under care of tutors—II Ki. 10:1; Acts 22:3; Gal. 4:1, 2. Inherited possessions of their fathers—Deut. 21: 16, 17; Lu. 12:13, 14. Received paternal blessing—Gen. 27:1-4; 48: 15; 49:1-33.

Female.—Drawers of water—Gen. 24:13; Ex. 2:16. Inheritors of property in default of sons—Num. 27:1-8; Josh. 17:1-16. Were given in marriage by father, eldest preferred—Gen. 29:16-29. Being debarred from marriage a reproach—Jer. 11:37; Is. 4:1.

Illegitimate.—Disregarded by father—Heb. 12:8. Despised by brothers—Ju. 11:2. Excluded from congregation—Deut. 23:2. Exiled from family—Gen. 21:14; 25:6. Had no inheritance—Gen. 21:10-14; Gal. 4:30.

Good children.—Obey parents—Gen. 28:7; 47:29-31; Ex. 20:12; Pr. 10: 1; 13:1; Col. 3:20. Observe the law of God—Ps. 119:9, 99; Pr. 28:7. Submit to discipline—Pr. 8:32-36; Heb. 12:9. Honor and care for parents—Gen. 45:9-11; 46:29; 47: 12; Pr. 10:1; 29:17. Respect the aged—Lev. 19:32.

Examples of.—Shem and Japheth. —Gen. 9:23. Isaac—Gen. 22:6. Judah—Gen. 4:32. Joseph—Gen. 37:13; 46:29. Jacob's sons—Gen. 50:12. Jephthah's daughter—Ju. 11:36. Samuel—I Sam. 3:19; 22: 6. David—I Sam. 17:20; Ps. 71:5. Solomon—II Ki. 2:19. Josiah—II Chr. 34:3. Esther—Esth. 2:20. The Rechabites—Jer. 35:5-10. Daniel—Dan. 1:6. Jesus—Lu. 2:51. Timothy—II Tim. 3:15.

Wicked children.—To their parents—
Gen. 26:34, 35; Deut. 27:16; I Sam.
2:25; II Sam. 15:10-15; I Ki. 1:5-
10; Pr. 15:5, 20; 19:26; 28:24; 29:
15; 30:11; Ez. 22:7. To their leaders
—II Ki. 2:23, 24; Job 19:18. Not
restrained by parents—I Sam. 3:11-
14. Sons of Belial—I Sam. 2:12-17,
22-25; 8:1-3.

Punishment of.—Ex. 21:15; Deut. 21:
18, 21; 27:16; II Ki. 2:23; Pr. 28:
24; 30:17; Mk. 7:10.

Fondness and care of mothers for.—
Ex. 2:2-10; I Sam. 2:19; I Ki. 3:27;
Is. 49:15; I Thess. 2:7, 8.

Grief occasioned by loss of.—Gen.
37:35; 44:27-29; II Sam. 13:37;
Jer. 6:26; 31:15.

**Consequences of sin entailed on chil-
dren in this world.**—Ex. 20:5; 34:
7; Lev. 26:39, 40; Num. 14:33;
Deut. 5:9; I Ki. 14:9-10; Job 5:3-7;
Ps. 21:10; 37:28; Is. 1-4; 13:16;
14:20-22; Jer. 32:18; Lam. 5:7; Mt.
23:32-36; John 9:2, 3, 34.

**Children not punished for sins of par-
ents.**—Deut. 24:16; II Ki. 14:6; II
Chr. 25:4; Jer. 31:29, 30; 32:18;
Ez. 18:2-4, 20; Mt. 19:13, 14; Mk.
10:13-15; Lu. 18:15-17.

Children of God.—Heb. 12:5-9; I Pet.
1:14.

Children of light.—Lu. 16:8; John
12:36; Eph. 5:8; I Thess. 5:5.

CONCUBINE. Hebrew concubinage
grew out of a desire for offspring as
associated with the hope of the promised Redeemer. The children were
adopted as if the wife's own offspring—Gen. 30:1-24. Husband
could take any of his own slaves as
concubines, but could not take any
of his wife's slaves without her consent—Gen. 16:2, 3; 30:3, 4, 9. Not
illegal, but supplementary. Abraham

sent Ishmael away to guard the rights
of Isaac—Gen. 17:20, 21.

Laws concerning.—Ex. 21:7-11; Lev.
19:20-22; Deut. 21:9-14. Concubines called wives—Gen. 37:2; Ju.
19:1-4. Children, but not heirs—
Gen. Ch. 49.

Incest with concubines.—Gen. 35:
22; 49:4; I Chr. 5:1; II Sam. 16:21,
22.

**Concubinage not right as we see it,
but permitted for the time.**—Acts
17:30; Mt. 19:3-12. Since Christ,
fornication a sin against one's own
body—I Cor. 6:15-20.

Examples in.—Abraham—Gen. 16:
3; 25:6; I Chr. 1:32. Nahor—Gen.
22:24. Jacob—Gen. 30:4; 35:22;
49:4; I Chr. 5:1. Eliphaz—Gen. 36:
12. Gideon—Ju. 8:31. Caleb—I
Chr. 2:46. Manasseh—I Chr. 7:14.
Saul—II Sam. 3:7; 21:11. David—
II Sam. 5:13; 15:16; 19:5; 20:3; I
Chr. 3:9. Solomon—I Ki. 11:3. Rehoboam—II Chr. 11:21. Belshazzar
—Dan. 5:3.

DIVORCE. Ex. 21:7-11; Deut. 21:
14; 22:13-19, 28, 29; 24:1-4; 28:
1-4; Mt. 5:31, 32; 19:3-9; Mk. 10:
2-12; Lu. 16:18; Rom. 7:2, 3; I
Cor. 7:10-17. Moses allowed divorce
because of the hardness of heart of
the Jew—Mt. 19:8. Adultery breaks
the marriage bond—Mt. 19:9.

FATHER (*Heb.* Ab; *Chald.* abba. Ancestor, source. Ab, when a prefix
to a name, signifies "father of").

As an ancestor.—Gen. 2:24; 9:18,
22; 10:21; 11:28, 29; 22:7, 21;
26:3, 15, 18, 24; 31:3; 47:3, 9, 30;
48:15; 49:29; Ex. 8:13; 10:6; 13:
5; Deut. 1:8, 11; Josh. 24:6; Ju.
2:10; I Sam. 12:6, 8, 15; II Sam.
7:12; I Ki. 11:12; 13:22; II Ki. 8:
24; I Chr. 29:18; II Chr. 9:31; Ezra

304

7:27; Neh. 9:2, 9; Ps. 22:4; 49:19; 106:7; Jer. 7:7; 11:10; Ez. 18:2; Zech. 1:4; 23:10; Mk. 11:10; Lu. 1:32, 73; 6:23, 26; John 7:22; Acts 7:2.

As chief or ruler.—Priest—Ju. 17:10; 18:19; Acts 22:1. Prophet—II Ki. 2:12; 6:21; 13:14. King—Josh. 15: 13; I Ki. 15:24. Apostle—I Cor. 4: 15. Syrian general—II Ki. 5:13.

Father of nations or tribes.—Gen. 17:4, 5; 19:37, 38; 36:9, 43; 45: 18; Num. 3:30; Josh. 17:1; I Chr. Chs. 2, 4; 9:19. (In Num. Ch. 17, *house* is used for *tribe.*

Father, as related to household.—Gen. 12:1; 20.13, 24:7, 23, 38, 40; 28:21; 31:14; 38:11; 41:51; 46:31; 50:8, 22; Lev. 22:13; Num. 2:2; 18:1; Deut. 22:21; Josh. 2:12; Ju. 6:15; 9:5, 18; 11:2, 7; I Sam. 2:31; 9:20; 18:2; 22:1, 11, 16, 22; II Sam. 3:29; 14:9; I Ki. 18:18; I Chr. 21:13; Neh. 1:6; Is. 7:17; 22:23, 24; Lu. 2:49; 16:27; Acts 7:20.

Father as source of inventor of.—Gen. 4:21; Job 17:14; 38:28; John 8:44; Rom. 4:11, 12; 9:5; I Cor. 4:15; II Cor. 1:3.

As an object of respect.—II Ki. 2:12; 5:13; 6:21; Jer. 2:27; Acts 7:2; 22:1.

In earliest times his jurisdiction was surpreme.—Gen. 22:31, 32; 38: 24; 42:37.

In later times jurisdiction was distributed.—Court of judges determine —Ex. 21:22, 15, 17; Lev. 20:9; Deut. 21:18-21. Power to sacrifice children, still his—II Ki. 16:3; Jer. 7:31; 19:5; Ez. 16:20; 20:26. Done in violation of law—Lev. 18:21; 20: 1-5; Deut. 12:31; 18:10.

Children treated by fathers as slaves or chattels.—Arbitrary marriages—

Gen. 38:6; Ju. 12:9; Ezra 9:2. Children pledged or sold—II Ki. 4:1; Is. 50:1. Harlotry of daughters forbidden—Lev. 19:29. Bonds of daughters disallowed—Num. 30:5. Wives divorced at pleasure—Gen. 21:9-10.

Blessing of father.—Gen. 27:4-38; 48:9-22; 49:1-28.

Malediction of father.—Gen. 9:25-27; 27:27-40; 48:17-19; 49:1-28. (In which blessing and curse mingle.)

Qualities of a father: To command—Gen. 18:19; 49:33; Deut. 32:46. To provide—Ju. 1:14-15; Mt. 7:9-11; Lu. 11:11-13; 12:32; 15:12. To renounce—Gen 22:2-3; Hos. 11:8; Lu. 15:11-12. To pity—Ps. 103:13. To grieve—Gen. 21:11-12; 37:34-35; 42:38; 44:29; II Sam. 18:33. To love—Gen. 25:28; 37:3; II Sam. 2:32. To protect—Job 29: 16; Ps. 27:10; 68:5; Deut. 32:6. To correct—Pr. 3:12; 23:13; 29:17; Heb. 12:9.

Duties of children to fathers: To obey —Gen. 27:8, 13, 43; Deut. 21:18-21; Jer. 35:14; Eph. 6:1; Col. 3: 20. To honor—Ex. 20:12; Lev. 19: 3; Mt. 15:4; 19:19. To love—Gen. 45:9-11; 46:29; 47:12, 29-30. To gladden—Pr. 10:1; 17:21; Phil. 2: 22.

Influence of fathers upon posterity: Evil influence—Ex. 20:5; 34:7; Lev. 26:39; Num. 14:18; Deut. 5:9; 8: 3; I Ki. 15:12; II Ki. 17:14, 41; II Chr. 30:7, 8; Neh. 9:2, 16; Ps. 78: 57; 106:6; Is. 14:21; 65:7; Jer. 2: 5-9; 6:21; 7:26; 9:16; 13:14; 14: 20; 16:12; 19:4; 44:9; Lam. 5:7; Ez. 20:30-32; Dan. 9:16. Amos 2: 4; Zech. 1:4-6; Mal. 2:10; Mt. 23: 29-32; Lu. 11:47-48; Acts 7:51-53. Good influence—Gen. 15:15; 47:9;

I Ki. 2:10; 15:11, 12, 23, 24; II Chr. 14:2-6; 32:32-33; Heb. 12:9.
Children not to suffer for sins of fathers.—Deut. 24:16; II Ki. 14:6; II Chr. 25:4; Jer. 31:29-30; Ez. Ch. 18.
Fatherless.—Abuse of—Ex. 22:22; Job 6:27; 22:9; 24:9; Ps. 94:6; 109:10-12; Is. 10:2; Jer. 7:6; 22:3; Ez. 22:7; Zech. 7:10. To be cared for—Deut. 14:29; 16:11, 14; II Sam. 9:3; II Ki. 11:1-2; Job 31:17 -18; Ps. 68:5; 146:9; Jer. 49:11; Jas. 1:27.
Father-in-law.—Gen. 38:13; Ex. 2: 18; 3:1; 18:1-27; Num. 10:29; Ju. 1:16; 4:11; 19:4, 7, 9; I Sam. 4: 19, 21.
New Testament references.—Whose son asks for a loaf—Mt. 7:9-11. To bury my father—Mt. 8:21; Lu. 9:59. He that loveth father more—Mt. 10: 37. Father give me the portion—Lu. 15:12. Devil is father of lies—John 8:34. Father of all that believe—Rom. 4:11, 17. As a child serveth father—Phil. 2:22. Father of our flesh—Heb. 12:9. Your father tried me—Heb. 3:9.
FORNICATION. Forbidden—Ex. 22: 16, 17. With bond-maiden—Lev. 19:20. Offering to be made on account of—Lev. 19:21-22. Midianitish woman—Num. 25:6, 8. Take a wife and hate her—Deut. 22:13-22. A betrothed virgin—Deut. 22:23, 29. No prostitutes in house of God —Deut. 23:17. Jerusalem's—Ez. 16:15, 29. Delivered from strange woman—Pr. 2:16; 5:3; 6:25, 26. Young men warned of—Pr. Ch. 7; 31:3. The foolish woman's entreaty—Pr. 9:13-18. Mouth of strange woman—Pr. 22:14; 23:27; 29:3. Out of the heart comes—Mt. 15:19; Mk. 7:21. Putting away wife

save for—Mt. 5:32; 19:9. Were not born of fornication—John 8:41. Abstain from—Acts 15:20, 29; I Cor. 6:9; I Thess. 4:3. Have no company with fornication—I Cor. 5:9. Shall not inherit Kingdom of Heaven—I Cor. 6:9. The works—Gal. 5:19; Eph. 5:3. Put to death your members—Col. 3:5. Law made for—I Tim. 1:10. God will judge—Heb. 13:4. To commit—Rev. 2:14. Second death for—Rev. 21:8. Without are fornicators—Rev. 22:15. Gentiles abstain from—Acts 21:25. Among the Jews—I Cor. 5:1. Body not for—I Cor. 6:13, 18. Let every man have his own wife, To avoid—I Cor. 7:2. Repented not of—II Cor. 12:21.
Examples of: Lot—Gen. 19:31. Reuben—Gen. 35:22. Judah—Gen. 38:1-24. Samson—Ju. 16:1. Eli's sons—I Sam. 2:22. Amnon—II Sam. 13:1-20. Gentiles—Eph. 4:17-19; I Pet. 4:3.
Spiritual (Idolatry).—Ez. 16:22. Take thee a wife of—Hos. 1:2, 3. Err because of—Hos. 4:11. Cities given over to—Jude 7. Wrath of—Rev. 14:8; 18:3. Kings of earth counted —Rev. 17:2, 4; 18:3. Repented not of—Rev. 9:21. Corrupted the earth with—Rev. 19:2.
GRANDMOTHER. II Tim. 5:4.
HARLOT. For hire.—Gen. 34:21; Num. 25:1, 6; Ju. 11:1; 16:1; 19: 2, 25; I Ki. 3:16; Amos 2:7.
In heathen worship.—Gen. 38:21; Ex. 34:15, 16; Hos. 4:14.
Legislation against.—Common—Lev. 19:29; Deut. 23:18. Religious—Ex. 34:12-16; Lev. 21:7, 9, 14; Deut. 23:17; Hos. 1:2; 4:12; Ez. 16:26.

Warnings.—Pr. 6:26; 7:7-23; 23:27; 29:3; Hos. 4:11-14.

Punishment.—Burned or stoned to death—Gen. 38:24; Lev. 20:10-12; Deut. 22:22-25; John 8:5.

The New Covenant demands purity of heart and life.—Mt. 5:8, 27, 28, 31, 32; Acts 15:20, 29; I Cor. 6:9, 10, 13-20; Eph. 5:3-5; Col. 3:5-8; Tit. 1:15; 2:12; Jas. 4:4, 8.

HUSBAND: Laws concerning.—Ex. 21:22; Lev. 19:20; 21:3, 7; Num. 30:6-16; Deut. 22:22, 23; 24:5; 25:11; 28:56; Ez. 44:25. Jealousy—Num. 5:13, 19, 29-31. Marriage of captive women—Deut. 21:13. Bishops—I Tim. 3:2. Elders—Tit. 1:6. Divorce—Deut. 24:3, 4; Mt. 5:31, 32; 19:3-9; Mk. 10:12; Lu. 16:18; Rom. 7:2, 3.

Duties of.—Deut. 24:5; Pr. 5:18; I Cor. 7:2-4, 10, 16, 34, 39; Eph. 5:23-33; Col. 3:19; I Tim. 5:8; I Pet. 3:7.

Exhortation to.—Eccl. 9:9; Eph. 5:23-33; Col. 3:19; I Tim. 5:8; I Pet. 3:7.

Making husbands contemptible.—Esth. 1:17.

Prophecy concerning.—Jer. 6:11.

Figurative.—Is. 54:5; Jer. 31:32; II Cor. 11:2; Gal. 4:27. Christ the husband of His people—Eph. 5:25-32; Rev. 19:7f.

Illustrative.—Jer. 3:1; Ez. 16:32, 45; Hos. 2:2, 7; Joel 1:8; Rev. 21:2.

Mention of.—Adam to Eve—Gen. 2:18, 23, 24; 3:6, 16. Abraham to Sarai—Gen. 16:3. Isaac to Rebekah—Gen. 24:67. Jacob to Leah—Gen. 29:32, 34; 30:15, 18, 20. Manoah—Ju. 13:6, 9, 10. Samson to Philistine woman—Ju. 14:15. Elimelech to Naomi—Ruth 1:3, 5, 12. Of Ruth—Ruth 1:9, 12; 2:11.

Of Orpah—Ruth 1:9, 12. Elkanah to Hannah—I Sam. 1:8, 22, 23; 2:19-21. Phinehas as—I Sam. 4:19, 21. Nabal to Abigail—I Sam. 25:19. Paltiel to Michal—II Sam. 3:15, 16. Uriah to Bathsheba—II Sam. 11:26. To woman of Tekoa—II Sam. 14:5, 7. To the Shunammite woman—II Ki. 4:9, 14, 22, 26. Sons of prophets were—II Ki. 4:1. Of a worthy woman—Pr. 12:4; 31:11, 23, 28. To Samaritan—John 4:16-18. Zacharias to Elizabeth—Lu. 1:5, 13, 39, 40. Joseph to Mary—Mt. 1:16, 19. To Anna—Lu. 2:36. Ananias to Sapphira—Acts 5:9, 10. Aquila to Priscilla—Acts 18:24 28; I Cor. 16:19.

Husband head of the house.—Esth. 1:22; Eph. 5:23; Col. 3:18.

LASCIVIOUSNESS. Mk. 7:22. Commited—II Cor. 12:21. Doings—II Pet. 2:2. Gave themselves up to—Eph. 4:19. Life—II Pet. 2:7. Turning grace of God into—Jude 4. Walked in—I Pet. 4:3. Works of the flesh—Gal. 5:19.

LUST: Worldly.—II Pet. 1:4; I John 2:16, 17. Of appetite—Num. 11:4, 34; Ps. 78:18, 30; 106:14. Of flesh—Ju. 3:29; Is. 59:10; Rom. 1:24, 27; 6:12; 13:14; I Cor. 10:6; Gal. 5:16, 17, 24; Eph. 2:3; I Thess. 4:5; II Tim. 3:6; 4:3; Tit. 3:3; Jas. 1:14; 4:2, 3; I Pet. 4:2, 3; II Pet. 2:10, 18; I John 2:16. Of the eyes—I John 2:16. Of deceit—Eph. 4:22.

Warnings against.—Pr. 6:25; I Tim. 6:9; II Tim. 2:22; Tit. 2:12; I Pet. 1:14; 2:11; 4:2, 3; II Pet. 3:3; Jude 16, 18.

Punishment for.—Jas. 1:15; Rev. 18:14.

Is of the world, and passes away.—I John 2:16f.

MALE AND FEMALE. Creation of male and female—Gen. 1:27; 5:2.

Laws concerning males.—Birth—Lev. 12:7; Lu. 2:23. Numbering of—Num. 1:2; 3:15, 22, 28, 39, 40; 26: 62. Men of war—Num. 1:20; Deut. 20:13. Unclean—Num. 5:3; 31:17. Circumcision of—Gen. 17:10-27; 34:15, 22, 24; Josh. 5:4. Laws of vows—Lev. 27:3-7. Tithes of—II Chr. 31:16, 19. Adultery of—Ju. 21:11. Males in priest's houses—Lev. 6:18, 29; 7:6; Num. 18:10; II Chr. 31:19.

Killed in war.—Gen. 34:25; Num. 31:7; I Ki. 11:15, 16.

List of males who went with Ezra.—Ezra 8:3-14.

Heirs of the covenants.—Deut. 7:14. Gen. 17:2.

Male children of Manasseh.—Josh. 17:2.

Male and female gods.—Deut. 4:16.

Neither male nor female.—Gal. 3: 28.

Animals.—Males and females in ark —Gen. 6:19; 7:2, 3, 9, 16. Used as offerings—Lev. 3:6. Of males: Sheep—Ex. 12:5; 34:19; Lev. 1:3, 10. Ox—Ex. 34:19. Bullock—Lev. 1:3, 10; 22:19. Goats—Lev. 3:6; 4:23. Herd—Mal. 1:14. Of females —Lev. 4:28, 32; 5:6.

Consecration of males.—Ex. 3:12, 15; 23:17; Deut. 15:19; 16:16. Circumcision and consecration of Jesus —Lu. 2:21-23.

MAN: Is created by God.—Gen. 2: 7; Deut. 4:32; Job 4:17; 10:3, 8; 14:15; 31:15; 32:22; 33:4; 34:19; 35:10; 36:3; Ps. 95:6; 100:3; 119: 73; 138:8; 139:15, 16; Pr. 14:31; 22:2; Eccl. 7:29; Is. 17:7; 45:12; Jer. 27:5; Hos. 8:14.

Man made in the image of God.—Gen. 1:26, 27; 5:1, 2; 9:6; I Cor. 11:7; Jas. 3:9.

Man formed from the dust of the earth.—Gen. 2:7; 3:19; Job 4:19; 10:9; 33:6; Is. 29:16; 45:9; 64:8; Jer. 18:6; Rom. 9:20, 21; II Cor. 4:7.

God gives to man the breath of life —The Father of his spirit—Gen. 2: 7; Num. 16:22; 27:16; Job 12:10; 27:3; 33:4; 34:14; Is. 42:5; 57:16; Dan. 5:23; Ez. 37:5, 6, 9, 10; Zech. 12:1; Acts 17:25; Heb. 12:9; Rev. 22:6.

Man consists of body (*Heb.* Basar. *Gr.* Soma).—**Soul** (*Heb.* Nephesh. *Gr.* Psuche). **Spirit** (*Heb.* Ruach, Neshama. *Gr.* Pneuma). Gen. 2:7; Job 32:8, 18; 34:14; Ps. 31:9; Is. 10:18; Mt. 10:28; II Cor. 5:6, 8; I Thess. 5:23; Heb. 4:12.

Man is the completion of creation. —Gen. 1:28; 2:4-7; Ps. 8:4-8; Heb. 2:6-8.

Made but a little lower than God.— Ps. 8:5. **Than angels.**—Heb. 2:7.

Granted dominion over the earth.— Gen. 1:26, 28; Ps. 8:6-8; 49:14; 72:8.

Wonderfully made.—Job 10:8-11; Ps. 149:14-16; Eccl. 11:5. A puzzled saint—Job 12:4-6; Rom. 7:15-24. Thwarted plans—Ps. 33:10-19.

Differs from everything else living. I Cor. 15:39.

Male and female represented in.— Gen. 1:26-28; 5:2; Mt. 19:4; Mk. 10:6.

Endowed with intellect.—Job 13:3, 15; Is. 1:18; 41:1, 21; 43:26; Jer. 12:1; Mt. 11:25; 16:7.

Endowed with affections.—Gen. 3: 16; Lev. 19:18; Deut. 18:6; I Chr. 29:3; Mt. 19:19; John 13:34; Rom. 12:10; 13:9, 10; Col. 3:12; I Thess. 4:9; Heb. 13:1; I Pet. 1:22; I John 3:14.

Man made to toil.—Gen. 1:28; 2:5, 15; 3:19; 31:42; Ex. 31:16; Ps. 104:23; Pr. 13:11; 14:23.

Full liberty granted with but one restriction.—Gen. 2:16, 17; 3:2, 3.

Fall of.—Gen. 3:1-8; Eccl. 7:27-29; Rom. 5:12-19; I Cor. 15:21, 22.

Enticed by the tempter.—Gen. 3:4, 5, 13; Pr. 1:10-19; 12:26; 16:29; John 8:44; II Cor. 11:3; I Tim. 2: 14; I Thess. 3:5; I Tim. 2:14; Jas. 1:13-15; I John 2:16, 17; Rev. 12: 9, 13.

Sinfulness of.—Gen. 6:5, 6, 12; 8: 21; I Ki. 8:46; Job 15:14-16; Ps. 14:1 3; 51:5; Pr. 20:9; Eccl. 7:20; 9:3; Is. 53:6; Jer. 17:9; Mk. 7:21 23; John 3:19; 7:7; Rom. 3:9-18; 7:18; Gal. 5:17; Jas. 1:13-15; I John 1:8.

Imperfection and weakness of.—Job 4:17-21; Ps. 39:5-13; Is. 41:21-24; Mt. 6:27; Rom. 9:16; II Cor. 3:5; Gal. 6:3.

Man subject to suffering.—Gen. 3: 17-19; Job 5:7; 14:1, 2; Rom. 8: 22, 23.

Man rebuked for perversity.—Is. 59: 1-15; John 8:21-24, 38-48.

Vanity of man's life.—Job 7:7-10, 16; Ps. 103:14-16; Eccl. Chs. 1; 2; 7:15; 12:1-8; I Pet. 1:24.

Equality of.—I Sam. 2:7; Job 21:23-26; Ps. 49:6-14; Pr. 22:2; 29:13; Acts 10:34-35; Gal. 3:28; Eph. 6: 5-9; Jas. 2:1-9.

The shortness of his life.—Job 14:1-22; Ps. 39:5; 49:6-14; 89:48; 90:5 -10; Eccl. 1:4; 12:1-8; Heb. 9:27.

Man is great, though in ruins.—Lu. 15:17-24; 19:7-10; Rom. 5:7-8.

Man honored in the assumption of humanity by Jesus.—I Cor. 15:45-49; Eph. 1:19-23; Phil. 2:5-9; Col. 1:12-20; Heb. 2:5-18.

Man's salvation provided for from the beginning.—Gen. 3:15; 12:3; Is. 53:1-12; Mt. 25:34; Rom. 16: 25; Eph. 1:3-14; 3:1-11; II Thess. 2:13, 14; II Tim. 1:9, 10; Tit. 1:2, 3; II Pet. 1:10-12, 18-20; Rev. 13: 8.

Man at his best when following Christ.—Mt. 4:19; 19:28, 29; II Cor. 3:18; 5:17; Eph. 2:4-7, 10; 4:11-13.

Man's individuality respected.—Lu. 12:57; John 8:15; 12:47; 15:14-16; Rev. 3:20, 21.

Man obtains enlargement of life.— John 1:4; 5:21 26; 6:33 35; 10: 10; 17:2, 3; 20:31; I John 3:1 3.

Endowed with will.—John 7:17; Rom. 7:18; I Cor. 9:17; Phil. 2:13; Rev. 22:17.

Value of.—Mt. 10:31; 12:12; 16:26; Mk. 2:27; John 3:16, I Cor. 11:7.

Whole duty of.—Deut. 10:12; Eccl. 12:13; Mic. 6:8; I John 3:18-22.

Man proposes, but God disposes.— I Sam. 17:47; II Chr. 20:15; Eccl. 9:11; Is. 10:11; 47:1-15; Jer. 9:23, 24; Amos 2:14-16; Lu. 12:16-21.

Obtains an advocate in time of trouble. —Rom. 8:34; I Tim. 2:5, 6; Heb. 7:25; 9:24-28; I John 2:1, 2.

Man the partaker of the divine nature. —John 1:16; Eph. 3:19; 4:13, 24; Heb. 3:1, 14; 6:4; 12:10; II Pet. 1: 4; I John 3:2.

He shall be recompensed according to his works.—Deut. Chs. 27; 28; Job 34:1, 12, 25; Ps. 62:12; Pr. 12:14; 24:12; Is. 3:10, 11; Jer. 32: 19; Mt. 7:15-27; 16:27; John 5:29, Rom. 2:5, 6; 6:20-23; 14:12; I Cor. 3:8; II Cor. 5:10; Eph. 6:8; Col. 3: 25; Rev. 2:23-27; 20:12, 13; 21:7, 8; 22:12.

MARRIAGE: Ordained of God.— Gen. 2:18, 24; Mt. 19:5, 6; Mk. 10: 7, 8; I Cor. 6:16; 11:11, 12; Eph. 5:31; Heb. 13:4.

Expressed by.—Joining together— Mt. 19:6; Mk. 10:9. Making affinity —I Ki. 3:1; 7:8; 9:16; II Chr. 8:11. Taking to wife—Ex. 2:1; Ruth 4:13. Giving daughters to sons, and sons to daughters—Deut. 7:2; Ezra 9:12.

Commended.—Pr. 18:22; 31:10-12; Jer. 29:6; I Tim. 5:14, 15.

For this life only.—Mt. 22:30; Mk. 12:23; Lu. 20:27-36.

Marriage of near relatives.—Abraham and Sarai were half brother and sister—Gen. 20:12. The mother of Moses and Aaron was the aunt of her husband—Ex. 6:20. Of cousins—Gen. 24:50-67; 28:2; Num. 36:1-12.

Marriages contracted by parents.— Gen. 21:21; 24:1-67; 34:4-10; 38: 6; Ex. 21:7; 22:17; Ju. 1:12; 14:2, 3; I Sam. 17:25; 18:17-27.

Father gave daughters in marriage. —Ex. 22:17; Deut. 7:3; Josh. 15: 16, 17; Ju. 14:20; 15:1-6; I Sam. 18:17-21; 25:44. Eldest daughter usually given first—Gen. 29:26. A dowry given to woman's parents before marriage—Gen. 24:53; 29:18; 34:12; Deut. 22:29; I Sam. 18:25-28; Hos. 3:2.

Consent of parties necessary.—Gen. 24:57, 58; I Sam. 18:20, 21; 25: 40, 41.

Marriage contract made at gate of city.—Ruth 4:1-11.

Marriage laws of the Jews: Concerning near relatives.—Lev. 18:6 -18, 24; 20:11-21; Deut. 22:30; 27: 20-23; Mk. 6:17-19. **After seduction.**—Deut. 22:28, 29; Ex. 22:16.

Levirate marriage.—In case a man died without an heir—Brother or near kinsman to marry widow—Gen. 38:8-11; Deut. 25:5-10; Ruth 2:1, 10-13; 3:2-18; 4:1-13; Mt. 22:24-28; Mk. 12:19-23; Lu. 20:28-33.

Marriages were to be between members of the same tribe.—Ex. 2:1; Num. 36:6-12.

Marriages of priests.—Lev. 21:7, 13, 14; Ez. 44:22.

Marriages with Gentiles forbidden because of idolatry.—Gen. 24:3-6; 27:46; 28:1, 2, 6-9; 34:13, 14; Ex. 34:13-16; Deut. 7:3, 4; Num. 25:6-15; Josh. 23:12, 13; I Ki. 11: 2; 16:31; Ezra 9:11, 12; Neh. 10: 30; 13:23-30.

Marriages made with Gentiles.— Jer. 14:1-5; I Ki. 11:1; Neh. 13:23 -30.

Marriage of captives.—Deut. 21:10-14.

Married man exempted from going to war for one year after marriage. —Deut. 20:7; 24:5.

Infidelity of those contracted in marriage same as if married.—Deut. 22:23, 24; Mt. 1:19. Tokens of virginity—Deut. 22:13-21.

Not to be married considered a calamity.—Ju. 11:37, 38; Ps. 78:63.

Weddings.—Celebrated with feasting —Gen. 29:22; Ju. 14:10-12; Esther 2:18; Jer. 16:8, 9; 33:11; John 2: 1-10. Feasting lasted seven days— Gen. 29:27; Ju. 14:12. Garments provided for guests at the wedding —Mt. 22:12. Christ attends the wedding feast in Cana—John 2:1-10.

The bride.—The bath and anointing— —Ruth 3:3. Receives presents— Gen. 24:53. Given a handmaid— Gen. 24:59; 29:24, 29. Adorned— Ps. 45:13, 14; Is. 49:18; Jer. 2:32;

Rev. 19:7, 8. *With jewels*—Is. 61:
10. Attended by bridesmaids—Ps.
45:9. Stood on right hand of bridegroom—Ps. 45:9. Receives bene-
diction—Gen. 24:60; Ruth 4:11,
12. Must forget father's house and
people—Ruth 1:8-17; Ps. 45:10.
Bridegroom.—Specially clothed—Is.
61:10. Attended by many friends—
Ju. 14:11; John 3:29. Crowned
with garlands—Song of Sol. 3:11;
Is. 61:10. Rejoices over bride—Ps.
19:5; Is. 62:5. Returns with bride
to his house at night—Mt. 25:1-6.
Paul's teaching concerning—Advises
marriage.—I Tim. 5:14, 15. For
the sake of chastity—I Cor. 7:1-6,
9. Lawful in all I Cor. 7:8 10; 9:5.
Rebukes those who advise against
marriage—I Tim. 4:3. Elders or bishops and deacons to be husbands of
one wife—I Tim. 3:2, 12.
Should be only in the Lord.—I Cor.
7:39. **Honorable in all.**—Heb. 13:
4.
Seems to think that to remain un-
married and virtuous is better, be-
cause of persecution of that time.
—I Cor. 7:8, 17, 25-40.
Be not unequally yoked with unbe-
lievers.—II Cor. 6:14, 17.
Marriage of widows.—Rom. 7:1-3; I
Cor. 7:39, 40.
Monogamy taught in the Bible.—
Wife singular number—Mt. 19:5.
God gave Adam one wife—Gen. 2:
18-24. Each man had one wife in
the ark—Gen. 7:13. See Gen. 2:
24; Mal. 2:15; Mt. 19:5, 65; Mk.
10:7, 8; I Cor. 11:11, 12; Eph. 5:
31; I Tim. 3:2, 12.
Polygamy and concubinage prac-
ticed.—Lamech the first polygamist
—Gen. 4:19. Abraham—Gen. 12:
5; 16:1-6; 25:1, 6. Jacob—Gen.

29:25-30. Esau—Gen. 36:2, 3.
Gideon the judge—Ju. 8:30, 31.
Elkanah the father of Samuel—I
Sam. 1:2. Saul—II Sam. 3:7. David
—I Sam. 27:3; II Sam. 5:13; I Chr.
14:3. Solomon—I Ki. 11:1-3; Song
of Sol. 6:8. Rehoboam—II Chr. 11:
21.
Marriage figurative.—Symbolizes:
Idolatry—Mal. 2:11. God's union
with the Jews—Is. 54:5; Jer. 8:14;
Hos. 2:19, 20. Christ's union with
the church—Mt. 22:1-14; 25:1-10;
Rom. 7:4; Eph. 5:23, 24, 32; Rev.
19:7.

MOTHER. Must honor her—Ex. 20:
12; Deut. 5:16; Pr. 1:8; 23:22; Mt.
15:4; 19:19; Mk. 7:10; 10:19; Lu.
18:20; Eph. 6:2. Eve, the mother
of all—Gen. 3:20. Love of mothers
contrasted with God's—Is. 49:15.
Sarah a mother of nations—Gen.
17:16. Punishment for maltreat-
ment of—Ex. 21:15, 17; Lev. 18:7;
20:9; Pr. 30:11; 30:17. Foolish son
heaviness of—Pr. 10:1. Despise not,
when old—Pr. 23:22. He that loveth,
more than Me—Mt. 10:37. Mother
of Lord come to Me—Lu. 1:43.
Mother of Jesus was there—John
2:1. Peter's wife's mother—Mt. 8:
13; Lu. 4:38. Who is my mother?
—Mt. 12:48; Mk. 3:34. Mary,
Mother of Jesus, steadfast—Acts 1:
14. Can a man enter second time,
etc.—John 3:4. Entreat elderly
women as mothers—I Tim. 5:2.
MOTHER-IN-LAW. Not to be defiled
—Lev. 18:17; 20:14; Deut. 27:23.
Ruth's affection for—Ruth 1:14-17.
Dwelt with—Ruth 2:23. Boaz provides for—Ruth 3:17. Rising up
against—Mic. 7:6; Mt. 10:35; Lu.
12:53. Peter's mother-in-law healed
by Jesus—Mk. 1:30-31.

311

NAKEDNESS. Sin discloses nakedness—Gen. 3:7; John 21:7; Rev. 3:18.
Shame of.—Noah's—Gen. 9:21-27. Of kin—Lev. 20:17-21. Jonathan's —I Sam. 20:30. Nineveh's—Nah. 3:5. Drunkard's—Hab. 2:15, 16. Children of Israel—Hos. 2:9, 10. The church—Rev. 3:17, 18; 16:15.
Laws concerning.—Lev. 20:10-23.
Spiritual nakedness.—Babylon—Is. 47:3. Jerusalem—Lam. 1:8-9; Ez. Ch. 16.
Inflicted as punishment. — Against Israel and Judah—Hos. 2:3; Mic. 1:7-9. The harlot of the church— Rev. 17:16.
Clothing the naked a proof of righteousness.—Job 22:5-7; 31:19-22; Mt. 25:35-40; Jas. 2:15.
Not able to separate from God.— Rom. 8:35, II Cor. 11:27.
References.—Job 1:21; Mk. 14:51, 52; II Cor. 5:3.
PARENTS: The father.—Father was the priest of the family group—Gen. 31:53; 32:9; I Sam. 20:6. As such, reverence due him—Ex. 21:15, 17; Mt. 15:4-6; Mk. 7:10-13.
House.—Fathers constituted elders of Hebrew communities—Ex. 3:16, 18; 4:29; 12:21; 17:5; 18:12; 24: 1, 9. Ruled the household—Gen. 18:19; Pr. 3:12; 13:24; I Tim. 3: 4, 5, 12; Tit. 1:6; Heb. 12:7. Decided on marriages of children— Gen. 24:4; 28:2; Ju. 14:2. Sold daughters to bridegrooms—Ex. 21: 7; Neh. 5:5.
Wives and mothers.—Wives were bought and paid for; thus legally property of husband—Gen. 29:18-30; 31:41; Ex. 20:17. Wife not a mere chattel. Wife largely the provider—Pr. 31:10:29. Superior to concubine in that her children were

preferred—Gen. 17:18-21. Law sympathetic to wife—Ex. 21:2, 12; Deut. 21:14.
Mother.—To be childless a disgrace —Gen. 30:1; I Sam. 1:5-7; Is. 4:1. To possess children a great joy— Gen. Ch. 30. Mother to be honored —Ex. 20:12; 21:15; Lev. 19:3; Mt. 15:4; 19:19; Eph. 6:2. Beloved by children—Pr. 31:28. Comforts her children—Is. 66:13.
Parents: Responsibilities of. — To maintain children—Pr. 19:14; II Cor. 12:14. To educate—Gen. 18: 19; Ex. 12:26, 27; 13:8; Deut. 6: 6, 7; Eph. 6:4. Sons depend on fathers after passing from mother's control—Pr. 1:8; 3:12; 4:1; 13:1.
Further duties of parents.—To love —Tit. 2:4. To train children up for God—Deut. 4:9; 11:19; Pr. 22:6; Is. 38:19; Eph. 6:4. To command obedience to God—Deut. 32:46; I Chr. 28:9. To teach them God's power—Ex. 10:2; Ps. 78:4. His judgments—Joel 1:3, 4. To pity them Ps. 103:13. To bless them—Gen. 48:15; Heb. 11:20. To provide for them—Job 42:15; II Cor. 12:14; I Tim. 5:8. To correct them—Pr. 13: 24; 19:18; 23:13; 29:17; Heb. 12: 7. Not to provoke them—Eph. 6: 4; Col. 3:21. Not to make unholy connections for them—Gen. 24:1-4; 28:1-2. To impress divine deeds and commands upon them—Deut. 4:9; 6:6; 11:19; 32:46; Ps. 44:2; 78:3-6.
PURITY, PURIFICATION (Clean, Cleansing). Correlative terms, Clean, Pure; Contrasted, Unclean, Impure.
Purification.—Removal of uncleanness; hence rendering clean (pure) what previously was unclean (defiled).

Clean and unclean (ceremonially).
(1) **Of animals:** respectively fit and unfit for food—Gen. 7:2, 8; 8:20; Lev. 20:25. Marks of distinction: Quadrupeds—Lev. 11:4, 5, 6, 7, 8; Deut. 14:7, 10. Birds—Lev. 11: 13-19; Deut. 14:11-20. Insects— Lev. 20:23. Reptiles—Lev. 11:29-31; Deut. 14:19. Fish—Lev. 11:9-12. Unclean may not be offered on the altar—Lev. 22:25.
(2) **Of persons,** qualified or disqualified to appear in worship before God; hence also to mingle in society —Lev. 11:24, 39, 40, 47; 12:2, 5; 13:3, 8ff.; 15:2ff.; Deut. 12:15, 22; 15:22.

The uncircumcised are unclean —Is 52:1.

Sources of personal defilement: Primary: Natural causes, issue out of one's flesh—Lev. 15:2, 3. Seed of copulation—Lev. 15:16. Sexual intercourse—v. 18. Issue from a woman in health—Lev. 15:9; in disease— v. 25ff.

Woman in childbirth—Lev. 12:1-5.

Contact with a corpse—Num. 19:11; Lev. 5:2; 21:1ff.

Touching a carcass—Lev. 11:39.

Eating that which died of itself—Lev. 17:15; 22:8.

Transmission by heredity—Job 14:4.

Secondary: Accidental, touching an unclean person or thing—Lev. 15: 4, 10; 22:5, 6. Sitting on anything that an unclean person has sat on —Lev. 15:4ff.; or lying down on a bed occupied by an unclean person —Lev. 15:24.

Moral cause of uncleanness: Unnatural sins of unchastity (abominations)—Lev. 18:6-18; 19:23, 30; Job 36:14 marg. Incestuous relations—Lev. 20:21, 25.

(3) **Of places, respectively free or not free of ceremonially unclean objects.**—Lev. 14:36, 40, 41. Leprous houses—Lev. 14:34-57. Foreign lands—Amos 7:17. Any land defiled by sin—Lev. 18:25-28; Num. 35: 33; Josh. 22:19; Ez. 9:11; Lam. 4: 15; Ez. 22:24.

Distinction between clean and unclean of vital importance.—Lev. 10:10; 20:25; Deut. 23:14.

Regulations affecting the unclean. —Animals must be redeemed—Lev. 27:11, 27; Num. 18:15. Persons may not eat of holy things—Lev. 7: 19-21; 22:4, 5. What they may eat —Deut. 12:15, 22. They may celebrate the passover at a special time —Num. 9:10. General disqualifications of—Is. 35:8. Priests especially must avoid defilement—Num. 6:7; Is. 52:11. Also a Nazirite's mother —Ju. 13:4, 7, 14. Duty of teaching distinctions devolves on priests —Ez. 44:23. The temple to be guarded against uncleanness—II Chr. 23:19. Application of distinctions by Haggai—Hag. 2:13. Uncleanness a hardship—Hos. 9:3.

Confession of uncleanness.—Is. 6:5; 64:6.

Duration of uncleanness.—For secondary causes, "until even"—Lev. 11: 32, 39, 40; 15:5, 6, 8, 18, 21, 27; 17:15; 22:6; Num. 19:22. Priests in preparing water of purification— Num. 19:8, 21. In applying the same —Num. 19:20.

For primary causes: Seven days— Woman after birth of a son—Lev. 12:2 (continued to forty days). Suspicion of leprosy—Lev. 13:4, 21, 26, 31, 50, 54. Contact with dead body—Num. 19:11, 14, 16. Two weeks—Woman after birth of a

313

daughter—Lev. 12:5 (continued to 80 days). Indefinite, depending on length of impurity—Lev. 15:25ff. Permanent. Leprosy pronounced incurable—Lev. 13:8, 15, 36, 44. In garments—Lev. 13:51, 55.

Modes of purification, Law of.— Num. 19:11-13. (1) Washing of one's clothes—Lev. 15:5, 6, 11, 13, 22. (2) Bathing the body with water —Lev. 15:5-7, 13. (3) Sacrifice of two turtle doves, one for a burnt-offering, the other for a sin-offering —Lev. 15:14, 15, 29, 30. Or a lamb in purification for childbirth, in case of wealthy mother—Lev. 12:6-8. (4) **Special ceremonials.**—Water of purification made by mixture of ashes, of red heifer, cedar wood and hyssop—Num. 19:2ff.; Heb. 9:13. (5) For leprosy—Lev. 14:21-32.

Applications of the law of purification.—Purging the altar—Lev. 8: 15; Ez. 43:20, 25; II Chr. 34:5. The temple—II Chr. 29:18; Neh. 13:9; Dan. 8:14. The Levites and priests —Num. 8:21; Ez. 6:20; Neh. 12: 30. Bathsheba—II Sam. 11:4.

Purification according to Persian rite.—Esth. 2:3, 9, 12.

Moral purification.—Essential to normal relations with God—Ps. 24:4; 18:26; Job 4:17 marg.; 8:6; II Sam. 22:27; Pr. 20:9; 21:8; 30:12. Prayer for—Ps. 51:7; 79:9.

Purification in the N. T.—Ritual elaborate—Mt. 15:2ff.; Mk. 7:3ff.; Heb. 9:10, 22; John 11:65. Provisions made for—John 2:6.

Discussion about.—John 3:25.

Attitude of Jesus towards.—Lu. 11: 38-41; Mt. 15:3-20; Mk. 7:6-23. Neglect by the disciples of Jesus—

Mk. 7:1-5; Mt. 15:1, 2; but practiced by Paul—Acts 21:26; and distinctions survive in Christian practice— Acts 10:10ff.; 11:8. Transfer of distinction to that between idol worship and spiritual worship—Acts 15:29; but with abolition of inherent values —Rom. 14:14-20; I Cor. 6:13; Col. 2:16, 20-22; Tit. 1:15; Heb. 10:2; and symbolic use—Rev. 16:13; 18:2.

Distinction spiritualized.—II Cor. 6: 17; Eph. 5:5; Heb. 9:23.

Spiritual purification through Jesus Christ.—I Pet. 1:22; II Pet. 1:9; Heb. 1:3; I John 3:3.

SEDUCTION, Leading astray.—Sexual seduction: Laws concerning—Ex. 22:16-17; Deut. 22:23-29.

Instances of: Lot—Gen. 19:30-35. Dinah—Gen. 34:2. Bilhah by Reuben—Gen. 35:22; 49:3; Deut. 27: 20; I Chr. 5:1, 2. Judah—Gen. 38: 13-18. Attempted seduction of Joseph—Gen. 39:7-12. Bathsheba —II Sam. 11:2-5. Warnings against —Pr. 6:23-35; 7:4-27; 9:13-18.

Political.—Israel—II Ki. 21:9-12; Ez. 13:10. Samson—Ju. 16:4-20. Egypt —Is. 19:13.

Spiritual.—Jer. 3:9; Mk. 13:22; I Tim. 4:1; II Tim. 3:13; I John 2:26; Rev. 2:20.

SODOMITE. This word describes those who practiced as a religious rite the unnatural vice of the people of Sodom and Gomorrah—Deut. 23: 17; I Ki. 14:24; 15:12; 22:46; II Ki. 23:7; Job 36:14 (margin). Women were also consecrated to this lewd religious rite—Gen. 38:21-23 (also margin); Deut. 23:17; Hos. 4:14; I Ki. 22:38.

UNMARRIED. Women—I Cor. 7:8, 11, 32, 34.

WIDOW. Under God's protection—Deut. 10:18; Ps. 68:5; 146:9; Pr. 15:25; Jer. 49:11. Laws relating to marriage—Deut. 25:5; Lev. 21:14; Ez. 44:22; Mk. 12:19.

Laws respecting: Not to be oppressed—Ex. 22:22; Deut. 27:19; Is. 1:17, 23; 10:2; Jer. 22:3; Zech. 7:10; Mal. 3:5. Creditors not to take raiment—Deut. 24:17. Bound to perform their vows—Num. 30:9. To be allowed to glean in fields—Deut. 24:19. To have a share of triennial tithe—Deut. 14:28-29; 26:12-13. To share in public rejoicings—Deut. 16:11-14.

When childless, to be married to husband's nearest kin.—Deut. 25:8-10; Ruth 3:10-13; 4:4-5; Mt. 22:24-26.

Widows to be cared for by church.—Acts 6:1; I Tim. 5:3-5, 9-16; Jas. 1:27.

WIFE: Laws concerning.—Ex. 20:17; 21:3-5; 22:16; Lev. 18:8, 11, 14-16, 18, 20; 20:10, 11, 14, 21; 21:7, 13, 14; Num. 5:11-31; 30:16; 36:8; Deut. 5:21; 13:6; 20:7; 21:11-14; 22:13, 30; 24:5. Divorce—Deut. 24:1, 3, 4; Mt. 5:31, 32; 19:3-10; Mk. 10:2-12; Lu. 16:18; I Cor. 7:32-40.

Proverbs concerning.—Pr. 12:4; 18:22; 31:10.

Duties of.—Gen. 3:16; Rom. 7:2; I Cor. 7:2-4, 10, 11, 13, 14, 16; Eph. 5:22, 24, 33; Col. 3:18; Tit. 2:4, 5; I Pet. 3:1. Honoring husbands—Esth. 1:20.

Illustrative.—Jer. 3:1, 20; Ez. 16:32; Eph. 5:25-27, 29, 33; Rev. 19:7; 21:9.

WOMAN, *i.e.,* **Taken out of man.**—Gen. 2:23. Created—Gen. 1:27; 2:21, 22. Blessed of God—Gen. 1:28. The function of—Gen. 1:28. A helpmeet to man—Gen. 2:18. Led astray by Satan—Gen. 3:1-7; II Cor. 11:3; I Tim. 2:14. Curse pronounced on—Gen. 3:16.

Had separate dwelling.—Gen. 24:67; 31:33. Esth. 2:9, 11.

Had a court in the tabernacle assigned to them.—Ex. 38:8; I Sam. 2:22.

Dress.—II Sam. 13:18; Is. 3:16-23; I Tim. 2:9; I Pet. 3:3-5. May not wear man's clothing—Deut. 22:5. Wore a veil—Gen. 24:65; 38:14; I Cor. 11:5-7, 13. Often went unveiled—Gen. 12:14; 24:16, 21. Wore long hair—I Cor. 11:5, 6, 14, 15. Wore hair plaited and adorned with gold and pearls—Is. 3:24; I Tim. 2:9; I Pet. 3:3. Had head covered—I Cor. 11:5-7, 13. Wore Ornaments—Is. 3:16-23; I Tim. 2:9. Earrings—Gen. 24:47; 35:4; Ez. 16:12. Nose jewels—Is. 3:21. Bracelets—Gen. 24:47; Ex. 35:22; Is. 3:9; Ez. 6:11. Armlets—Is. 3:18. Signet rings—Ex. 35:22. Anklets—Is. 3:18. Amulets—Is. 3:20.

Abiding as virgins.—I Cor. 7:25-38. Spared in war—Num. 31:18, 35; Deut. 21:14. Wives for the tribe of Benjamin—Ju. 21:12-14. Apparel of king's daughters—II Sam. 13:18. Nurtured for kings' wives—Esth. 2:8-13. No marriage without father's consent—Gen. 34:6-8; Ex. 22:17. Non-marriage a calamity—Ju. 11:37; Ps. 78:63. Punishment for corrupting betrothed—Deut. 22:23, 24. When not betrothed—Ex. 22:16, 17; Deut. 22:28, 29. Kingdom of heaven likened to—Mt. 25:1-12. Typify saints in heaven—Rev. 14:4.

Duties of women.—Subject to husband—Gen. 3:16; I Cor. 7:39; 11: 8, 9; Eph. 5:22-24; Col. 3:18; Tit. 1:5; I Pet. 3:1-6. Helper of husband —Pr. 31:11-29. Housekeeping— Gen. 18:6; Pr. 31:15-21, 27. Spinning—Ex. 35:25, 26; Pr. 31:19. Tending flocks and herds—Gen. 29: 9; Ex. 2:16. Gleaning—Ruth 2:7, 8, 15-23. Drawing and carrying water—Gen. 24:11-16; I Sam. 9: 11; John 4:7. Work in fields—Is. 27:11; Ez. 26:6, 8. Grinding corn —Mt. 24:41; Lu. 17:35.

Social status of.—Esth. 1:10-22; Dan. 5:1, 2, 10-12; Acts 8:27; 24:24; 25: 13, 23. Take part in public affairs— Ex. 15:20, 21; Ju. 4:4-22; 9:50-54; 11:24; I Sam. 18:6, 7; II Sam. 20: 14-22; I Ki. 1:15-21; 10:1-13; 21: 7-15; II Ki. 11:1-3; II Chr. 9:1-9; 21:6; 22:3; Ps. 68:25; Dan. 5:9-13.

In business.—I Chr. 7:24; Pr. 31:14, 16; Acts 16:14.

Required to attend the reading of the law.—Deut. 31:12; Josh. 8:35.

Celebrants of victories.—Ex. 15:20-21; I Sam. 18:6-7.

Mourners at funerals.—Jer. 9:17, 20.

Property rights.—Num. 27:1-9; Josh. 17:3-6; Ruth 4:3-9; Job 42: 15. Wife sold for husband's debts— Mt. 18:25. Aid to widows—Deut. 14:29; II Ki. 4:1-7; Ps. 146:9; Acts 6:1; I Tim. 5:3, 16.

Characteristics.—Fair and graceful— Gen. 12:11; 24:16; Song of Sol. 1:8. Haughty—Is. 3:16. Ambitious —Mt. 20:20, 21. Wise—II Sam. 14: 2; Pr. 31:26. Weaker than man— I Pet. 3:7. Timid—Is. 19:16; Jer. 51:30; Nah. 3:13. Silly and easily led into error—II Tim. 3:6. Loving and affectionate—II Sam. 1:26.

Clings to her children—Is. 49:15. Virtuous—Ruth 3:11. Fond of dress and ornaments—Is. 3:17-21; I Tim. 2:9. Mirthful—Ju. 11:34; 21:21; Jer. 31:13. Patriotic—Ex. 15:20-21; Ju. 4:4-22; 5:24-27; 9:53, 54; I Sam. 18:6; II Sam. 20:16-22; Esth. 5:1-8; 7:1-4; Prophetic: *Deborah*—Ju. 4:4. *Hannah*—I Sam. 2:1-10. *Huldah*—II Ki. 22:14-20. *Elizabeth*—Lu. 1:41-43. *Philip's daughters*—Acts 21:9.

Women's vows.—Num. 30:3-16.

Woman, charged with adultery, to be tried.—Num. 5:12-31.

Taken captive.—Num. 31:9, 15, 17, 18, 35; Deut. 28:32, 41; Ju. 5:30; Lam. 1:18; Ez. 30:18.

Treated with cruelty in war.—Is. 13: 16; Lam. 5:11. Zech. 14:2.

Purification of.—Lev. Ch. 12; 15:19-33; II Sam. 11:4; Lu. 2:22-24.

Punishment of.—Ex. 22:16, 17; Deut. 22:23-27, 28, 29.

Religious privileges in N. T.—Lu. 2: 36-38; Acts 1:14; 12:12-17; 21:9; I Cor. 11:5; 14:34, 35; Gal. 3:28; Phil. 4:3; I Tim. 2:12; 5:2-11; Tit. 2:3-5.

Church workers.—Phil. 4:3. Lydia— Acts 16:14-15. Dorcas—Acts 9:36. Priscilla—Acts 18:26. Phebe—Rom. 16:1, 2. Julia—Rom. 16:5. Mary— Rom. 16:6.

Paul's teaching concerning.—I Cor. 11:5-15; Eph. 5:22-24; Col. 3:18; I Tim. 3:11; 5:2-16; Tit. 2:3-5. Concerning public speaking—I Cor. 11:13; 14:34, 35; Gal. 3:28; I Tim. 2:12, 13. Paul welcomes women as church workers—Acts 16:13-15; 18:2, 3; Rom. 16:1-16.

First at the sepulchre.—Mk. 15:46, 47; 16:1-6; Lu. 23:55, 56; 24:1-10; John 20:1.

316

Christ appears to the.—Mt. 28:8, 10; Mk. 16:8, 10; Lu. 24:9, 10, 22; John 20:2, 18. To Mary Magdalene —Mk. 16:9; John 20:14-17.

Precepts concerning: Seduction—Pr. 2:16, 19; 5:3-11; 6:25-29; 7:4-27; 23:27. Housekeeping—Pr. 14:1; 18:22; 31:10-31; Lu. 10:38-42. Keepers at home, sober—Tit. 2:1-5; Virtue—Pr. 12:4; 31:10-31. Contentiousness—Pr. 19:13; 21:9, 19; 25:24; 27:15, 16; I Cor. 14:34. Prudence—Pr. 19:14. Idlers and tattlers—I Tim. 5:13. Examples to the younger—Tit. 2:3-5. Modesty —I Cor. 11:5, 6; 14:34, 35.

Two remarkable conversions.—Samaritan woman—John 4:7-39. Lydia—Acts 16:13-15.

Noted women—Good: Deborah—Ju. 4:5-16; 5:1-31; Mother of Samson —Ju. 13:23; Naomi—Ruth 1:1-22; 2:1-3, 18-22; 3:1; 4:14-17. Ruth —Ruth 1:4-22; Chs. 2-4. Hannah, the mother of Samuel—I Sam. 1:2-28; Abigail—I Sam. 25:14-37. Widow of Zarephath, who fed Elijah—I Ki. 17:8-24. The Shunammite woman—II Ki. 4:8-38. Vashti —Esth. 1:9-22; 2:1-4. Esther— Esth. 2:5-23; 4:4-17; 5:1-14; 7:1-10; 8:1-17. Mary, mother of Jesus —Mt. 1:18-25; 2:11-15; 12:46, 47; Mk. 3:31; Lu. 1:26-56; 2:4-7, 16-19, 34, 35; 8:19; John 2:3-5; 19:25-27; Acts 1:14. Mary Magdalene—Mt. 27:56, 61; 28:1-10; Mk. 15:40, 47; 16:1-9; Lu. 8:2, 3; 23:55, 56; 24:1-7; John 19:25; 20:1, 11-18. Mary, sister of Lazarus— Mt. 26:7-13; Mk. 14:3-9; Lu. 10:38-42; John 11:1, 2, 5, 29; 12:3. Mary, wife of Clopas—Mt. 27:55; Mk. 15:47; John 19:25. Mother of John Mark—Acts 12:12. Elizabeth —Lu. 1:6, 41-45. Anna—Lu. 2:37, 38; Widow with two mites—Mk. 12:41-44; Lu. 21:2-4. Joanna and Susanna—Lu. 8:3. Martha—Lu. 10:38-42; John 11:1-5, 17-40. Pilate's wife—Mt. 27:19. Dorcas—Acts 9:36-39. Lydia—Acts 16:14, 15. Priscilla—Acts 18:26; Rom. 16:3, 4. Phebe—Rom. 16:1, 2. Julia— Rom. 16:15. Lois and Eunice—II Tim. 1:5.

Wicked women: Eve—Gen. 3:6; I Tim. 2:14. Lot's wife—Gen. 19:26; Lu. 17:32. The daughters of Lot— Gen. 19:31-38. Tamar—Gen. 38:14-24. Potiphar's wife—Gen. 39:7-21. Samson's wife—Ju. 14:15 19. Delilah—Ju. 16:4-22. Michal —II Sam. 6:16-23. Jezebel—I Ki. 18:4; 19:1, 2; 21:1-29; II Ki. 9:30; Rev. 2:20. Athaliah—II Ki. 11:1-16. Herodias and her daughter— Mt. 14:3-11; Mk. 6:17-28; Lu. 3:19, 20. The woman of Samaria— John 4:7-29. Woman taken in adultery—John 8:1-11. The woman who was a sinner—Lu. 7:36-49. Sapphira—Acts 5:2-10.

WOMB. Barren—Pr. 30:16; Lu. 23:29; Rom. 4:19. Formed from—Job 31:15; Is. 44:2, 24; 49:5. Fruit of —Gen. 30:2; Is. 13:18; Hos. 9:16. Jesus concerned in—Lu. 1:31, 41, 42, 44; 2:21, 23. Lame from—Mt. 19:12; Acts 3:2; 14:8. Miscarrying —Hos. 9:14. Nazirite from—Ju. 13:5, 7; 10:17. Open—Gen. 29:31; 30:22; Ex. 13:2; Num. 8:16; Ez. 20:26; Lu. 2:23. Second time in— John 3:4. Shut—Gen. 20:18; I Sam. 1:5, 6; Is. 66:9. Sons in—Ruth 1:11. Two nations in—Gen. 25:23, 24; 38:27.

317

Scripture Index

Subject Index